PRENTICE HALL
LITERATURE

PENGUIN EDITION

Reader's
NOTEBOOK
TEACHING GUIDE

Grade 7

PEARSON
Prentice
Hall

Upper Saddle River, New Jersey
Boston, Massachusetts

Copyright © 2007 by Pearson Education, Inc., publishing as Pearson Prentice Hall, Boston Massachusetts 02116. All rights reserved. Printed in the United States of America. This publication is protected by copyright, and permission should be obtained from the publisher prior to any prohibited reproduction, storage in a retrieval system, or transmission in any form or by any means, electronic, mechanical, photocopying, recording, or likewise. For information regarding permission(s), write to: Rights and Permissions Department, One Lake Street, Upper Saddle River, New Jersey 07458.

ISBN 0-13-165406-3

2 3 4 5 6 7 8 9 10   10 09 08 07 06

© Pearson Education, Inc.

Contents

How to Use the *Reader's Notebooks* v

To the Teacher vi

Reader's Notebook

Answers to Part 1

Unit 1 1

Unit 2 12

Unit 3 23

Unit 4 33

Unit 5 42

Unit 6 53

Answers to Part 2

Turbo Vocabulary 163

Reader's Notebook Adapted Version

Answers to Part 1

Unit 1 63

Unit 2 72

Unit 3 81

Unit 4 89

Unit 5 97

Unit 6 104

Answers to Part 2

Turbo Vocabulary 167

Reader's Notebook English Learner's Version

Answers to Part 1

Unit 1 113

Unit 2 122

Unit 3 131

Unit 4 139

Unit 5 147

Unit 6 154

Answers to Part 2

Turbo Vocabulary 170

How to Use the *Reader's Notebooks*

Share the same selection with all your students!

STEP 1

Introduce instruction using *Prentice Hall Literature* Student Edition

- Use the Background information
- Introduce the Literary Analysis and Reading Skill
- Preview the vocabulary words

STEP 2

Develop instruction with targeted reading support

Choose the *Reader's Notebook* that meets each student's needs

Reader's Notebook
- For average readers
- Full-length selections
- Interactive reading support for all selections
- Vocabulary and pronunciation guides
- All selections on audio CD

Adapted Version
- For struggling readers
- Selection adaptations and authentic text
- Enhanced design for easier readability
- All adapted selections on audio CD

English Learner's Version
- Specialized vocabulary and reading support
- Focus on idioms, colloquialisms, and cultural information
- All adapted selections on audio CD

STEP 3

Conclude instruction using *Prentice Hall Literature* Student Edition

- Present the unabridged selection and instruction in the student edition
- Have students read along with the audio CDs
- Use the scaffolded Thinking About the Selection questions

To the Teacher

As you face the challenge of heterogeneous classes, you will find a wide variety of abilities and strengths among your students. The *Reader's Notebook*, the *Reader's Notebook Adapted Version*, and the *Reader's Notebook English Learner's Version* that accompany your *Prentice Hall Literature* anthology are aimed at students who have difficulty with their grade-level textbook. You can use the *Notebooks* to keep your classes reading the same selections but getting the instruction and reading support at the appropriate level. These books provide extended support for those students who need more guidance with reading skills and strategies, literary analysis, and critical thinking skills.

Factors that Affect Reading Success

Four key factors influence students' ability to achieve reading success. These factors, alone and in combination, determine how well a student will learn, grow, and succeed as a reader. To understand the students in your classroom, consider these factors:

(a) **Kinds of Learners** Consider each student's background, previous learning experiences, and special needs. In addition to students who read fluently at grade level, you may find a mix of the following learning characteristics in your classroom:

- *Students who speak a language other than English at home* Unlike their fully fluent counterparts, these students often speak English only at school. This situation leaves them limited hours in which to learn the grammar, vocabulary, idioms, and other intricacies of English.

- *Students who have recently moved to this country* These students may be highly capable students without the specific language skills to function academically in English.

- *Students with learning disabilities* These students may have cognitive, behavioral, social, or physical challenges that make reading more difficult.

(b) **Kinds of Skills and Instruction** Students' reading ability is influenced by the skills they bring to the task. Students must master the skills of decoding, activating and building prior knowledge, and making connections among experiences and new information. Other factors include a student's knowledge of the English language and vocabulary and a student's ability to apply reading comprehension strategies.

Active reading, including the practice of summarizing, questioning, setting a purpose, and self-monitoring, is key to successful reading. For those students who have not yet developed such skills, your classroom instruction is critical. You should model such skills and encourage students to practice them. Through practice, students should be able to internalize the strategies of active reading.

(c) **Kinds of Texts** Just as students and their backgrounds and skills vary, so do the texts presented in a language arts curriculum. The grade-level language arts classroom curriculum traditionally addresses fiction, nonfiction, poetry, and drama. Each of these forms presents unique challenges to students. Each writer and selection also presents challenges in the difficulty of the concepts addressed or in the coherence of the writing. For example, you may find that students are more comfortable with narratives than with expository writing. Focused reading strategies that you model and reinforce can help students tackle texts that are more dense or difficult for them to master.

(d) **Classroom Environment** The classroom environment affects everything and everyone within it. Research suggests that students learn best in a friendly, respectful setting categorized by these criteria:

- Students feel a sense of safety and order.
- They feel comfortable taking risks.
- They understand the purpose and value of the tasks presented.
- They have high expectations and goals for learning.
- They feel accepted by their teachers and peers.

Students performing below grade level may be especially self-conscious. Therefore, these criteria are key to helping students take full advantage of the opportunities the classroom affords. Set up your classroom as a caring yet on-purpose environment that helps students achieve.

Researchers encourage teachers to be truthful with students about the work it will take to build and master abilities in the language arts. Tell your students that improving reading, writing, speaking, and listening takes a great deal of practice. You need to be prepared to provide direct instruction, guided practice, specific feedback, coaching, and more. Then, encourage your students to understand their responsibilities as active, self-directed learners as well.

The Special Education or Special Needs Student

Your classroom may have a number of special education or special needs students—young people who begin the year three or more years below grade level and yet do not qualify for special education services. Special education and special needs students have difficulty in organizing and categorizing new information during instruction. They may have trouble in the following areas:

Memory
- ordering or arranging information
- classifying information
- grasping a main idea or "big picture"
- using long-term memory to make meaningful connections or connecting to prior knowledge

Attention
- focusing attention on the most important elements of a presentation or a selection

By presenting specific focused strategies and interactive review and extension activities, you can provide these students with full access to the language arts curriculum.

Another category of deficiency in special education readers is the ability to apply learning strategies to a variety of situations. Special education and special needs students often have these weaknesses:

Learning Strategies
- a lack of effective or efficient strategies for completing academic tasks such as taking notes, responding to literature, or writing a focused paragraph
- a limited set of learning strategies from which to draw
- difficulty in self-monitoring—they often don't know which strategies to use or when a strategy is not working

Many of these students are underprepared; their deficiencies are generally based on their lack of experience, not on any biological difference. When these students learn effective strategies, they can improve their academic performance. You need to provide direct instruction to explicitly show them how, when, and why to use each strategy.

Overview of Components for Differentiated Instruction

Prentice Hall Literature: Penguin Edition includes an array of targeted resources for special needs students. Fully integrated, these materials help teachers identify student needs or deficiencies, teach to the varying levels in a classroom, and provide the quality that literature teachers expect.

As your main resource, the *Annotated Teacher's Edition* provides a lesson plan for every selection pairing. In addition to teaching notes and suggestions, the *Annotated Teacher's Edition* also includes cross-references to ancillary material such as the *Reader's Notebook,* the *Reader's Notebook Adapted Version,* and the *Reader's Notebook English Learner's Version. Differentiated Instruction* notes help teachers direct lessons to the following groups of students: special needs students, less proficient readers, English learners, gifted and talented students, and advanced readers.

The **Reading Kit** has three parts, each designed to help you address the needs of students with varying ability levels.

- *Part 1: Practice and Assess* includes worksheets for every selection to build reading proficiency.

- *Part 2: Everyday Reading Strategies* provides direct instruction to improve students' comprehension and interpretation.

- *Part 3: Classroom Management for Differentiated Instruction* presents research-based, classroom-tested strategies for engaging students of all ability levels in learning activities and class discussions.

Success Tracker is an online intervention system that allows you to monitor progress and intervene before students take your state standardized test.

- *Assess:* Students take a Diagnostic or Benchmark test online.

- *Diagnose:* Based on assessment results, Success Tracker automatically diagnoses student mastery level for each skill tested.

- *Remediate:* Customized assignments are made for each student based on the skills mastered. Assignments can be made automatically or customized by the teacher.

- *Report:* Color-coded reports make it easy for you to monitor progress on your standards.

Several components—**Vocabulary and Reading Warm-Ups, Selection Tests,** and **Graphic Organizer Transparencies**—are offered in two versions, Level A and Level B. This allows you to customize to the individual ability levels of your students.

- *Vocabulary and Reading Warm-Ups* for every selection include word lists, exercises, and reading passages.

- *Selection Tests* for every selection include multiple choice and essay questions.

- *Graphic Organizer Transparencies* support the skills taught in the student edition.

The **Reader's Notebook** is a consumable component. The book contains instructional support for all the selections and the full text of approximately half of the selections from the student book. Questions prompt students to interact with the text by circling, underlining, or marking key details. Write-on lines in the margins also allow for students to answer questions. You can use this book in place of the student book to help students read interactively.

The **Reader's Notebook Adapted Version** is another consumable component. This book uses the same format and contains the same selections as the *Reader's Notebook*. However, the selections are abridged and appear in a larger font size. The questions are targeted toward special education students. You can use this book as a supplement to or in place of the student book for certain selections to enable special education students to experience the same literature and master the same skills as on-level students.

The **Reader's Notebook English Learner's Version** is a third consumable component. This book uses the same format and contains the same selections as the *Reader's Notebook*. Again, the selections are abridged and appear in a larger font size. The questions are targeted toward English learners. You can use this book as a supplement to or in place of the student book for certain selections to enable English learners to experience the same literature and master the same skills as students who are native English speakers.

Listening to Literature Audio CD This component features professional recordings of every selection in the *Reader's Notebook*. To support student reading, you can play the selections, in part or in full, before students read them.

Reader's Notebook Adapted and English Learner's Version Audio Program These components feature professional recordings of every adapted selection in the *Reader's Notebook Adapted* and *English Learner's Versions*. The recordings include the explanatory bridges along with the lines of original text. As with the *Listening to Literature Audio CD*, you can support student reading by playing selections, in part or in full, before students read them.

The Listening to Literature Audio CD and the *Reader's Notebook Adapted and English Learner's Version Audio Program* can be used to support reading fluency. As you play the CDs, have students read along, either silently or aloud.

Spanish/English Summaries Audio CD Audio summaries in both English and Spanish are provided for every selection. You can play these selection summaries for struggling readers, special education students, and English learners before they read the actual texts.

About the *Reader's Notebook*, the *Reader's Notebook Adapted Version*, and the *Reader's Notebook English Learner's Version*

The *Reader's Notebook* is designed to support students who are reading on level or one grade level below level. The *Reader's Notebook Adapted Version* and the *Reader's Notebook English Learner's Version* are designed to support your special needs and special education students.

Part 1: Skills Instruction and Complete Selections (Reader's Notebook)

Part 1 will guide students as they interact with the selection from *Prentice Hall Literature*. Skills instruction is included for every selection that appears in *Prentice Hall Literature*. In addition, many of the selections from *Prentice Hall Literature* appear in the *Reader's Notebook* in their entirety. The selections that appear include the more accessible selections, the most frequently taught selections, and many examples of narrative and expository writing.

Part 1: Skills Instruction and Selection Adaptations with Excerpts of Authentic Text (Reader's Notebook Adapted and English Learner's Versions)

Part 1 will guide special needs students and English learners as they interact with the selections from *Prentice Hall Literature*. Part 1 in the *Reader's Notebook Adapted Version* and the *Reader's Notebook English Learner's Version* provides larger print summaries of literature selections with passages from the selections.

Prereading pages

The **Build Skills** page is based on its parallel in *Prentice Hall Literature*. It introduces the same literary element and reading skill addressed in the textbook and provides a graphic organizer to make the information more accessible.

The **Preview** page will help your students get the general idea of the selection and therefore be better equipped to understand it. A written summary, along with an image or illustration, previews the selections before students read. The Reading/Writing Connection provides sentence starters that help students think about the big idea behind the selection. It also helps build student vocabulary by using vocabulary that is introduced in the student edition. The Note-taking Guide helps students organize the main ideas of the selection, and helps them track their understanding.

Selection pages

The **selection** pages in the *Reader's Notebook* present the selections as they appear in the student edition. The selection pages in the *Reader's Notebook Adapted Version* and the *Reader's Notebook English Learner's Version* present the text in a larger font size. Interspersed among blocks of authentic text, these two Notebooks also provide summaries of episodes or paragraphs to make the selections more accessible to your students.

The *Take Notes* feature provides questions to accompany the selections. These questions make active reading strategies explicit, asking students to look closely at the text to analyze it in a variety of ways. Notes with a pencil icon prompt students to underline, circle, or otherwise note key words, phrases, or details in the selection. Notes with write-on lines offer students an opportunity to respond in the margin to questions or ideas. These notes offer focused support in a number of ways:

Literary Analysis notes provide point-of-use instruction to reinforce the literary element introduced on the Build Skills page. By pointing out details or events in the text in which the literary element applies, these notes give students the opportunity to revisit and reinforce their understanding of literature.

Reading Skill notes help students practice the skill introduced on the Build Skills page. These notes guide students to understand when, how, and why a skill is helpful.

Stop to Reflect notes ask students to reflect on the selection or on a skill they are using. By encouraging students to solidify their own thinking, these notes help to develop active reading skills.

Reading Check notes help students confirm their comprehension of a selection. These notes help to make explicit a critical strategy of active reading.

Read Fluently notes provide students with concrete, limited practice reading passages aloud with fluency.

THESE INSTRUCTIONAL NOTES ARE SPECIFIC TO THE READER'S NOTEBOOK ENGLISH LEARNER'S VERSION:

Vocabulary and Pronunciation notes guide students in understanding prefixes, suffixes, roots, and words with multiple meanings. In some cases, they explain how specific words are pronounced in English.

Culture notes explain an aspect of American culture that might be unfamiliar to English Learners. They may focus on an aspect of popular culture or on an event or a concept of historical significance.

Build English Skills notes help students in understanding the nuances of the English language, such as idioms, contractions, verb tenses, and difficult sentence constructions.

Post-reading Pages

The *Apply the Skills* pages ensure students' comprehension of the selection. Written in simple language, they assess students' understanding of the literary element and the reading skill. In addition, they offer a scaffolded guide to support students in an activity based on the writing lesson in the student edition of the grade-level textbook. Students are also provided with additional support for an extension activity based on either the Listening and Speaking activity or the Research and Technology activity in the student edition.

Using the *Notebooks*

Classroom Management:

When you are planning lessons for heterogeneous classes, the *Reader's Notebooks* offer you an opportunity to keep all the students in your class reading the same selection and studying the same vocabulary, literary element, and reading skill but also to get the support they need to succeed. At the outset, assign appropriate *Notebooks* to the students and have them write their names in them. Students very quickly assume ownership as they complete the interactive format of the *Notebooks*. The books become a personalized "response journal" and study guide for tests as they move through the selections.

Here are some planning suggestions for using these books in tandem with the grade-level volume of *Prentice Hall Literature:*

Use the *Annotated Teacher's Edition* and the *Student Edition* of the grade-level textbook as the central text in your classroom. The *Annotated Teacher's Edition* includes *Differentiated Instruction* notes throughout each selection. In addition, it identifies when use of the *Notebooks* is appropriate.

Accountability:

Collect the *Notebooks* at intervals that you choose. For example, you may decide to review students' work in the *Notebooks* once weekly. Have students mark a page completed during that time period with a sticky note, which can be used as a tab. This tab makes it easy for you to open the *Notebook* quickly to the specific page, check for the accuracy and thoroughness of the work on selected questions, and award points or a grade.

Absent students:

Use the *Reader's Notebook* for students who will be absent during discussions or for homebound students. These students will be in step with the rest of the class in terms of concepts, strategies, and standards covered during their absence.

Teaching the Genre

At the beginning of each unit of the *Reader's Notebook*, the *Reader's Notebook Adapted Version*, and the *Reader's Notebook English Learner's Version* are two pages devoted to genre instruction. These pages

- describe the most important elements of a particular genre.

- provide definitions for key terms, such as *mood* or *setting*.

Teachers can use these pages as an overview for the Model Selection and for the other selections that follow. Use these steps:

- Review the key terms with students before they read.

- Then, ask them to locate these elements in the selections as they read.

- Finally, reinforce the genre instruction by using the questions on the Apply the Skills page following the first selection in each unit. Each of these questions has students apply their knowledge of genre to the specific selection.

The graphic organizers on the genre page single out certain characteristics of the genre and present them in an easy-to-read format. A sample genre page and graphic organizer are shown here.

A concise definition is provided for setting, *a key term.*

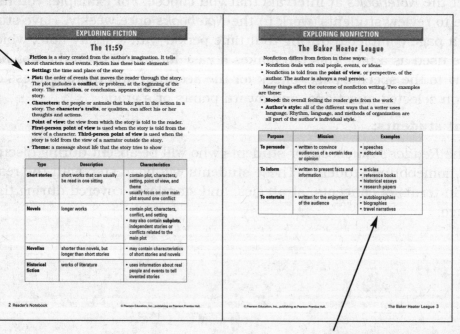

This chart ties the main purposes of nonfiction to real-life examples.

Teaching the Penguin Authors

Penguin Selections

In the student edition of *Prentice Hall Literature: Penguin Edition*, a contemporary Penguin author serves as a guide for each unit. This author introduces the genre or theme of the unit, introduces his or her selection in the unit, annotates and answers questions about that selection, and introduces and annotates a sample of his or her writing. Penguin authors also discuss literature, writing, and their own lives on the DVD that accompanies the textbook.

In the section entitled "Teaching the Penguin Selections," you will find ideas for using the commentary by Penguin authors as you teach their selections in the *Reader's Notebook*, the *Reader's Notebook Adapted Version*, and the *Reader's Notebook English Learner's Version*. The Penguin selections, which are the Model Selections, appear in their entirety in the *Reader's Notebook* and in abridged form in the *Reader's Notebook Adapted Version* and the *Reader's Notebook English Learner's Version* together with almost all the same features that accompany other selections:

- **Preview page**, with a Summary of the selection and a Note-taking Guide

- **Interactive questions** in the margin of the selection

- **Vocabulary words** defined (with pronunciations) where they first appear

- **Reader's Response** question at the end of the selection

- **Apply the Skills** page, with critical thinking questions

However, instead of the page headed Support Your Writing and Extend Your Learning, Penguin selections have a special Research the Author page, which guides students in learning more about the Penguin author:

RESEARCH THE AUTHOR
Oral Report

- Richard Peck's other fiction includes many novels for both adults and young adults. He says that in fiction, "you can go anywhere and be anybody." He also believes that his experience as a junior high school teacher helped make him a writer. He decided that he wanted to write for the students he taught. In many cases, his novels teach about life. They help show young adult readers about problems they face and people they meet.

What I learned from Peck's writing:

- Search the Internet. Use search terms such as "Richard Peck" + and "interview." Choose reliable sites from your list of hits. Reliable sites include sites that end in *.gov*, *.edu*, or *.org*.

What I learned from my own Internet research about Peck:

- Watch the video interview with Richard Peck. List something you learned in the interview that you did not learn in your research.

© Pearson Education, Inc., publishing as Pearson Prentice Hall.   The Fall of the Hindenburg 17

Teaching the Penguin Selections

You can use the commentary by Penguin authors in the student edition to help students read the Penguin selections in the *Reader's Notebook*, the *Reader's Notebook Adapted Version*, and the *Reader's Notebook English Learner's Version*.

Before students begin reading the Penguin selection, show them the interview with the author on the DVD. You might want to guide their viewing by asking individuals or groups to focus on different topics. These topics might include the author's

- life experiences,
- ideas about writing,
- ideas about literature, or
- perspectives on the selection that he or she wrote.

Then, have students summarize for the class the information they learned about their topic.

As students read the selection, use the Penguin author's commentary in the student edition to motivate them and reinforce their learning. Following are some suggestions for using this material with specific pages in the *Reader's Notebook*, the *Reader's Notebook Adapted Version*, and the *Reader's Notebook English Learner's Version*.

Preview page

- Explain to students that the Penguin author introduces his or her selection in the student edition. Point out to them that in this introduction, the author often explains how, why, and when he or she wrote the selection.

- Read this introduction—or passages from it—aloud to students before they read the Summary on the Preview page in the *Reader's Notebook*, the *Reader's Notebook Adapted Version*, and the *Reader's Notebook English Learner's Version*.

- Briefly discuss with students some of the author's insights. If appropriate, ask students to look for evidence to support these insights as they read the selection.

Selection

- Tell students that the author comments on specific passages in his or her selection. These comments appear in notes headed by the author's name and located in the margin of the selection.

- Have students mark in the *Reader's Notebook*, the *Reader's Notebook Adapted Version*, and the *Reader's Notebook English Learner's Version* the passages where the author's comments appear in the student edition.

- Ask students to pause in their reading when they reach the marked passage and refer back to the student edition to read the author's comment.

- If appropriate, ask students to circle or underline in the *Reader's Notebook*, the *Reader's Notebook Adapted Version*, and the *Reader's Notebook English Learner's Version* words or phrases that illustrate or support what the author says.

- When students have finished reading the selection, read aloud one or more of the questions and author responses on the page that follows the selection in the student edition. Then, have students formulate their own questions for the author. Consider having students work in pairs to pose and answer these questions. First, one student can pose a question and the other can answer *as* the author. Next, they can switch roles.

Research the Author

- Introduce this page in the *Reader's Notebook*, the *Reader's Notebook Adapted Version*, and the *Reader's Notebook English Learner's Version* by reviewing with students the sources of information about the author on the DVD and in the student book. Do not forget to mention the Writing Workshop page on which the Penguin author introduces and annotates a draft of his or her writing.

- Questions on the Research the Author page sometimes require Internet research. Review with students the use of key words to do such research. Also, remind them that the most reliable Web sites are sponsored by universities, encyclopedias, and other reputable organizations. Sites created by individuals may not have accurate information.

- To achieve closure, have students relate what they have learned about the author to the selection they have just read. Also, if they are not already prompted to do so by a question on this page, have them use their research to create a list of Further Readings by the same author.

Teaching Part One: The Selections and Informational Materials

The Selections

PRETEACH with the Full Class

Anticipate the reading. Use the *Motivation* activity provided for the selection in the *Annotated Teacher's Edition*. These activities vary and may include discussion questions, anticipation guides, or graphic organizers that will help students focus their attention on the important ideas presented in the selection.

Preview the selection. To help students see the organization of a selection, or to help them get a general idea of the text, lead a quick text prereading or "text tour" using the textbook. Focus student attention on the selection title, the art accompanying the text, and any unusual text characteristics. To build connections for students, ask them to identify links between the selection and other works you have presented in class or to find connections to themes, activities, or other related concepts.

Build background. Use the Background information provided in the *Student Edition*. Whether explaining a historical time period, a scientific concept, or details about an idea that may be unfamiliar to students, this instruction presents useful information to help all students place the literature in context.

Build connections. Use the *Connecting to the Literature* feature in the *Student Edition* to help students find relationships between their own life experiences or reading and the selection they are about to read. Direct average students to complete the *Expressive Vocabulary* task in the Connecting to the Literature section. Direct struggling readers, special education students, special needs students, and English learners to the *Preview* page of the *Notebooks*. Work with them to complete the *Reading/Writing Connection* task on that page.

Focus vocabulary development. The *Student Edition* provides a list of vocabulary words included in each selection. Instead of attempting to cover all of the vocabulary words you anticipate your students will not know, identify the vocabulary that is most critical to talking and learning about the central concepts. However, for the words you do choose to teach, work to provide more than synonyms and definitions. Using the vocabulary notes in the *Annotated Teacher's Edition*, introduce the essential words in more meaningful contexts: for example, through simple sentences drawing on familiar issues, people, scenarios, and vocabulary. Guide students in internalizing the meanings of key terms through these familiar contexts and ask them to write the definitions in their own words. Look at the following examples of guided vocabulary instruction:

> Point out the word *serene* and explain that it means "calm or peaceful." Then, provide the following scenarios and ask students to determine whether the situations are *serene* or not: an empty beach at sunset *(yes)*; a basketball playoff game *(no)*. You might also ask students to provide their own examples of *serene* situations.

Point out the word *interval* and explain that it means "the period of time between two events or points of time." Ask students to identify the interval between Monday and Wednesday *(two days)* and the interval between one Monday and the next Monday *(one week)*.

You might also take the opportunity to teach the prefix *inter-*, meaning "between." Then, discuss with students the following group of words:

> *interview* (a meeting between two or more people);
> *interstate* (between two or more states);
> *international* (between nations);
> *intervene* (to come between two sides in a dispute).

Separate the class to introduce the skills. For average students, introduce the *Literary Analysis* and *Reading Skills* using the instruction in the *Student Edition* and the teaching support in the *Annotated Teacher's Edition*. Have struggling readers, special education students, special needs students, and English learners put their textbooks aside. Direct these students to the *Notebooks* to begin study of *Literary Analysis* and *Reading Skills*.

PRETEACH Using the *Notebooks*

Introduce skills. All versions of the *Reader's Notebooks* provide the same literary analysis and reading skills concepts as the *Student Edition*. The *Adapted* and *English Learner's* versions do so with simplified language and basic sentence structures. Use the *Build Skills* page in the *Notebooks* along with teaching support from the *Annotated Teachers' Edition* to introduce the skills to struggling readers, special education students, special needs students, and English learners.

Reinforce the key ideas. Use the *Summary* presented on the *Preview* page for every selection in the *Notebooks*. The summary will give students a framework to follow for understanding the selection. Use this tool to build familiarity, but do not use it as a replacement for reading.

Introduce note taking. Prepare the students to use the *Note-taking Guide* that appears on the *Preview* page for every selection. Each note-taking guide focuses on a specific aspect of the selection. For example, the guide may help students keep track of details in a poem, trace the plot of a story, or track the line of reasoning in an essay. Tell students that taking notes can help them focus their reading and better understand a selection. It will also allow them to gather information that will help them later as they answer questions or write about a particular selection.

Present audio summaries. The *Spanish/English Summaries on Audio CD* can reinforce the main idea of a selection and provide extra support for students whose first language is Spanish.

Provide decoding practice. Because many struggling readers, special education students, and English learners lack strategies for decoding bigger words, give them guided practice with the vocabulary words for the selection. Using the list from the *Student Edition*, model a strategy for decoding polysyllabic words. First, show students how to break the word into parts and then put the parts back together to make a word.

> For the words *mimic* and *frightening,* ask students to draw a line under each word part as they pronounce it.

> *mim ic*   *fright en ing*

Using this strategy, you can encourage students to look for familiar word parts and then break the rest of the word down into its consonant and vowel sounds. By building this routine regularly into your preteaching instruction, you reinforce a key reading skill for your students.

Prepare for lesson structure. To build students' ability to complete classroom activities, examine your lesson to see what types of language functions students will need to participate in. Look at these examples:

> If students are being asked to make predictions about upcoming paragraph content in an essay, review the power of transition words that act as signals to meaning. Rather than teaching all transitions, limit your instruction to the ones in the passages. Identify the key transition words and point out their meaning. In addition, teach students some basic sentence patterns and verbs to express opinions. Model for students statement patterns such as the following:

> *I predict that . . .*

> *Based on this transition word, I conclude that . . .*

TEACH Using the *Notebooks*

Read the selection. The three versions of the *Reader's Notebook* allow you to teach the same selections to students who demonstrate differing levels of achievement. Average achieving students in your class may read the selection in the *Student Edition*. The *Reader's Notebooks* provide a range of other options as you work with struggling readers, special education students, special needs students, and English learners:

- Students reading just at or below grade level may benefit from the extra guidance provided in the *Reader's Notebook* version of the selection.

- Have your special education and special needs students and English learners read the adapted version of the selection in the

Reader's Notebook Adapted Version or *Reader's Notebook English Learner's Version.*

- If the *Reader's Notebook* does not include the selection, have students read the text in the *Student Edition.*

Whenever possible, give your struggling readers, special education and special needs students, and English learners individualized attention by pairing them with aides, parent volunteers, or student peers.

Set purposes and limits. To keep students focused and motivated and to prevent them from becoming overwhelmed as they read a selection, clearly establish a reading purpose for students before assigning a manageable amount of text. Once you identify a focus question or a purpose, revisit the question occasionally as students read. You can do this with a brief whole-group dialogue or by encouraging students in pairs to remember the question. In addition, your effective modeling will also provide the scaffolding for students to begin internalizing these strategies for effective reading.

Model your thinking. Describe and model strategies for navigating different kinds of text. Use the questions raised in the side notes as a starting point. Then, explain how you arrive at an answer. Alternatively, ask a student to explain his or her responses to classmates.

Reinforce new vocabulary. Present key words when they occur within the context of the reading selection. Review the definition as it appears on the page. Then, make the words as concrete as possible by linking each to an object, a photo, or an idea.

Build interactivity. The side notes in the *Notebooks* are an excellent way to encourage student interactivity with the selections. To build students' ability to use these notes, model several examples with each selection. These are not busy work; they are activities that build fluency and provide the scaffolding necessary for student success.

Whenever possible, get students physically involved with the page. Many side-note questions invite students to use highlighters or colored pencils to circle, underline, or number key information. In addition, some students may find that using a small piece of cardboard or heavy construction paper helps to focus and guide their reading from one paragraph or page to the next.

Vary modes of instruction. To maintain student attention and interest, monitor and alternate the mode of instruction or activity. For example, alternate between teacher-facilitated and student-dominated reading activities. Assign brief amounts of text at a time, and alternate between oral, paired, and silent reading.

Monitor students' comprehension. As students use the side notes in the margins of the *Notebooks*, build in opportunities to ensure that students are on purpose and understanding. Consider structured brief conversations for students to share, compare, or explain their thinking. Then, use these conversations to praise the correct use of strategies or to redirect students who need further support. In addition, this is an excellent chance for you to reinforce students' use of the *Note-taking Guide* and provide models of effective study notes for students to emulate.

Reinforce the reading experience. When students read the selection for the first time, they may be working on the decoding level. If time allows, students should read the selection twice to achieve a greater fluency and comfort level.

APPLY THE SKILLS: Post-reading Activities

Invite reader response. Have students using the *Reader's Notebooks* complete the *Reader's Response* question following the selection.

Conduct a full-class discussion. When students have finished reviewing the selection—whether in the *Notebook* or in the grade-level textbook—include all students in your class in a post-reading analysis. To guide an initial discussion, use the *Respond* question in the *Thinking About the Selection* section in the textbook. You will find that questions such as the following examples will provide strong springboards for classroom interaction:

> **Respond:** What advice would you have given the mother and daughter? Why?
>
> **Respond:** What questions would you like to ask the writer about her experience?
>
> **Respond:** Do you find the boy's actions courageous, touching, or silly? Explain your response.

Encourage students to support their answers to these questions with evidence from the text or their own lives. In addition, invite students to respond appropriately to classmates' ideas. These questions will lead students from simply getting the gist of a selection to establishing a personal connection to the lesson content.

Direct student analysis with scaffolded questions. When you are ready to move students into more challenging critical thinking questions, have your average-achieving students use the instruction and questions in the grade-level textbook. Have students performing just at or one grade below reading level use the questions in the *Reader's Notebook*. Have struggling readers, special education students, special needs students, and English learners use the questions on the *Apply the Skills* page in the *Reader's Notebook Adapted Version* and *Reader's Notebook English Learner's Version*.

- Questions in the *Notebooks*, written in simpler language and providing more explicit support, will be more accessible to students currently achieving below grade level. Students will be able to apply concepts at their own level.

- Some special education or special needs students or English learners may be prepared to answer questions in the grade-level text. The two-part questions in the *Thinking About the Selection* section are written to build and support student analysis. For the first part of the question, students use lower-level thinking skills to identify information or to recall important details in a selection. For the second part, students use a higher-level thinking skill based on the answer to the first part.

Look at these examples of scaffolded questions from the grade-level textbooks:

(a) Recall: Why does the boy tell his father to leave the sickroom?
(b) Infer: What does this reveal about the boy?

(a) Recall: Why does the boy think he will die?
(b) Interpret: What is the meaning of the story's title?

Reinforce literary analysis and reading skills. Have students complete the *Literary Analysis* and *Reading Skills* questions on the *Apply the Skills* pages. Depending on the students' individual capabilities, determine whether students will use the questions in the grade-level textbook or the simplified versions in the *Notebooks*.

Reinforce writing, listening and speaking, or research and technology skills. Once students have completed the *Literary Analysis* and *Reading Skills* questions, assign the *Writing Lesson* and *Extend Your Learning* activities. Based on the activities presented in the grade-level text, the versions in the *Notebooks* provide guided, step-by-step support for students. By giving students supported opportunities to show their reading comprehension, writing, and listening and speaking or research and technology skills, you maintain reasonable expectations for their developing academic competence.

Model expectations. Make sure that students understand your assessment criteria in advance. Provide models of student work, whenever possible, for them to emulate, along with a non-model that fails to meet the specified assessment criteria. Do not provide exemplars that are clearly outside of their developmental range. Save student work that can later serve as a model for students with different levels of academic preparation.

Lead students to closure. To achieve closure, ask students to end the class session by writing three to five outcome statements about their experience in the day's lesson, expressing both new understandings and needs for clarification.

Encourage self-monitoring and self-assessment. Remember to provide safe opportunities for students to alert you to any learning challenges they are experiencing. Consider having students submit anonymous written questions (formulated either independently or with a partner) about confusing lesson content. Later, you can follow up on these points of confusion at the end of class or in the subsequent class session.

EXTEND Using the Student Edition

Present the unabridged selection for students who read the adapted version. Build in opportunities for students to read the full selection in the grade-level textbook. This will allow them to apply familiar concepts and vocabulary and stretch their literacy muscles.

Play an audio reading of the unabridged selection. Use the *Listening to Literature Audio CDs.* Students who read the adapted version may benefit from reading along while listening to a professional recording of the selection. Encourage students to use their fingertips to follow the words as they are read.

Revisit and reinforce strategies. Recycle pre- and post-reading tasks regularly so that students can become more familiar with the task process and improve their performance. If they are constantly facing curricular novelty, special education and special needs students never have the opportunity to refine their skills and demonstrate improved competence. For example, if you ask them to identify a personality trait of an essential character in a story and then support this observation with relevant details in an expository paragraph, it would make sense to have them write a similar paragraph in the near future about another character.

Show students how to transfer skills. Consider ways in which students can transfer knowledge and skills gleaned from one assignment/lesson to a subsequent lesson. For example, discuss with students the ways in which they can apply new vocabulary and language strategies outside of the classroom. In addition, demonstrate the applicability of new reading and writing strategies to real-world literacy tasks. Include periodic writing tasks for an authentic audience other than the teacher, such as another class, fellow classmates, local businesses, family, etc.

Offer praise and encourage growth. Praise students' efforts to experiment with new language in class, both in writing and in speaking.

Reading Informational Materials

The *Reader's Notebook*, the *Reader's Notebook Adapted Version*, and the *Reader's Notebook English Learner's Version* present unabridged versions of all of the Reading Informational Materials features from the student book. As with other selections, questions prompt students to interact with the text in a variety of ways, helping them gain competence in reading informational materials such as newspaper articles, business documents, and product directions and warranties.

The prereading page for each selection previews the type of informational material in the lesson and presents the reading skill that is addressed in the student edition.

The selection pages include many of the same types of side notes that appear with other selections. Additional **Reading Informational Materials** notes focus on specific features of informational materials.

In the *Reader's Notebooks*, an **Apply the Skills** page follows each selection. This page provides additional support for students by focusing on reading comprehension, reading skills, and timed writing activities.

Part 2: Helping Students Use the Turbo Vocabulary Pages

The Turbo Vocabulary pages are located in Part 2 at the end of each *Notebook*. These pages provide ways for students to work with the vocabulary in the selections and to record new vocabulary words they come across in their reading. The Turbo Vocabulary section contains the following types of worksheets.

Word Roots, Prefixes, and Suffixes

Two-page charts give roots, prefixes, and suffixes that will help students improve their vocabulary. The chart gives the meaning of the word part and an example. Space is provided in the chart for students to write in other word parts that they come across in their reading. Point out to students words that contain these word parts as you read in class.

Using a Dictionary

These pages teach students how to read a dictionary entry. Practice working with dictionary entries is provided.

Word Study Cards

Use these word study cards to break big words into their parts. One card is filled out as an example and the rest are blank for students to write in words they want to examine more closely. Make sure that the words students choose to break down can be broken down. Help students choose words with meaningful prefixes and suffixes.

Academic Vocabulary Words

The *Reader's Notebook* lists ten academic vocabulary words for each unit. The *Adapted* and the *English Learner's* versions list five words for each unit. Exercises are provided that will help students learn to spell and use the academic vocabulary words. Most units have a place where students can write other academic words that they come across in their reading. Make sure that students pick high-use academic words to add to their lists.

Words in Other Subjects

This page provides students with a place to write down academic words that they come across in other subjects. Many academic words can be used across disciplines. Help students record and define important words for study in other subjects. An example sentence will help reinforce the meaning.

Vocabulary Flash Cards

The first set of these cards gives Vocabulary Builder words from Unit 1. The front of the card shows the word. The back shows the definition, the part of speech, and an example sentence. Students should use the blank cards provided to study words from other units. Students can test themselves using these cards or test each other.

Vocabulary Fold-A-List

The first list uses Vocabulary Builder words from Unit 1. Students can test themselves by filling in the definition of each word and then folding the paper over to check their definitions. The other side of the list provides definitions for which students can fill in the appropriate words. Once again, by folding the paper over, they can check their answers. Blank Vocabulary Fold-A-List pages are provided for studying words in other units.

Commonly Misspelled Words

The words listed on these pages cause problems for many people. You may wish to assign some of the words to be studied with flash cards or fold-a-lists. The pages can also serve as a reference for students to look up words before writing them. Blanks are provided on the second page for students to add words that they frequently misspell.

Word Attack Skills

This section helps students to look for vowel-consonant patterns in words. Learning these patterns will enable to students to read longer words. Guide students to find the appropriate patterns to fill in the chart.

Mnemonics

Mnemonic devices can be very helpful in remembering how to spell words. They can also aid in remembering meaning. Work with students to make up mnemonic devices for words they have trouble with. Divide students into groups so that they can work together to create mnemonic devices.

Communication Strategies (*Adapted* and *English Learner's Versions*)

Learning how to communicate in a classroom setting does not come naturally to most students. Give them these sentence starters and phrases to help them discuss more effectively. Prompt students to use these phrases when answering or asking questions so that they become more natural.

Idioms (*English Learner's Version*)

An idiom is one of the hardest things for a non-native speaker to learn in a foreign language. Point out idioms in the readings for your English Learner students. Have them record and write sample sentences for the idioms in the chart provided.

Vocabulary Bookmarks

Students can cut out these bookmarks and use them to mark their place in their reading. They should record unfamiliar words that they come across on the bookmarks. Students can review those words using Flash Cards or Fold-A-Lists.

Vocabulary Builder Cards

These pages provide a place for students to record new vocabulary words that they encounter in the selections. Remind students to use these pages. Periodically, you may want to allow volunteers to share original sentences that contain the vocabulary words they have chosen.

ANSWERS TO UNIT 1

"The Three-Century Woman"
Richard Peck

"The Fall of the Hindenburg"
Michael Morrison

p. 4 Note-taking Guide
Sample response:
Setting: The setting is Whispering Oaks Elder Care Facility, New Year's Day 2001.
Narrator: The narrator is a young girl named Megan.
Events of the Plot: Media people want to interview Great-grandma Breckenridge; Great-grandma allows them to come into her room; she makes up stories about her life, including ones about having lived through the San Francisco earthquake and the Hindenburg disaster; the news team leaves, and Great-grandma admits to having learned her facts by reading.
Ending: In the end, Megan feels new appreciation for her great-grandmother.

p. 5 Activate Prior Knowledge
Some students might say that the stories are boring and always the same. Other students might say that they enjoy the stories because they like to learn about life in the past.

p. 5 Fiction
Students should circle "We were heading for Whispering Oaks to see my great-grandmother Breckenridge, who's lived there since I was a little girl."

p. 5 Fiction
Sample response: Facts about Great-grandmother Breckenridge include that she lives at Whispering Oaks, that she has lived there since the narrator was a little girl, and that she was born in 1899.

p. 6 Fiction
Students should circle the words "I" and "we."

p. 6 Fiction
Mom is upset; she does not want the news reporters to interview Great-grandma.

p. 6 Reading Check
Students should underline "camera crews" and "woman from the suburban newspaper" or "the newspaperwoman."

p. 7 Stop to Reflect
Sample response: No. Aunt Gloria is wrong. Great-grandma is aware of her surroundings. She seems bright and alert. She makes a joke by saying, "At least you know who you are. Plenty around this place don't."

p. 7 Fiction
Sample response: The TV anchor is interviewing Great-grandma.

p. 7 Reading Check
Students should circle, "Nothing to it," and "Let's do this in one take."

p. 8 Fiction
Sample response: Megan's mom seems nervous, perhaps because she is unsure of what Great-grandma Breckenridge will say next.

p. 8 Fiction
Sample response: Yes. The narrator notices that "a tiny smile played around Great-grandma's wrinkled lips."

p. 8 Reading Check
Students should circle "the San Francisco earthquake."

p. 9 Fiction
Students should circle "Mom moaned, and the cameraman was practically standing on his head for a close-up."

p. 9 Stop to Reflect
Sample response: "Standing on his head" means that the cameraman is so excited about getting a good shot that he has positioned himself very uncomfortably to see Great-grandma.

p. 9 Fiction
Sample response: Great-grandma is in control of the interview. She is giving the anchor the story he wants and playing to the camera.

p. 9 Reading Check
Students may circle "the Hindenburg when it blew up" or any other reference on the page to the Hindenburg disaster.

p. 10 Stop to Reflect
Sample response: Mom's words tell that the stories are made up. Great-grandma has not actually experienced the events she recalls.

p. 10 Fiction
Sample response: People can be clever and have a sense of humor, no matter what their age.

p. 10 Stop to Reflect
Sample response: In some ways, Great-grandma thinks the future will be negative. She tells the reporter that taxes will be higher. In other ways, Great-grandma thinks the future will be positive because more people will live longer.

p. 11 Stop to Reflect
Sample response: Great-grandma asks all of the questions, and she makes the decision to throw out the suburban newspaperwoman.

p. 11 Fiction
Sample response: "The Three-Century Woman" is a short story because it tells a made-up series of events. All of the action is contained in a few pages, rather than in many chapters.

p. 11 Reading Check
Students should circle "No, but I can read" and "You can pick up all that stuff in books."

p. 12 Fiction
Sample response: Great-grandma's lesson is that older people should not be stereotyped, and they should be valued.

p. 12 Stop to Reflect
Sample response: Megan loves her Great-grandma and enjoys being with her. An example from the text is, "But I felt like giving her a kiss on her little wrinkled cheek, so I did."

p. 12 Reader's Response
Students may like the way Great-grandma "directed" the interview, which went the way she wanted it to go. She played with the newspeople and had her own kind of fun with them.

p. 13 Note-taking Guide
Sample response:
Where: The Hindenburg disaster took place in Lakehurst, New Jersey.
What Happened: Thirty-five people on board and one ground crewperson died; people have tried to learn what caused the disaster, but the cause is still uncertain.
Why: The cause may have been the varnish on the fabric on the outside of the vessel.

p. 14 Activate Prior Knowledge
Sample response: The German-built *Hindenburg* was a huge gas balloon called a zeppelin. It exploded just as it was landing in New Jersey.

p. 14 Nonfiction
The work deals with the Hindenburg disaster. Herb Morrison, a radio reporter, is the real person discussed in the work.

p. 14 Nonfiction
Sample response: This is an article because it is about an event, and it presents facts, details, and other true information.

p. 14 Reading Check
Students should circle "Frankfurt, Germany."

p. 15 Nonfiction
Sample response: The Nazi party in Germany was becoming an enemy of the United States at the time of the Hindenburg disaster.

p. 15 Stop to Reflect
Sample response: The Hindenburg is so famous because it was the subject of tragedy and because the cause of the disaster is still uncertain.

p. 15 Reader's Response
Students may describe people running around and panicking, the smell and heat from the flames, and the terrible noises coming from the explosion and the screams of people.

p. 16 Apply the Skills
1. Sample response: Yes, she is very lively and interesting. She has a sense of humor. She knows how to have fun. She also knows a lot of stories.

2. Graphic Organizer

Sample response:

Her Comments: "Let's do this in one take"; "Last night I fell off the bed pan"; "I was on the Hindenburg when it blew up, you know."

Her Character: She is in control; she has a sense of humor; she makes up stories.

Message/Theme: Older people like Great-grandma can have a lively imagination and a great sense of humor.

3. Sample response: It has made-up characters and some made-up events. It has a narrator who is a character inside the story. It has a series of events that make up a plot. It has a theme.

4. Sample response: The fictional account is much shorter, contains far fewer facts and details, and has some made-up information. The nonfiction article consists only of details about what really happened and who was really there.

"Papa's Parrot"
Cynthia Rylant

"mk"
Jean Fritz

p. 18 Graphic Organizer

Sample response:

"Papa's Parrot"

Beginning: Harry and his friends stop going to Papa's store.

Middle: Papa buys a parrot.

End: Harry realizes that Papa missed seeing him at the store.

"mk"

Beginning: Jean finishes sixth grade at the British School in Wuhan.

Middle: Jean goes to the Shanghai American School.

End: Jean moves to America. She goes to a school in America for the first time.

p. 19 Reading/Writing Connection

Sample response:

1. Age might help a teenager appreciate any extra time that he or she has.

2. He or she might learn to react more calmly to problems.

3. A more mature person might be more likely to act in a responsible way.

p. 19 Note-taking Guide

Sample response:

Before Harry Starts Junior High: Harry brings his friends to visit the store and to eat nuts and candy.

After Harry Starts Junior High: His father embarrasses Harry by talking to the parrot.

After Harry's Father Gets Sick: Through the parrot, Harry realizes how much his father misses him; Harry decides to spend more time with his father.

p. 20 Activate Prior Knowledge

Students may say that their feelings for someone close to them changed after they had an argument with that person. They no longer felt as close to that person after the fight.

p. 20 Reading Skill

Students should circle the phrase, "people with whom you enjoy spending time" and the sentence "Mr. Tillian looked forward to seeing his son and his son's friends every day."

p. 20 Literary Analysis

Sample response: Harry and his friends like the kinds of things that real kids of that age enjoy.

p. 21 Stop to Reflect

Sample response: Harry had fun with his father at home because he was not embarrassed to be with him there. Seeing his father talking to a parrot embarrassed Harry, so Harry did not want people to see him in his father's store.

p. 21 Reading Skill

Sample response: The detail that Harry and his Mr. Tillian joked with each other shows that "teasing" can mean joking around in a gentle or nice way.

p. 21 Literary Analysis

Sample response: Early in the story, Harry is young and spends a great deal of time with his father. Now that Harry is older, he spends his time doing other things. His father now embarrasses Harry.

p. 21 Reading Check

Students should circle this text "Harry told his father that he would go to the store every day after school and unpack boxes. He would sort out all the candy and nuts. He would even feed Rocky."

p. 22 Literary Analysis

Sample response: If Harry had not forgotten about the bird, he would not have been scared by it. If Harry had not been scared, he might not have listened to what the bird was saying.

p. 22 Stop to Reflect

Sample response: 1. Rocky asks where Harry is. This means that Harry does not come to the store often. 2. Rocky repeats Harry's insult. This shows that Harry can be mean when he is frightened or embarrassed by something.

p. 22 Reading Check

Students should circle this sentence: "Harry jumped, spilling a box of jawbreakers."

p. 23 Literary Analysis

Sample response: Harry realizes that his father misses him. The problem between father and son is about to be resolved.

p. 23 Stop to Reflect

Some students may say that Harry should tell his father what happened with Rocky. Harry can say that he now knows how much his father misses him.

p. 23 Reading Check

Students should circle this sentence: "Then he left to go visit his papa."

p. 23 Reader's Response

Some students may think that Harry will change the way he thinks about his father because he understands why his father talks to the parrot. Harry will probably also spend more time with his father. His father may embarrass him less. He could realize that his actions have hurt his father.

p. 24 Apply the Skills

1. Sample response: Harry and friends are interested in things such as video games. They are no longer interested in candy.
2. Sample response: Mr. Tillian buys Rocky because he is lonely; Harry and his friends no longer visit at the store.
3. **Graphic Organizer**
Sample response:
Context Clues: on his way somewhere else; walking.
Possible Meaning: *Stroll* might mean "to walk slowly."

Context Clues: "so the bird wouldn't get cold."
Possible Meaning: A *furnace* might be a machine that produces heat.

p. 26 Reading/Writing Connection

Sample response:
1. Kids in other countries might imitate American styles of clothing.
2. People overseas often observe things that people in America do not see.
3. Living in another country would allow a person to explore that country's natural wonders.

p. 26 Note-taking Guide

Sample response:
Character's Name: Jean
What Character Says: Jean "talks" to Priscilla about hardships. Jean says, "I always felt a tingling when I saw the American flag flying over the American consulate."
What Character Thinks: Jean thinks that the Shanghai American school will help her feel more American. Jean thinks that American children are ignorant.
What Character Does: Jean is shy and sensitive. She keeps the name of her hometown a secret so that the other students won't laugh at it.
What Others Say about Character: Mrs. Barrett asks whether Jean is all grown up. Fletcher says that Jean is pretty. Paula, the American roommate, says that Jean looks like an MK.

p. 27 Apply the Skills

1. Sample response: The school is not exactly as Jean thinks it will be. She does not get a tingling feeling from the flag when she walks into the school. She does not feel more American at the school. She does enjoy the tea dances, though.
2. Sample response: Both Jean and Priscilla look forward to a new life in America. They are excited and interested in learning about America.
3. **Graphic Organizer**
Sample response:
Context Clues: "more than a tingling"
Possible Meaning: *Overwhelm* might mean "overpower."

4. Sample response: A narrative is any type of writing that tells a story. It can be fiction or nonfiction, and it is often told in chronological order. "MK" is a nonfiction story told in chronological order.

Reading Informational Materials: Reference Materials

p. 32 Apply the Skills
Thinking About the Reference Material
1. Sample response: The climate, landscape, and soil are better in the eastern area than in the other parts of the country. That area is also closer to the East China Sea.
2. Shanghai is located on the east coast of China. It touches the East China Sea. Jiaxing and Wuxi are near Shanghai.

Reading Skill
3. Sample response: A *booming* economy is one that is thriving. The context clue is that Taiwan "exports its products around the world."
4. The context clue is an example: Exporting is one reason that the economy is thriving.

from An American Childhood
Annie Dillard

"The Luckiest Time of All"
Lucille Clifton

p. 33 Graphic Organizer
Sample response:
from An American Childhood
Unfamiliar Word in Context: Any normal adult would have quit, having *sprung* us into flight and made his point.
Word's Function in Sentence: *Sprung* is a verb that describes what happens to Dillard and her friends.
Meaning of Word: *Sprung* probably means "thrown" or "hurled."

"The Luckiest Time of All"
Unfamiliar Word in Context: Her grand-daughter brought her a big bunch of dogwood blooms.
Word's Function in Sentence: Dogwood is the name of the blossoms.
Meaning of Word: Dogwood is probably a type of tree, shrub, or plant.

p. 34 Reading/Writing Connection
Sample response:
1. I have always enjoyed the <u>challenge</u> of building something new.
2. It will be hard to win the game unless I <u>exert</u> all my energy.
3. Sometimes I <u>exceed</u> my own goals.

p. 34 Note-taking Guide
Sample response:
Conflict: The driver wants to teach the children a lesson. The children want to escape.
Climax: An angry driver chases Dillard and her friends.
Second Event: The driver catches Dillard and Mikey.
Third Event: The driver lectures Dillard and Mikey.
Resolution: Dillard is excited that she had to try so hard to get away.

p. 35 Activate Prior Knowledge
Students may describe a time when they played a certain sport or performed well in a play. Because they really enjoyed the activity, they wanted to perform to the best of their ability.

p. 35 Literary Analysis
Students should underline this sentence: "Some boys taught me to play football."

p. 35 Reading Check
Students should circle " . . . so the boys and I threw snowballs at passing cars."

p. 36 Reading Skill
Sample response: 1. The words, "I started making an iceball" suggest the meaning of *embarked.* 2. The word *started* means "to have begun something." So, *embarked* means "started" or "began."

p. 36 Literary Analysis
Students should circle four instances of "us," two of "we," one of "I," and one "our."

p. 36 Reading Check
Students should underline ". . . the only time in all of life, the car pulled over and stopped. Its wide black door opened; a man got out of it, running."

p. 37 Literary Analysis
Sample response: The narrative is told from the first-person point of view. Only the narrator's thoughts are known.

p. 37 Stop to Reflect

Sample response: He knows that you have to fling yourself at what you are doing. You have to forge ahead and complete your task.

p. 37 Reading Skill

Students may draw a box around "simultaneously." They should circle "We kept running . . . we kept improvising."

p. 37 Reading Check

Students should underline "The driver of the Buick sensibly picked the two of us to follow."

p. 38 Literary Analysis

Students should underline "I was cherishing my excitement." Dillard seems to be happy rather than upset or afraid; this is not the reaction many students might have expected.

p. 38 Reading Skill

Students should draw a box around "redundant." Students should circle "a mere formality" and "beside the point."

p. 38 Reading Check

Students might underline "I wanted the glory to last forever."

p. 39 Reading Check

Students should underline "skinny" and "red-headed."

p. 39 Stop to Reflect

Sample response: She has done something that required her to use everything she had. She is thrilled from the effort.

p. 39 Reader's Response

Many students will say they would like to have Dillard as a friend because she would be fun to be with. She is enthusiastic and positive.

p. 40 Apply the Skills

1. Sample response: Dillard admires his commitment to flinging himself into the chase and not giving up.
2. Sample response: The words "redundant, a mere formality, and beside the point" suggest the meaning of *perfunctorily*.
3. Sample response: It could mean "without excitement."
4. **Graphic Organizer**
Sample response:
Situation: The author describes playing football with the boys.

Thoughts or Feelings: She says that "Nothing girls did could compare with it." She feels that throwing herself completely into a task is more fun than playing as the girls do.
Situation: The man from the Buick yells at her and Mikey.
Thoughts or Feelings: She wants "the glory to last forever." She thinks that being pursued by a grown-up who throws himself into the chase is glorious.

p. 42 Reading/Writing Connection

Sample response: Many people define luck as good fortune. Many of us cannot interpret right away whether an event will bring good luck. We may need to wait for the outcome of an event to confirm whether or not the event was lucky.

p. 42 Note-taking Guide

Sample response:
Cause: Elzie goes to the show.
Effect/Cause: Elzie throws her lucky rock at the dancing dog.
Effect/Cause: The dog chases Elzie.
Effect/Cause: A young man chases the dog.
Effect/Cause: Elzie and the man meet.
Effect: The man later marries Elzie.

p. 43 Apply the Skills

1. Sample response: Elzie seems to be looking for adventure.
2. Sample response: Mr. Pickens saves Elzie from the dog and checks the dog to see whether it is hurt.
3. Sample response: *Lit out* may mean "to chase or run at top speed."
4. Sample response: Context clues are "I flew," "Round and round we run," and "a runnin dog."

5. **Graphic Organizer**
Sample response:
Situation: Elzie goes to the show.
Thoughts or Feelings: She feels adventurous.
Situation: Elzie meets a man who helps her.
Thoughts or Feelings: She feels lucky.

"All Summer in a Day"
Ray Bradbury

"Suzy and Leah"
Jane Yolen

p. 45 Graphic Organizer
Sample response:
"All Summer in a Day"
Entertain: ". . . the gigantic sound of the rain . . ."
Teach: "A thousand forests had been crushed under the rain and grown up a thousand times to be crushed again."
Reflect: "The silence was so immense and unbelievable that you felt your ears had been stuffed. . . ."

"Suzy and Leah"
Entertain: The story is told entirely through diary entries.
Teach: It is wrong to judge others.
Reflect: Suzy's comments in her diary show how comfortable her life has been, compared with Leah's life.

p. 46 Reading/Writing Connection
Sample response: I don't know whether I could survive in a rainy climate. It would require that I adjust to losing many things that I love. I am sure that there is some benefit to living in a rainy climate, but I don't know what it is!

p. 46 Note-taking Guide
Sample response:
What Happens: 2. Margot writes a poem. 3. Margot refuses to play games with the other children. 4. The sun shines.
What is the Result? 2. William says that Margot did not write the poem. 3. Margot does not have many friends. 4. The children laugh and play.

p. 47 Apply the Skills
1. Sample response: The children have never seen the sun. They cannot imagine how it feels or why Margot misses it.
2. Sample response: The children go along because they do not feel that Margot is one of them. They may feel less responsibility because the prank is William's idea.
3. Sample response: The author's main purpose is to show that people can be cruel and that we should think carefully about what we do.

4. Sample response: The rain on Venus makes the story sad and dark. The mood is happier when the sun comes out. If the story were set on Earth, the conflict would not be about the weather or the sun.
5. **Graphic Organizer**
Sample response:
Setting: 1. Venus is sunless. 2. Venus is sun-filled.
Character's Mood: 1. Margot is sad. 2. The sun makes the children happy.

p. 49 Reading/Writing Connection
Sample response: To communicate with others might be difficult in a new country. The person would have to adapt to a new language and a different culture. It might be hard to participate in activities and events in a strange country.

p. 49 Note-taking Guide
Sample response:
Leah Beginning: Leah says that Suzy has a "false smile," makes her feel terror, and treats her "like a pet." She says that Suzy laughed at Leah's friend, has a meaningless name, and "wants to feed [Leah] like an animal."
Leah End: Leah says that Suzy is friendly, honest, generous, and understanding.
Suzy Beginning: Suzy says that Leah is strange, "prickly as a porcupine," unfriendly, stuck-up, and mean. Suzy also says that Leah never smiles, has a permanent frown, doesn't eat enough, has a funny accent, and knows nothing about America.
Suzy End: Suzy says that Leah is strong, has been through a lot, and is scared rather than stuck-up. Suzy thinks that she and Leah might yet be able to become friends.

p. 50 Activate Prior Knowledge
Students may name themselves, friends, or family members as people who keep diaries. One famous person who kept a diary was Anne Frank.

p. 50 Literary Analysis
Students may underline any of the following details: ". . . ugly," "A line of rickety wooden buildings," "a fence lots higher than my head," "With barbed wire on top," and "all those kids just swarmed over to the fence, grabbing."

p. 50 Reading Check

Students should underline "two candy bars" or "sweets."

p. 51 Stop to Reflect

Students may realize that the refugee children probably do not recognize oranges. Students may suggest that it was wrong for Suzy to laugh. They may also suggest that she should be more understanding.

p. 51 Reading Skill

Sample response: These details help the author teach readers. The details show that Leah was not always a refugee. She had a happy life before the war.

p. 51 Literary Analysis

Sample response: Leah was used to a pleasant life, perhaps on a farm, with her family and plenty of good food to eat.

p. 52 Literary Analysis

Students may underline any of the following passages: "there you and baby Natan were killed"; "he was hidden away in a cupboard by his grandmother who was taken by the Nazis"; and "he was almost three days in that cupboard without food, without water, without words to comfort him."

p. 52 Stop to Reflect

Sample response: Avi stopped speaking when his grandmother hid him from the Nazis. He stayed in a cupboard for three days without food and water and without words to comfort him. He did not speak again.

p. 52 Reading Skill

Sample response: The detail helps readers reflect on Leah's situation. In the refugee camp, she is still behind barbed wire. Because she cannot speak English, she feels that she is fenced in another way, too.

p. 53 Reading Skill

Sample response: The author wants readers to reflect on how Suzy and Leah are different and how they are alike. The two girls are connected because Leah is wearing Suzy's dress.

p. 53 Literary Analysis

Sample response: Leah's setting is strange because the school is new to her, and it is the first time she has gone to school with boys.

p. 53 Reading Check

Students should circle "They even had hair bows, gifts from the teachers."

p. 54 Reading Skill

Sample response: Leah calls Suzy "the yellow-haired girl." This name shows how different Suzy and Leah are from each other.

p. 54 Stop to Reflect

Sample response: Leah is not a grouch, but she sometimes seems that way because her experiences have made her cautious and quiet.

p. 54 Reading Check

Students should underline the following sentences: "I wish she would wear another dress." "I wish I had another dress." "I wish I had a different student helping me and not the yellow-haired girl." "I wish Mr. Forest would let me trade."

p. 55 Literary Analysis

Sample response: The village is a very important place for Leah. She is proud to be from there, and she is proud of her family's history there. This is an important setting for Leah.

p. 55 Reading Skill

Sample response: The author wants to teach readers about the terrible experiences Leah has lived through and to show how Leah is skeptical and afraid of people. Leah feels certain that people will not continue to be nice to her. The author also wants to show that people can survive terrible experiences, as Leah did.

p. 55 Literary Analysis

Students should mark the following passages: "I wonder if she eats enough." "And she saves the school lunch in her napkin, hiding it away in her pocket." "I'm sure they get dinner at the shelter." "Mom says we have to eat everything on our plates."

p. 56 Reading Skill

Students may underline any of the following passages: "Leah knows a lot about the world and nothing about America," "She thinks New York is right next to Chicago," "She can't dance at all," "She doesn't know the words to any of the top songs," and "she only talks in class to answer questions." These details point out that Leah does not know as much about America and its culture as Suzy does. Suzy is more outgoing and confident than Leah is in her surroundings.

p. 56 Literary Analysis
Sample response: Suzy's mother reminds Leah of her own mother the last time Leah saw her. Leah has to "steel her heart" because she is afraid of loving Suzy's mother. If she loves Suzy's mother, she might forget about her own.

p. 56 Reading Check
Students should underline the following sentences: "Avi loves the food I bring home from school."

p. 57 Reading Skill
Sample response: The author includes this detail to show how much Leah misses her little brother, Natan.

p. 57 Stop to Reflect
Sample response: Leah probably didn't tell anyone she was sick because she was afraid. She might have been afraid to admit she was weak in any way. Maybe she was afraid she would be punished for being sick.

p. 57 Reading Check
Students should circle "She had to have her appendix out and nearly died."

p. 58 Reading Skill
Students should underline the following passages: "the Nazis killed people. . . . in places called concentration camps" and "all the Jews . . . had to wear yellow stars on their clothes."

p. 58 Literary Analysis
Sample response: Germany during the war is a very important part of the story. German leaders and their followers had done terrible things to people, especially the Jews, during World War II. Leah's mother and brother were killed in German concentration camps. The setting is part of the conflict because it is a secret that Suzy does not understand until now.

p. 58 Stop to Reflect
Sample response: Avi helps Leah by telling the guards that she is sick. His action is important because he saves Leah's life. It's also important because it's the first time that Avi speaks aloud to anyone but Leah.

p. 59 Reading Skill
Students may say that the author has young people tell the story because they can reach young readers. A young American like Suzy might not know what happened in Europe during World War II. A young refugee like Leah would not know about America. Readers learn along with the characters.

p. 59 Reading Check
Students should underline "diary."

p. 59 Reader's Response
Students may say that they would welcome people from other cultures into their homes, invite them to play sports and other games, share meals with them, or take them to American movies.

p. 60 Apply the Skills
1. Sample response: Suzy has lived a comfortable, sheltered life. She does not like Leah because Leah is strange to her.
2. Sample response: Leah has survived a terrible experience. She is afraid of strangers. She detects Suzy's "false smile." Leah is afraid to be Suzy's friend.
3. Sample response: One of the author's purposes is to teach people about what happened to the Jews in Germany when the Nazis were in control.
4. **Graphic Organizer**
Sample response:
Setting: Leah is in a refugee camp.
Character's Mood: Leah feels afraid and suspicious.
Setting: Suzy visits Leah in the hospital.
Character's Mood: Suzy is sorrowful and friendly.

"My First Free Summer"
Julia Alvarez

"My Furthest-Back Person"
(The Inspiration for *Roots*)
Alex Haley

p. 62 Graphic Organizer
Sample response:
"My First Free Summer"
What I Know About the Author: She spent her early life in the Dominican Republic. Words make her feel "complete."

What I Know About the Topic: The Dominican Republic was ruled by a dictator for thirty-one years. Many families fled the country during a rebellion.

Author's Purpose: The author writes to describe a personal experience.

"My Furthest-Back Person"

What I Know About the Author: He grew up hearing stories about his family's history. He later wrote a book about his family's past.

What I Know About the Topic: Slavery is part of the history of the United States and of parts of Africa.

Author's Purpose: The author writes to describe a personal experience.

p. 63 Reading/Writing Connection

Sample response: Most people would respond to this news with complaints or grumbling. A person might react by feeling sad or upset. It would take time and effort to adjust.

p. 63 Note-taking Guide

Sample response:

Conflict: Julia does not want to learn English.

Event: Julia goes to summer school.

Event: Julia decides to try harder to learn English.

Event: Julia and her family try to leave the country.

p. 64 Activate Prior Knowledge

Students should describe at least one positive experience and at least one negative or disappointing experience. Positive experiences could include taking trips with their families, making new friends, or learning a new sport or hobby. Disappointments could include being bored or being required to do something they don't enjoy. Students who have been to summer school may describe it as a disappointment—or as a positive experience.

p. 64 Literary Analysis

Students should underline this sentence: "For thirty years, the Dominican Republic had endured a bloody and repressive dictatorship."

p. 64 Reading Check

Students should circle "my friends . . . were often on holiday to honor the dictator's birthday, the dictator's saint day . . . the day the dictator's oldest son was born, and so on."

p. 65 Reading Skill

Sample response: The author's purpose is to add humor by including funny details here, such as the "funny witch hats" and the "picture of a man wearing a silly wig." The humor helps illustrate the narrator's frustration with summer school.

p. 65 Literary Analysis

Sample response: Most Dominicans have to go to Dominican schools, but Julia is one of the few Dominicans who goes to an American school.

p. 65 Reading Check

Students should circle "my grandmother."

p. 66 Literary Analysis

Students should underline the sentence, "The plot had unraveled" or "Every day there were massive arrests."

p. 66 Stop to Reflect

Sample response: Julia is not enjoying her summer. She says that all of her friends are gone and she has no one to play with. She says that even summer school would be better than this kind of freedom.

p. 66 Reading Skill

Students should recall that Julia doesn't think she needs to learn English. Her mother can stop Julia's questioning and complaining just by giving her a sharp look. Knowing this, students may say that Julia's mother is giving her a look that says, "Just do as I say and don't ask questions."

p. 67 Reading Skill

Sample response: The author does not tell what happens to those people because what happens to them is a mystery. That mystery shows how dangerous the situation is.

p. 67 Literary Analysis

Sample response: By sharing these facts about the dictator, Julia reveals that her whole family is in great danger. The danger of being taken away by the secret police and led to an unknown fate builds the tension of the scene.

p. 67 Reading Check

Students should underline the sentences: "Freedom and liberty and justice for all . . . I knew that ours was not a trip, but an escape. We had to get to the United States."

p. 68 Reading Skill

Sample response: Julia has learned to speak English and to be an eager student, so she says "Yes, sir!" to the American official. She is also eager to answer the official because she is afraid of being sent back. The scene shows that the author's purpose is to show that Julia's family is afraid of being sent back to the Dominican Republic. They escape to America in order to save their lives. The author also wants to show that learning and school are part of being free.

p. 68 Reading Check

Students should underline "'Welcome to the United States,' he said with a smile."

p. 68 Reader's Response

Most students will say they were surprised by the family's experience. Many students will not be aware that people in countries such as the Dominican Republic could not just leave when they wanted to. For these students, the details will be new and unexpected.

p. 69 Apply the Skills

1. Sample response: The American school teaches English and American history. The other schools on the island teach about the dictator and have many days off in honor of the dictator.
2. Sample response: Julia improves her attitude. She improves her English. She becomes more attentive and cooperative in class.
3. Sample response: The author is sharing information about the Dominican Republic as it was during the time when the author was growing up. The author's family left the country during this time.
4. **Graphic Organizer**
Sample response:
Author's Actions: 2. Packs her things and prepares to leave the country

p. 71 Reading/Writing Connection

Sample response:
1. Many people want to acquire information about their ancestors.
2. They want to identify their roots.
3. They are curious about the circumstances surrounding major events in their family history.

p. 71 Note-taking Guide

Sample response:
What: Haley found the names of his relatives in census records from just after the Civil War.
Whom: Haley told his cousin, Georgia Anderson, who used to tell him stories about his ancestors.
Why: Haley thought that Dr. Vansina might know where in Africa Haley's ancestors came from.
Where: Haley went to a village in Gambia to hear the *griot*.
How: Haley linked the *griot's* tale to his family history through certain details that were common to both stories.

p. 72 Apply the Skills

1. Sample response: Both the sounds and the writing had to be translated. The African sounds in Haley's family were spoken; the words on the Rosetta Stone were written.
2. Sample response: The *griot* tells what happened before Kunte Kinte left Africa. Haley's family stories begin after Kunta Kinte's arrival in America. Together, these stories complete the family history.
3. Sample response: The author's purpose is to tell the story of his ancestor, who was one of the many Africans brought to America as slaves.
4. Sample response: Haley searches for his family's African roots.

Reading Informational Materials: Web Sites

p. 77 Apply the Skills
Thinking About the Web Site

1. Sample response: The *About Us* link on the home page and the *Biography of John Carlin* link on the Welcome page should lead to more information about NARA and its director.
2. Sample response: Clicking on the links to related government Web sites should lead to sites with similar information.

Reading Skill

3. Sample response: The purpose of the NARA Welcome page is to persuade readers to make use of the documents that NARA provides.
4. Sample response: The purpose of this Web site might be to inform people about the history and development of airplanes.

ANSWERS TO UNIT 2

"The Treasure of Lemon Brown"
Walter Dean Myers

p. 80 Note-taking Guide
Sample response:
Event: The bad men go after Lemon Brown.
Event: Lemon Brown tells Greg about his treasure.
Event: Greg understands a new meaning for treasure.
Climax: Lemon Brown and Greg scare off the men.
Resolution: Greg goes home with a better understanding of his father.
Conflict: Greg cannot accept what his father has to say.

p. 81 Activate Prior Knowledge
Students may write about a time when their parents were upset with them but were really just concerned about their safety.

p. 81 Short Story
Students should underline "Greg" and "his father." Greg is remembering the time when he asked to play ball with the Scorpions. Greg's father had said it depended on Greg's next report card.

p. 81 Short Story
Sample response: Greg and his father have trouble understanding one another. This fact may relate to a theme about getting along in families.

p. 82 Stop to Reflect
Students may circle words such as "graffiti-scarred," and "grim shadows." Students may say that they would not enter because it does not look safe.

p. 82 Short Story
Sample response:
Characters: Greg and his father
Time: The story takes place at night.
Place: The story takes place inside an old tenement building.

p. 82 Reading Check
Students should underline "He stood up to go upstairs, thought of the lecture that probably awaited him if he did anything except shut himself in his room with his math book, and started walking down the street instead."

p. 83 Short Story
Sample response: Someone else will be in the building with Greg.

p. 83 Short Story
Students should underline the words "Don't" and "nothin.'"

p. 83 Stop to Reflect
A razor that could cut a week into nine days would be very sharp. A week is only seven days long. It would take something very sharp to cut a week that precisely.

p. 84 Short Story
Students may underline "old man"; "black, heavily crinkled face"; "halo of crinkly white hair and whiskers"; "layers of dirty coats"; "smallish frame"; "pants were bagged to the knee"; "rags that went down to the old shoes"; "rope around his middle"; "picking through the trash"; and "pulling clothes out of a Salvation Army box." These examples are direct characterization because they describe how Lemon Brown looks and acts.

p. 84 Stop to Reflect
Sample response: Lemon Brown is probably a homeless person. The building is supposed to be empty, but it would give Brown a place to sleep that is out of the rain.

p. 84 Reading Check
Students should circle "He had seen the man before, picking through the trash on the corner and pulling clothes out of a Salvation Army box."

p. 85 Short Story
Sample response: Lemon Brown means that hard times are just an ordinary part of life.

p. 85 Stop to Reflect
Sample response: Lemon Brown at first seemed dangerous, but now he seems friendly and talkative.

p. 85 Reading Check
Students should underline "They used to say I sung the blues so sweet that if I sang at a funeral, the dead would commence to rocking with the beat."

p. 86 Reading Check
Students should underline "We heard you talking about your treasure. We just want to see it, that's all."

p. 86 Short Story

Sample response: Three bad men are coming into the building. Lemon Brown and Greg are hiding.

p. 86 Short Story

Sample response: Lemon Brown probably squeezed Greg's hand to make Greg feel better. This might be part of the theme of the importance of mutual care between people of different generations.

p. 87 Short Story

Students may underline "'Hey, old man, are you up there?'" Sample response: This shows that the bad men are disrespectful.

p. 87 Stop to Reflect

Sample response: The men are probably planning to steal Lemon Brown's treasure.

p. 87 Reading Check

Students should underline "Lemon Brown stood at the top of the stairs, both arms raised high above his head."

p. 88 Short Story

Students should underline "A rush of warm air came in as the downstairs door opened."

p. 88 Stop to Reflect

Sample response: Greg deserves credit because he acted bravely too. He helped Lemon Brown scare the bad men away even though he could have been hurt if the men had found him.

p. 88 Short Story

Sample response: Lemon Brown's treasure is very important to him. He fought the bad men so that they would not steal his treasure.

p. 89 Short Story

Sample response: Yes, there is still the conflict between Greg and his father.

p. 89 Short Story

Sample response: The news clippings and harmonica are a treasure to Lemon Brown because they remind him of happy times in the past.

p. 89 Stop to Reflect

Sample response: They show a father who values passing something on to his children. Greg's father wanted to pass on his own values about hard work to Greg.

p. 90 Short Story

Sample response: They are a treasure to him because his son valued them. They connect him to his son.

p. 90 Short Story

Sample response: Lemon Brown downplays his affection for Greg, but this affection relates to the theme of the older generation caring for the younger one.

p. 90 Stop to Reflect

Sample response: Lemon Brown's treasure was worth fighting for because it is a reminder of his son.

p. 91 Short Story

Sample response: Greg leaves Lemon Brown and heads home.

p. 91 Reading Check

Students should underline "The night had warmed and the rain had stopped."

p. 91 Reader's Response

Sample response: It could happen. The setting is a real place. A man like Lemon Brown could be homeless and lose his son in a war. Children like Greg often have conflicts with parents over grades and homework. The theme of the story also reveals what's important in life.

p. 92 Apply the Skills

1. Some students may say that Greg should not tell his father. Greg's father might not understand why Greg was in an abandoned building. Other students may suggest that Greg should tell his father about the lesson he learned from Lemon Brown. Doing so might resolve the conflict between them.

2. **Graphic Organizer**

Sample response:

Column 1: Brown's treasures are his harmonica, his newspaper clippings, and his memories.

Column 2: These were Brown's legacy to his son.

Column 3: Greg realizes that his father's lectures are his legacy.

3. Sample response: The main conflict is between Greg and his father.

4. Sample response: Details about the stormy weather and the inside of the tenement building could be real.

"The Bear Boy"
Joseph Bruchac

"Rikki-tikki-tavi"
Rudyard Kipling

p. 94 Graphic Organizer
Sample response:

"The Bear Boy"
Exposition: Kuo-Haya's father mourns the death of his wife. He does not teach his son to wrestle or to run.
Event: Kuo-Haya follows bear tracks.
Event: Kuo-Haya plays with bear cubs.
Event: The villagers and Kuo-Haya's father find Kuo-Haya with the bears and try to get him back.
Climax: Kuo-Haya's father treats the bears with respect. He gives them honey.
Event: Kuo-Haya's father promises to be friendly with bears.
Event: Kuo-Haya agrees to go back with his father.
Resolution: Kuo-Haya becomes the best wrestler and greatest runner in the village.

"Rikki-tikki-tavi"
Exposition: A flood destroys Rikki's home.
Event: Teddy's family adopts Rikki.
Event: Rikki rescues Teddy by killing a small snake.
Event: Teddy's father and Rikki kill Nag.
Climax: Rikki chases Nagaina into a hole and kills her.
Event: The coppersmith announces that Rikki has killed Nagaina.
Event: Rikki eats a large meal.
Resolution: Teddy's family and Rikki are safe.

p. 95 Reading/Writing Connection
Sample response:
1. At the zoo, people appreciate seeing unusual animals.
2. Scientists observe wild animals to learn how these animals find food.
3. Lions might teach people how to survive when they are in danger.

p. 95 Note-taking Guide
Sample response:
Column 2, row 1: timid
Column 2, row 2: sad
Column 3, row 1: He learns to wrestle.

Column 3, row 2: He learns how to treat his son.
Column 4, row 1: He is confident.
Column 4, row 2: He is proud of his son.

p. 96 Activate Prior Knowledge
Sample response: They probably will not get along. Bears and people are usually enemies.

p. 96 Literary Analysis
Students should underline "But Kuo-Haya had never been told about this. When he came upon the tracks of a bear, Kuo-Haya followed them along an arroyo, a small canyon cut by a winding stream, up into the mesas." and "There, he came upon some bear cubs."

p. 96 Stop to Reflect
Kuo-Haya's father should have told him to avoid bear tracks.

p. 96 Reading Check
Students should underline "In his heart he still mourned the death of his wife, Kuo-Haya's mother, and did not enjoy doing things with his son."

p. 97 Reading Skill
Sample response: The mother bear will attack Kuo-Haya because she is afraid that he will hurt her cubs.

p. 97 Literary Analysis
Sample response: This paragraph shows that a conflict will arise between the bears and the humans.

p. 97 Reading Check
Students should circle "But as soon as the mother bear caught their scent, she growled and pushed her cubs and the boy back into the cave."

p. 98 Reading Skill
Sample response: People use weapons to hunt and kill animals. The father is probably planning to kill the bears.

p. 98 Literary Analysis
Students should circle "As he sat there, a bee flew up to him, right by his face. Then it flew away. The father stood up. Now he knew what to do! 'Thank you, Little Brother,' he said. He began to make his preparations."
Sample response: You know that this part of the story is the climax because it is the point

at which the reader may be able to predict the resolution of the story.

p. 98 Reading Skill
Sample response: Kuo-Haya's father no longer plans to attack the bears. Instead, he will give the bears honey. While the bears are eating the honey, he hopes to get his son.

p. 99 Stop to Reflect
The father is beginning to learn to respect others. Violence will not get him what he wants.

p. 99 Literary Analysis
No, this scene is part of the falling action. It follows the climax.

p. 99 Reading Check
Students should underline (1) "The bears have taught me a lesson. I shall treat you as a father should treat his son." (2) "But I, too, have learned things from the bears. They have shown me how we must care for one another."

p. 100 Literary Analysis
Students should note that Kuo-Haya is no longer timid; he is the best wrestler, and his father helped him become the best runner.

p. 100 Reading Check
The story reminds parents to love their children. Students should circle "To this day, his story is told to remind all parents that they must always show as much love for their children as there is in the heart of a bear."

p. 100 Reader's Response
Sample response: This story is for both children and adults because it has a message that reminds all people to honor responsibilities and to solve problems in peaceful ways.

p. 101 Apply the Skills
1. Sample response: Because the mother bear encourages Kuo-Haya and teaches him to be strong, Kuo-Haya feels that he belongs with the bears. In the village, he is neglected by his father and sees himself as an outsider.
2. Seeing the bee gives the father the idea to use honey as part of his plan to get back his son.
3. **Graphic Organizer**
Sample response:
Story Details: The father decides to get his son back.

My Prior Knowledge: Bears like honey.
Prediction: The father will use honey to get his son back.
4. Sample response: These two plot events increase the tension of the story: the mother bear's approach and the father's hunt for weapons.

p. 103 Reading/Writing Connection
Sample response:
1. Firefighters demonstrate bravery when they put out fires.
2. Police officers exhibit courage when they protect people from harm.
3. Acrobats in the circus display courage when they jump from one bar to another.

p. 103 Note-taking Guide
Sample response:
Why does Rikki leave his home? Rikki leaves his home because it has been flooded.
Where does Rikki go to live? Rikki lives with Teddy's family in India.
What creatures does Rikki meet in his new home? Rikki meets a tailorbird named Darzee, Darzee's wife, a muskrat named Chuchundra, Karait the dusty brown snakeling, and Nag and Nagaina, the cobras.
How does Rikki protect his adopted family? Rikki fights the cobras.

p. 104 Apply the Skills
1. Sample response: Rikki and the cobras are alike because they want to protect their families. They are different because Rikki is brave and good. The cobras are greedy and evil.
2. Students may say that this story deserves to be popular because its plot is suspenseful and exciting. Also, its hero is likable and its villains are evil.
3. **Graphic Organizer**
Sample response:
Story Details: Rikki hears the cobras' plot.
My Prior Knowledge: Cobras kill people.
Prediction: Rikki will protect Teddy and his family against the cobras.
4. Sample response: The tension between Rikki and Nag increases after Rikki bites Nagaina and after Rikki overhears Nag and Nagaina plotting to kill Teddy's family.

Reading Informational Materials: Magazine Articles

p. 106 Graphic Organizer
Sample response:
Clue: The title is "Mongoose on the Loose."
Clue: A subhead reads "Population Explodes."
Clue: Another subhead reads "Scientist Studies Problem."
Prediction: The article will be about mongoose overpopulation and what a scientist is doing to solve the problem.

p. 107 Reading Magazine Articles
Mongooses were imported to eat the rats that were feeding on the crops in Jamaica.

p. 107 Reading Informational Materials
Students should predict that the article will be about mongoose overpopulation.

p. 107 Reading Check
The huge mongoose population is now threatening other animals. Students should underline ". . . the mongoose population exploded, and within a few years, they were killing not just rats, but pigs, lambs, chickens, puppies, and kittens."

p. 108 Stop to Reflect
Students may be interested in the project. Volunteers can see mongooses while helping to solve a problem.

p. 108 Reading Skill
It tells readers that the article refers to a unique situation.

p. 108 Reading Check
Students should underline "'I want to know what happens when you take a small animal and put him in an area with no competition.'"

p. 109 Stop to Reflect
Sample response: Yes, it is a good idea. Implanting tracking devices in animals can help scientists learn more about animal behavior.

p. 109 Reading Informational Materials
Students should underline the caption "A mongoose is tagged."

p. 109 Reading Check
Students should underline "Among them: mongooses have a life expectancy of six to ten years, much longer than the previously accepted figure of three years."

p. 110 Apply the Skills
Thinking About the Magazine Article
1. Sample response: The title, subheads, and photos and captions help the reader predict what a magazine article is about.
2. Sample response: The information tells how and why mongooses were brought to the Caribbean. It also explains their value to farmers.

Reading Skill
3. The subhead tells the reader that a problem exists with the mongooses and that a scientist is studying this problem.

from Letters from Rifka
Karen Hesse

"Two Kinds" *from* The Joy Luck Club
Amy Tan

p. 111 Graphic Organizer
Sample response:
from **Letters from Rifka**
Prediction: Something bad will happen.
Details: There is talk of death, prison, and escape.
Revised or Confirmed Prediction: Rifka and her family will make it to Poland.
New Details: They work together, take precautions, and are determined.
Actual Outcome: Their fate is still undetermined at the end of the story.

"Two Kinds" *from* The Joy Luck Club
Prediction: Jing-mei will become a prodigy.
Details: Jing-mei is just as excited as her mother at the idea of being a prodigy. Jing-mei thinks that she will become perfect.
Revised or Confirmed Prediction: Jing-mei will not become a prodigy.
New Details: Jing-mei does not learn the capitals. She cannot pass her mother's tests. She begins to hate the tests.
Actual Outcome: Jing-mei does not become a prodigy. She and her mother argue about this fact.

p. 112 Reading/Writing Connection
Sample response: Most people could adjust to life without television. They would adapt their lives without it by reading books. Some children might feel that their parents deprive them of their favorite television shows.

p. 112 Note-taking Guide
Sample response:
Beginning: Rifka's brother leaves the army.
Event: The family decides to leave the country.
Event: The family packs to leave.
Event: The family hides in a cellar.
Event: Rifka distracts the guards so that her family can hide.
Event: The guards search the train.

p. 113 Activate Prior Knowledge
Sample response: People write letters to share family news. They also write to keep in touch with relatives and friends who live far away.

p. 113 Literary Analysis
Sample response: She loves and respects her grandmother and uncle.

p. 113 Reading Check
Students should circle "My Dear Cousin Tovah."

p. 114 Stop to Reflect
Sample response: They are hiding from the guards. They are also hiding in separate places; if one is caught, the others may still escape.

p. 114 Literary Analysis
The book is a special gift from her cousin, and she doesn't want to lose it.

p. 114 Reading Skill
Sample response: Nathan has committed a crime.

p. 115 Literary Analysis
Sample response: He has courage, and he loves his family. He took a great risk to come and warn Saul.

p. 115 Reading Skill
Sample response: The family will take actions to protect Saul and Nathan.

p. 115 Reading Check
Students should circle "I am ashamed, Tovah, to admit that at first hearing Nathan's news made me glad. I wanted Saul gone. He drives me crazy. From his big ears to his big feet, I cannot stand the sight of him. Good riddance, I thought." Sample response: Rifka may not like the things that Saul does, but she probably loves him because he is her brother.

p. 116 Stop to Reflect
The family will be traveling illegally.

p. 116 Reading Skill
Sample response: She will feel even more worried about her family. She probably will feel fear for her own life, too.

p. 116 Literary Analysis
Students should circle "I must not let them find Nathan."

p. 116 Reader's Response
Sample response: By writing the story as a series of letters, the author builds suspense but lets the reader know that Rifka survives. Also, the letters allow Rifka to reveal details in a creative way.

p. 117 Apply the Skills
1. Sample response: He probably felt scared because he took a risk in leaving the army to warn his family.
2. Some students may say that because she is young, Rifka is more afraid of what might happen. Others may say that Rifka's youth helps her get caught up in the excitement of the journey.
3. Students probably determined that the family was leaving Russia when they read that the Russian army shoots deserters. Students should have made the connection between Rifka's brothers and the army.
4. Students may identify Rifka as young, brave, small, poor, and loving.
Graphic Organizer
Sample response:
Rifka is young: She is twelve years old.
She is brave: She distracts the guards so that her family can hide.
She is small: The guards do not notice her at first.
She is poor: She does not have many things.
She loves her family: She wants everyone to be safe, even the brother she says she dislikes.

p. 119 Reading/Writing Connection
Sample response:
1. One day, I would like to <u>achieve</u> success as a great Olympic diver.
2. To <u>pursue</u> a Nobel Prize is another day-dream I have.
3. Sometimes I dream that I can <u>attain</u> the status of a legendary actor.

p. 119 Note-taking Guide
Sample response:
Mother's Plans: [row 2] She wants her daughter to be remarkable and smart. [row 3] She wants her daughter to play the piano well.
Daughter's Response: [row 1] Jing-mei looks forward to her future fame. [row 2] Jing-mei begins to hate the tests her mother gives her. [row 3] Jing-mei does not put in the effort necessary for playing the piano well.

p. 120 Apply the Skills
1. Sample response: The daughter believes she can never meet her mother's expectations, and the mother is angry because her daughter refuses to try.
2. Students may suggest that the mother pushed her daughter too hard. The mother's efforts backfired. Her daughter believed that she would never be good enough to meet her mother's expectations and stopped trying.
3. **Graphic Organizer**
Sample response:
sad, angry, powerful, willful, bored, lazy
She is sad and angry when she cries in the bathroom. She becomes powerful and willful after she realizes that she does not have to do as her mother says. She is bored and lazy when practicing the piano.
4. Sample response: The daughter will perform poorly because she is not interested in playing, and her teacher is not a good one. The prediction was accurate.

"The Third Wish"
Joan Aiken

"Amigo Brothers"
Piri Thomas

p. 122 Graphic Organizer
Sample Response:
"The Third Wish"
Details: Mr. Peters offers to turn Leita's sister into a human. Mr. Peters uses his second wish to turn Leita back into a swan.
Inference: Mr. Peters loves his wife and wants her to be happy.

"Amigo Brothers"
Details: Antonio waves to Felix from the dressing room. The boys stop in mid-punch as the bell rings.

Inference: Antonio still thinks of Felix as a friend. The two respect the match and play by the rules.

p. 123 Reading/Writing Connection
Sample response:
1. A person would be wise to maximize three wishes by asking for more wishes.
2. Some students might want teachers to grant them freedom from homework.
3. Some people might want money, but I want to obtain happiness.

p. 123 Note-taking Guide
Sample response:
1. Wish: Mr. Peters wishes for a wife.
Result: His wife loves him, but she misses her swan sister.
2. Wish: Mr. Peters uses his second wish to turn his wife back into a swan. **Result:** The swans keep Mr. Peters company when he grows old.
3. Wish: Mr. Peters does not make a third wish. **Result:** The unexpected effects of another wish do not disappoint him.

p. 124 Activate Prior Knowledge
Students may wish for money, good friends, happiness, or other things of value.

p. 124 Reading Skill
Sample response: Mr. Peters is curious, brave, and kind. He is curious when he hears a strange noise. He is brave and kind enough to try to free the trapped swan.

p. 124 Reading Check
Students may circle "Presently the swan, when it was satisfied . . . long beard, standing by the water."

p. 125 Stop to Reflect
Students may say that they would have talked to the little man because they would have been curious about who he was.

p. 125 Literary Analysis
Mr. Peters wants a reward for saving the King of the Forest. The King is upset that Mr. Peters knows that he should have a reward.

p. 125 Reading Check
Students should circle "three dead leaves."

p. 126 Literary Analysis
Mr. Peters's internal conflict of feeling lonely and having no one to grow old with will be solved if he has a wife.

p. 126 Stop to Reflect

Sample response: Mr. Peters's choice is wise because he does not base his wish on greed or pride; instead, he simply wishes for companionship.

p. 126 Reading Check

Students should underline "Taking a thorn he pricked his tongue with it."

p. 127 Stop to Reflect

Sample response: Someone is unhappy when he or she cries or cannot enjoy fun things.

p. 127 Literary Analysis

Leita wants to make Mr. Peters happy. She also misses her swan sister.

p. 127 Reading Skill

Sample response: The marriage will not work out because both people cannot be happy.

p. 127 Reading Check

Students should put an arrow next to the sentence that begins "Now he understood that Leita was really a swan from the forest. . . ."

p. 128 Literary Analysis

Students should underline *grief* and *cheerful*. Sample response: Mr. Peters loves his wife. He wants her to be with him always, yet he knows that she longs to be a swan again. He struggles with loving her but letting her go.

p. 128 Stop to Reflect

Students may say that they like both characters. They may feel sorry for Mr. Peters and Leita. Students may also feel that Leita is brave to stay human.

p. 128 Reading Skill

Leita wants to stay near the river. She wants to be close to her sister.

p. 128 Reading Check

Students should number as follows: 1. "taking her for drives in the car"; 2. "finding beautiful music for her to listen to on the radio"; 3. "buying clothes for her"; 4. "suggesting a trip round the world."

p. 129 Literary Analysis

He uses his second wish to turn Leita back into a swan. He decides not to use his third wish. Instead, he lives near the swans for the rest of his life.

p. 129 Reading Skill

The two swans are Leita and her sister. They watch out for Mr. Peters.

p. 129 Stop to Reflect

Sample response: Mr. Peters spent all of his time with the swans, which is not something people usually do.

p. 129 Reading Check

Students should circle "then came up to him and rested her head lightly against his hand."

p. 130 Literary Analysis

Mr. Peters's situation is the same because he is alone again at the end of the story. Sample response: He does not have the same conflict. He does not seem to be lonely. He says that he will stay faithful to Leita.

p. 130 Reading Skill

Sample response: The feather is probably one of Leita's feathers that Mr. Peters kept.

p. 130 Reader's Response

Students are likely to say that they would have made different wishes than Mr. Peters did. Most students will probably say that they would have used all three wishes.

p. 131 Apply the Skills

1. He is already content with the material things he has.
2. Sample response: Mr. Peters uses his second wish for Leita instead of for himself. He does not take another wife.
3. Sample response: She spends a great deal of time with him. She protects him and mourns his death.
4. **Graphic Organizer**
Sample response:
Smaller Conflict: Mr. Peters suffers from loneliness. Leita is unhappy as a human.
Resolution: Mr. Peters wishes for and receives a wife. He wishes that his wife be turned back into a swan.
Main Conflict: Mr. Peters has to decide whether to use a wish to turn Leita back into a swan (to make her happy) or keep her to alleviate his loneliness.

p. 133 Reading/Writing Connection

Sample response:
1. Fighting against a friend for the same prize involves being determined to win.
2. You must isolate yourself from troublesome people.
3. To accomplish your goal, you may have to make difficult decisions.

p. 133 Note-taking Guide
Sample response:
Physical traits/ Felix: dark, short, and husky
Fighting style/ Felix: short, muscular frame (better slugger)
Fighting gear/ Felix: sky-blue trunks, red socks, white shoes
Physical traits/ Antonio: fair, lean, and lanky
Fighting style/ Antonio: lean form, long reach (better boxer)
Fighting gear/ Antonio: white trunks, black socks, black shoes

p. 134 Apply the Skills
1. Sample response: The advantages are that training apart helps them focus on their training and not on fighting each other. The disadvantage is that they cannot enjoy their friendship and are only postponing the moment of the fight.
2. Some students may say that the solution was a good one because the boys remained friends. Other students may believe that the solution was not good because the boys did not really want to fight.
3. **Graphic Organizer**
Sample response:
Smaller Conflict: The boys need to focus on their fight; the boys want to remain friends.
Resolution: They decide to train apart; they agree to fight as hard as they can. Each accepts that the other will fight hard but remain a friend.
Main Conflict: Both Antonio and Felix want to win, but only one can win.
4. Sample response: Each boy is bothered by the thought of hurting the other. The boys leave the fight together, arm in arm, without caring to learn who won.

Reading Informational Materials: Government Publications

p. 136 Graphic Organizer
Sample response:
Evidence: Walking is a popular form of exercise.
Evidence: Walking is popular with older people.
Evidence: Walking has been popular for a long time.
Generalization: Many older people enjoy walking, an exercise that has never lost popularity.

p. 137 Reading Government Publications
Students should circle "The President's Council on Physical Fitness and Sports."

p. 137 Reading Informational Materials
Students should underline "Walking for Exercise and Pleasure" and "Walking: An Exercise for All Ages."

p. 137 Stop to Reflect
Sample response: Students may say that they could walk to more places, such as to school or the library.

p. 137 Reading Check
Students should draw an arrow next to 39.4%. Men who are 65 and older make up the highest percentage of regular walkers.

p. 138 Reading Skill
Sample response: People who walk are almost always healthier than people who do not walk. Walking can improve the body's ability to use oxygen, lower the resting heart rate, lower blood pressure, and increase the efficiency of the heart and lungs.

p. 138 Reading Informational Materials
Students may circle "It also helps burn excess calories."

p. 138 Reading Check
Students may underline "improve the body's ability to consume oxygen during exertion," "lower the resting heart rate," "reduce blood pressure," and "increase the efficiency of the heart and lungs." Students may also underline "burn excess calories." Some students may underline "Almost everyone can do it," "You can do it almost anywhere," "You can do it almost anytime," and "It doesn't cost anything."

p. 139 Reading Skill
Students should underline "You can do it almost anytime."

p. 139 Reading Informational Materials
Sample response: Pay attention to your body when you walk.

p. 139 Reading Check
Students should underline "The variety of settings available is one of the things that makes walking such a practical and pleasurable activity."

p. 140 Apply the Skills
Thinking About The Government Publication

1. Sample response: When done briskly on a regular schedule, walking can improve the body's ability to consume oxygen during exertion.
2. You should slow down if you develop dizziness, pain, nausea, or any other symptoms. These symptoms tell you that your body is working too hard.

Reading Skill

3. You can make the generalization that most people walk because it is good for them.
4. Sample response: It is possible to develop dizziness, pain, nausea, or other symptoms when walking.

"Zoo"
Edward D. Hoch

"Ribbons"
Laurence Yep

p. 141 Graphic Organizer
Sample response:
"Zoo"
Why Does the Writer tell the ticket price and the number of people who see the zoo?
Answer (inference): to suggest that Professor Hugo makes a lot of money from the zoo
Why Does the Writer describe the behavior of the horse-spider people of Kaan?
Answer (inference): to compare it with the behavior of the humans at the zoo

"Ribbons"
Why Does the Writer keep what happened to the grandmother's feet a secret?
Answer (inference): to make the reader wonder what happened to her feet
Why Does the Writer have the grandmother show affection to Ian but not to Stacy?
Answer (inference): to develop a conflict for the story

p. 142 Reading/Writing Connection
Sample response:
1. The border around my elephant habitat <u>minimizes</u> outside contact.
2. One <u>benefit</u> of being in the zoo is that animals cannot attack one another.
3. Overall, the people who run my zoo like to <u>emphasize</u> animal safety.

p. 142 Note-taking Guide
Sample response:
The Earth People: They walk on two legs. They walk on the ground. They wear clothes.
The Horse-Spider People: They walk on many legs. They walk in any direction. They wear no clothes.
Same: They have families. They like to see new things. They think that other ways of living are strange.

p. 143 Activate Prior Knowledge
Sample response: Zoos have animals from far-off places. People visit zoos to see these animals.

p. 143 Reading Skill
Sample response: The zoo is very popular, and children want their parents to take them there.

p. 143 Reading Check
Students should underline "In them were some wild breed of nightmare—small, horse-like animals that moved with quick, jerking motions and constantly chattered in a high-pitched tongue."

p. 144 Reading Skill
Sample response: Professor Hugo's home is his ship. He is always traveling.

p. 144 Reading Check
Students should underline "horrified and fascinated" and "'This is certainly worth a dollar,' one man remarked, hurrying away. 'I'm going home to get the wife.'"

p. 144 Reading Skill
Sample response: The people of Kaan are part of the traveling zoo because the zoo is an opportunity for them to see the creatures of other worlds.

p. 145 Reading Skill
Sample response: They are not part of a zoo, but tourists.

p. 145 Literary Analysis
Students may underline "It is well worth the nineteen commocs it costs" or "It was the very best zoo ever. . . ." Sample response: The creatures are telling what is unusual about Earth creatures, just as Earth people remarked about the unusual space creatures.

p. 145 Stop to Reflect

Students may say that Hoch successfully made the point that as different as things can seem, they can still be alike.

p. 145 Reader's Response

Sample response: Most students would probably like to visit the Interplanetary Zoo because it exhibits creatures that they would not be able to see anywhere else.

p. 146 Apply the Skills

1. Sample response: The crowd views the creatures as a nightmare because the creatures are totally unfamiliar.
2. Sample response: This label says that humans fail to accept or be open-minded when faced with live creatures that look different from themselves.
3. Sample response: The children behave themselves so that their parents will let them go to the Interplanetary Zoo.

4. **Graphic Organizer**

Sample response:

Theme: People view foreign creatures as strange or weird.

Setting: People in Chicago see the spaceship as a zoo, and the creatures on the spaceship see Chicago as a zoo.

Character: People on Earth are frightened of and curious about the horse-spider people. Horse-spider people are wary of and curious about Earth people.

p. 148 Reading/Writing Connection

Sample response:

1. A way to <u>maximize</u> your learning is to study other cultures.
2. <u>Ignore</u> your differences and pay attention to your similarities.
3. <u>Rely</u> on good manners to break down cultural barriers.

p. 148 Note-taking Guide

Sample response:

What does . . . Ian? She teaches him to speak Chinese.

What does . . . Stacy? She takes away Stacy's ribbons. She tells Stacy that she (Stacy) can dance.

p. 149 Apply the Skills

1. Students may suggest that the hardest changes for Stacy come when she has to change her behavior and give up her ballet lessons.
2. Sample response: Stacy's mother explains Grandmother's behavior to Stacy, and Stacy is finally able to explain her love of dancing to Grandmother.
3. Sample response: Why does the author include the detail about Grandmother's carrying her daughter on her back? Why does he include the detail about Grandmother's walking such a great distance?

4. **Graphic Organizer**

Sample response:

Theme: The theme might be understanding and overcoming differences.

Traits: Stacy tries hard and is loving and dedicated.

Motives: Stacy wants to dance and wants her grandmother to like her.

"What Makes a Rembrandt a Rembrandt?"
Richard Mühlberger

p. 153 Note-taking Guide
Sample response:
Circle 1: shows love of old clothes
Circle 2: highlights person's rank
Circle 3: leads viewers to center of painting

p. 154 Activate Prior Knowledge
Students may say that they would make the scene more interesting by painting different expressions on people's faces, rather than smiles.

p. 154 Nonfiction
Students should underline "In all of these group portraits, the men were evenly lined up so that each face got equal attention, just as they had been in traditional anatomy lesson paintings." Rembrandt's solution was to add extra people and a dog to the scene to add realism. He showed the excitement and activity before a military parade began.

p. 154 Reading Check
Students should underline "his militia company."

p. 155 Nonfiction
The officers are illuminated, or in the light. Everything else is in shadow. Students should underline "Rembrandt links him to Banning Cocq by contrasting the colors of their clothing and by painting the shadow of Banning Cocq's hand on the front of Van Ruytenburgh's coat."

p. 155 Nonfiction
Students should circle "Van Ruytenburgh turns to listen to him, which shows his respect for his commander."

p. 155 Reading Check
Students should underline "darkness" or "Rembrandt knew that darkness makes faces shine!"

p. 156 Stop to Reflect
Students may say that the way Rembrandt highlights figures in the background shows his greatness.

p. 156 Nonfiction
Sample response: The girls are dressed in yellow and blue. They carry the emblems of the company. One girl is holding the chicken's claws.

p. 156 Reading Check
Students should underline "While Rembrandt did not pose him in bright light, he made him important by placing him high up on the stairs, by showing the sheen in his costume, and by giving him the large flag to unfurl."

p. 157 Nonfiction
Sample response: These facts are about clothing and military equipment. Students should underline "What an opportunity for Rembrandt, perhaps the greatest lover of old clothes in Amsterdam!"

p. 157 Stop to Reflect
Sample response: Students may say that uniforms worn by the military today are much more practical. Many have colors that let soldiers blend in with their surroundings. The uniforms are similar in that they both show the rank of the men.

p. 157 Reading Check
Students should underline "there is daylight in the scene."

p. 158 Stop to Reflect
Students may think that "Washington Crossing the Delaware" is a great painting because it shows the bravery of General Washington and the difficult conditions of crossing the icy river.

p. 158 Reading Check
Students should circle "when he was thirty-six years old."

p. 158 Reader's Response
Students may say that they would like to see the contrasts in light and dark and whether they could tell who are the most important people.

p. 159 Apply the Skills
1. Sample response: *The Militia Parade, Citizen Soldiers*. The title *The Night Watch* does not describe the painting. The title should express that the painting is about a parade and the militia.

2. Sample response: Military portraits used to be painted with the men lining up evenly so that every man got the same attention. Rembrandt wanted to make his painting more realistic. He wanted to show the excitement before a parade, so he included people moving and doing things.

3. The two highest-ranking men are at the front of the portrait. One officer's face is illuminated against a dark background. The other's entire figure is painted in bright colors.

4. **Graphic Organizer**
Sample response:

Examples of Description: describing Banning Cocq; describing Van Ruytenburgh; describing the blonde girl; describing Visscher.

Examples of Exposition: describing how the background images are made visible by painting the paths; the use of color to create contrasts between light and dark.

"Life Without Gravity"
Robert Zimmerman

"Conversational Ballgames"
Nancy Masterson Sakamoto

p. 161 Graphic Organizer
Sample response:
"Life Without Gravity"
Column 3, row 1: weightlessness
Column 3, row 2: "Our inner ears use gravity to keep us upright."
Column 3, row 3: spines

"Conversational Ballgames"
Column 3, row 1: "A western-style conversation between two people is like a game of tennis."
Column 3, row 2: "If I introduce a topic, a conversational ball, I expect you to hit it back."
Column 3, row 3: elaboration

p. 162 Reading/Writing Connection
Sample response: Gravity will require you to be careful when you are jumping on a trampoline. Gravity forces you to react if you were to fall off your bicycle. Can you predict what would happen without gravity?

p. 162 Note-taking Guide
Sample response:
Effects on Blood: Blood flows to head and not to legs.

Effects on Stomach: Stomach gets upset; astronauts may throw up.
Effects on Eating: Astronauts must drink out of a special straw.

p. 163 Activate Prior Knowledge
Students may say that they would like to be an astronaut. They may think it would be exciting to go places where few people have been before.

p. 163 Literary Analysis
Being weightless in space is the topic of this essay.

p. 163 Reading Skill
Students should underline "the Red Planet."

p. 163 Reading Check
Students should underline "Our inner ears use gravity to keep us upright."

p. 164 Stop to Reflect
Sample response: A person should be active and in very good shape to be an astronaut. An astronaut has to exercise in space or their muscles become so weak that they cannot walk when they come back to Earth.

p. 164 Reading Skill
Students should underline "After about a week people usually get used to it."

p. 164 Literary Analysis
Students should circle "process." The essay explains how lack of gravity affects the lives of astronauts and it lists the steps they take to meet the challenge.

p. 165 Reading Skill
Sample response: Eating and drinking is not easy without gravity.

p. 165 Literary Analysis
It explains the process of how to drink from a straw in space.

p. 165 Reading Check
Students should circle "they will float away."

p. 166 Literary Analysis
The author ends the essay with the example of how astronaut Jerry Linenger adapted to weightlessness and recovered from its discomforts.

p. 166 Reading Skill
Students should underline these supporting details: "almost two dozen astronauts have

lived in space for more than six months, and four have stayed in orbit for more than a year" and "These men and women faced the discomforts of weightlessness and overcame them."

p. 166 Stop to Reflect
Students may say that they would miss their families, pets, or miss eating their favorite foods while in space.

p. 166 Reading Check
Students should circle "Your weight in pounds is actually the measure of the downward force of gravity on you."

p. 167 Stop to Reflect
Students may say that they would prefer to live on Earth where they are with their family and friends, can eat normal foods, and not put their bodies through the stress of changing gravity.

p. 167 Reading Check
Students should circle "surface gravity on the moon is one-sixth of Earth's gravity."

p. 167 Reader's Response
Students may say that reading this essay has caused them to not want to be an astronaut. They may explain that they thought weightlessness would be fun, but now they know how hard it is on the body.

p. 168 Apply the Skills
1. Without gravity to cause the muscles to push and pull on the bones, the body decides to stop laying down as much bone as before. Without gravity to tell the inner ear which way is up, people get dizzy and feel sick to their stomachs. Without gravity to work against the body, the muscles get weak.
2. An astronaut can choose to move up or down, or left or right, just by moving his or her head. He or she must also choose to tie down tools or let them float way and possibly get lost.
3. The main idea is that weightlessness has negative effects, but these effects can be overcome.
4. **Graphic Organizer**
Sample response:
Column 2: It is fun to float around. A person can float up to the ceiling. A person can change direction just by moving his or her head.

Column 3: Weightlessness can make a person feel dizzy and sick to his or her stomach. It causes the head to swell and the muscles to weaken.
Column 4: Weightlessness can be fun, and its effects are quickly reversed on Earth. It is important to know about the effects of weightlessness if astronauts are going to explore outer space.

p. 170 Reading/Writing Connection
Sample response: Newcomers to American culture may not comprehend that *cool* means "cold" or "very good." They may try to communicate using formal language. Americans may respond to them with confusion.

p. 170 Note-taking Guide
Sample response:
Column 2, row 3: Players take their own turn to hit the ball; the game does not stop for them to take their turn.
Column 3, row 3: People speak one at a time.
Column 4, row 1: bowling ball
Column 4, row 2: A player bowls and his or her turn ends.

p. 171 Apply the Skills
1. The author did not understand that she should wait her turn to speak, and that she should not respond to other people's comments.
2. Sample response: The newcomer should respect the rules of the other culture; the native speakers should be tolerant of the newcomer's style.
3. The main idea is that Western and Japanese-style conversations are very different.
4. **Graphic Organizer**
Sample response:
Describe Polite Conversation in the United States: It includes passing the topic back and forth, like a tennis ball or volleyball; it is exciting and fun; it involves all the members of the conversation in no particular order.
Describe Polite Conversation in Japan: It allows only one speaker at a time, according to his or her social standing. While the speaker talks, the others listen quietly. When it is time for a new speaker, he or she starts with a new topic.

Author's Conclusion: Western-style conversation is like tennis or volleyball, and Japanese-style conversation is like bowling, but both are valid forms of conversation.

"I Am a Native of North America"
Chief Dan George

from In Search of
Our Mothers' Gardens
Alice Walker

p. 173 Graphic Organizer
Sample response:

"I Am a Native of North America"
Main Idea: People of Chief Dan George's culture and people of white culture must love one another.
Left Key Point: Love is necessary for human life.
Detail 1: George's culture taught him to love and respect people.
Detail 2: George's father taught him to love and respect animals and nature.
Right Key Point: George wonders whether people from white culture know how to love.
Detail 1: White culture justifies hating and killing people.
Detail 2: White culture abuses Earth.

from In Search of Our Mothers' Gardens
Main Idea: Throughout history, women have often been forced to express their creativity in modest ways, such as storytelling, gardening, and quilting, but they have passed down the creative spirit to the next generation of women.
Left Key Point: The stories people tell are often the ones they heard and absorbed from their parents.
Detail 1: Many of the stories Walker has written are her mother's stories.
Detail 2: Through the years of listening to her mother's stories, Walker absorbed her mother's manner of storytelling.
Right Key Point: Gardening was an important means of self-expression for Walker's mother.
Detail 1: Whatever Walker's mother planted grew as if by magic.
Detail 2: In searching for her mother's garden, Walker found her own.

p. 174 Reading/Writing Connection
Sample response:
1. My cultural background has helped <u>enrich</u> my ability to respect others' opinions.
2. Many cultures stress that it is important to <u>cooperate</u> with one another.
3. People should <u>evaluate</u> how their cultural backgrounds influence their lives.

p. 174 Note-taking Guide
Sample response:
Native American Culture: values community; has learned much from white American culture
White American Culture: overtaking Native American culture; has not learned from Native American culture
[overlapping circle] Both groups must forgive each other.

p. 175 Activate Prior Knowledge
Students may suggest goals such as ending hunger, cleaning up the environment, or ending crime.

p. 175 Reading Skill
Students may circle "communal house," "All my grandfather's sons and their families lived in this large dwelling," and "one open fire in the middle served the cooking needs of all."

p. 175 Reading Check
Students should draw a box around "eighty feet long."

p. 176 Literary Analysis
The writer's culture taught him to respect nature and animals.

p. 176 Stop to Reflect
Students may say that they invite their neighbors for dinner or meet neighbors at neighborhood parties.

p. 176 Reading Skill
Students should circle "It is hard for me to understand a culture that not only hates and fights its brothers but even attacks nature and abuses her."

Students should underline "blotting out nature from his cities," "strip the hills bare, leaving ugly wounds on the face of mountains," "tearing things from the bosom of mother earth," "throw poison in the waters, indifferent to the life he kills there," "chokes the air with deadly fumes."

p. 177 Reading Skill

Sample response: Students should circle the word *love*. The repetition of the word *love* and the sentence "Love is something you and I must have" help determine the main idea. The repetition of *love* stresses its importance that Native Americans and white Americans must learn to love each other.

p. 177 Literary Analysis

Sample response: His Native culture respected people and Earth. White culture separates people, treats Earth badly, and is lacking in love.

p. 177 Reading Check

Students should underline "Man must love fully or he will become the lowest of the animals."

p. 178 Reading Skill

The author states that his culture did not cling to privacy. His culture lived in big family communities and learned to live with others.

p. 178 Stop to Reflect

Students may say that they could maintain their cultural identity while living in a different culture. To do this, they would need to remain faithful to the most important values in their culture.

p. 178 Reading Check

Students should underline the sentence, "But my culture did prize friendship and companionship."

p. 179 Literary Analysis

He feels that the white culture does not respect the earth and separates its people. His native culture loves the earth and learned for years to live together.

p. 179 Reading Check

Students should underline "You must truly love us, be patient with us and share with us. And we must love you—with a genuine love that forgives and forgets . . . ."

p. 179 Reader's Response

Students may say that the power to love is the most important quality. Without love, people become isolated and bitter.

p. 180 Apply the Skills

1. Sample response: By "brotherhood," Chief Dan George means love, patience, trust, acceptance, peace, and forgiveness among all people.

2. Sample response: He means that his "white brothers" have been more successful in spreading their values than his culture has been.

3. Sample response: The author believes it is important for all Americans to love, respect, care for, and forgive one another and to live in peace.

4. **Graphic Organizer**

Sample response:

Chief George's Reflections: How his culture is fading.

My Responses: Students' responses may include empathy or confusion.

After Rereading: Students may agree that the world would certainly benefit from people of different cultures showing more love, respect, and forgiveness to each other.

p. 182 Reading/Writing Connection

Sample response: I do not think that I can fully appreciate everything that my mother has done for me. She is the first person to contribute help when I need it. She has demonstrated love to me.

p. 182 Note-taking Guide

Sample response:

Anonymous Women: names unknown; lived hard lives; created beauty from everyday things: quilts, songs, and so on.

Alice Walker: very famous; lives much easier life; uses words and ideas to write

p. 183 Apply the Skills

1. Sample response: She represents women's creative spirits and mothers across the centuries who have passed on the spirit of creativity.

2. It is a tribute to all mothers, not just her own.

3. Sample response: The main idea is that throughout history, women have often been forced to express their creativity in modest ways. They garden, quilt, or tell stories. By doing so, they have passed down the creative spirit to the next generation of women.

4. **Graphic Organizer**

Sample response:

Walker's Reflection: The quilt by the "anonymous" black woman in Alabama is a work of art; Mother created beautiful gardens that were greatly admired.

My Responses: Students responses may include memories of quilts, stories, or gardens created by women in their families, or memories of other ways in which the women in their families have expressed creativity.
After Rereading: Students should identify ways their thinking has changed. For example, they may not have thought that quilts or gardens were creative outlets. After reading the essay, they may think otherwise.

Reading Informational Materials: Problem-and-Solution Essays

p. 186 Reading Problem-and-Solution Essays
Students should underline "As many as 9 million Americans have hearing loss caused by noise."

p. 186 Reading Skill
Students should circle "prevent hearing loss" and should number "using ear protectors," "buy quieter machines," "avoid using lawn-mowers or power tools at quiet times of the day," and "turning down the volume on headphones for radios and CD players."

p. 186 Stop to Reflect
Sample response: Students can turn down volume on radios, TVs, and CD players.

p. 186 Reading Check
Students should draw a box around "120 decibels."

p. 187 Reading Skill
Students may choose "What Can Communities Do?" Students may number "locate airports away from dense populations," "prohibit late-night flights," "have laws against noise that exceeds a certain decibel level," and "give fines to people who use noisy equipment."

p. 187 Reading Problem-and-Solution Essays
Communities can locate airports away from dense population and prohibit late-night flights. Students may say that these solutions are not realistic because space for airports is limited and restricting flight times can cause problems that airline companies would not agree to.

p. 187 Reading Informational Materials
The last paragraph tells about things that the government can do that affect everyone. It says the federal government could bring back laws that set limits on noise. It says the best way to fix the problem of noise pollution is to have the government pay for research to make machines quieter.

p. 188 Apply the Skills
Thinking About the Problem-and-Solution Essay
1. Cars, trains, trucks, and planes are the largest source of noise pollution. About 15 million Americans live near an airport or under a flight path.
2. Noise that does not cause pain can still damage your hearing. Household appliances such as a kitchen blender can slowly damage the hair cells in your cochlea.

Reading Skill
3. Noise pollution is a serious concern in the United States, but this problem can be lessened.
4. Sample response: Yes, this detail does support the main idea because the statistic emphasizes how important it is to solve the problem of noise pollution.

"The Eternal Frontier"
Louis L'Amour

"All Together Now"
Barbara Jordan

p. 189 Graphic Organizer
Sample response:
"The Eternal Frontier"
Appeals to Emotion: "And today is the past."
Appeals to Reason: "The computer age has arisen in part from the space effort."

"All Together Now"
Appeals to Authority: "President Lyndon B. Johnson pushed through the Civil Rights Act of 1964, which remains the fundamental piece of civil rights legislation in this century."
Appeals to Emotion: "I care about you because you are a fellow human being and I find it okay in my mind, in my heart, to simply say to you, I love you."
Appeals to Reason: "Each of us can decide to have one friend of a different race or background in our mix of friends."

p. 190 Reading/Writing Connection

Sample response:

1. People will have to invest too much time and money for space exploration.
2. The decision to undertake more space exploration could benefit the world.
3. Scientists will obtain new knowledge as a result of space exploration.

p. 190 Note-taking Guide

Sample response:

Circle 3: ". . . nor is the mind of man bound by any limits at all."

Circle 4: "Humans would still be hunter/gatherers if they had not looked beyond their immediate needs"

Circle 5: "It is our destiny to move out."

p. 191 Activate Prior Knowledge

Sample response: In the future people may live on other planets, travel in outer space on space shuttles, or spend time at space stations.

p. 191 Reading Skill

Students should circle "We have been preparing ourselves mentally for what lies ahead" and "if we can avoid a devastating war we shall move with a rapidity scarcely to be believed." Students should underline "Many problems remain," "In the past seventy years we have developed the automobile, radio, television, transcontinental and transoceanic flight, and the electrification of the country, among a multitude of other such developments," "In 1900 there were 144 miles of surfaced road in the United States," and "Now there are over 3,000,000."

p. 191 Reading Check

Students should circle "Our frontier lies in outer space."

p. 192 Literary Analysis

The author uses an appeal to emotion.

p. 192 Stop to Reflect

Sample response: The author means that it is in our nature to take on new challenges.

p. 192 Reading Check

Students should circle "If that had been the spirit of man we would still be hunters and food gatherers, growling over the bones of carrion in a cave somewhere."

p. 193 Literary Analysis

Students should number three factual statements in the paragraph, such as "The computer age has arisen in part from the space effort," "Transistors, chips, integrated circuits, Teflon, new medicines, new ways of treating diseases, new ways of performing operations, all these and a multitude of other developments . . . are linked to the space effort.

p. 193 Reading Skill

The words *must* and *all* are clues that indicate an opinion. The author supports his opinion with these facts: the space effort drove the development of computing devices, new medicines, new ways of treating diseases, and new ways of performing operations.

p. 193 Reader's Response

Students may say that this essay has not changed the way they think or will act because they already think that there should be more exploration of outer space and that people will live, travel, and work in outer space in the future.

p. 194 Apply the Skills

1. Sample response: The leaders may vote for legislation and funding that support space travel.
2. Sample response: The essay conveys the message that exploring outer space is our human destiny. It paints a noble picture of humankind.
3. **Graphic Organizer**

Row 1: "all"
Row 2: "always"
Row 3: "must"

4. Sample response: Appeal to emotion: "It is our destiny to move out, to accept the challenge, to dare the unknown." Appeal to reason: "The computer age has arisen in part from the space effort, which gave great impetus to the development of computing devices."

p. 196 Reading/Writing Connection

Sample response: Many laws help integrate our society. However, it is impossible to legislate people's feelings. Each person must promote tolerance in the community. Then, people will begin to understand one another.

p. 196 Note-taking Guide
How can we achieve it? through laws and personal actions
Why is it important? It brings peace to the world and helps us appreciate differences among people.

p. 197 Apply the Skills
1. Sample response: Jordan means that a baby has not yet been influenced by society.
2. Sample response: Jordan's ideas could work if all people were as optimistic as Jordan.
3. **Graphic Organizer**
Sample response:
Opinion 3: "Today the nation seems to be suffering from compassion fatigue"
Clue 2: "best way"
Clue 3: "seems to be"
4. Sample response: Appeal to authority: "President Lyndon B. Johnson pushed through the Civil Rights Act of 1964." Appeal to emotion: "I care about you because you are a fellow human being." Appeal to reason: "Each of us can decide to have one friend of a different race or background in our mix of friends."

"The Real Story of a Cowboy's Life"
Geoffrey C. Ward

"Rattlesnake Hunt"
Marjorie Kinnan Rawlings

p. 199 Graphic Organizer
Sample response:
"The Real Story of a Cowboy's Life"
atlas or map: route of a typical cattle drive
dictionary: difficult words, such as *occurrence*
encyclopedia: information about cattle drives
reliable Web site: information about the author, Geoffrey C. Ward

"Rattlesnake Hunt"
almanac: the burning of the countryside at that time of year in order to create cattle forage
atlas or map: the location of Big Prairie, the rattlesnake hunting ground
biographical dictionary: "Ross Allen, a young Florida herpetologist, invited me to join him on a hunt in the upper Everglades—for rattlesnakes."
dictionary: difficult words, such as *herpetologist*

encyclopedia: information about rattlesnakes
reliable Web site: information about the author, Marjorie Kinnan Rawlings

p. 200 Reading/Writing Connection
Sample response: You can identify a stampede at night by its low, rumbling sound. You can presume that getting out of the way will be important. A cattle drive can evoke hostility in farmers whose crops had been trampled in the past.

p. 200 Note-taking Guide
Inconveniences: no alcohol or gambling; dust in mouth; difficult landscapes
Dangers From Animals or Nature: dragged to death in a nighttime stampede; prairie dog holes
Benefits: beautiful views; payment; life in town

p. 201 Activate Prior Knowledge
Sample response: Students may list herds of cattle, riding horses, dusty ground, cowboy hats and boots, and so on.

p. 201 Stop to Reflect
Sample response: There were thousands of cattle to handle, many jobs to do, and long distances to travel.

p. 201 Literary Analysis
Students should underline "chair," "workbench," and "pillow."

p. 202 Reading Skill
Both sentences should be marked "O" for Opinion.

p. 202 Literary Analysis
Sample response: Settlers and cowboys on the trail did not get along.

p. 202 Reading Check
Students should circle "if one shot another he was to be tried by the outfit and hanged on the spot, if found guilty."

p. 203 Reading Skill
Students should circle "dictionary" and "encyclopedia"; the encyclopedia but not the dictionary; an atlas or a map.

p. 203 Literary Analysis
The author uses informal word choice. Students should circle "monkeyed as long as I want."

p. 203 Reading Check

Students should circle "liquor" and "gambling."

p. 204 Literary Analysis

Students should circle "funny," "informal," and "personal"; students may underline the following: "bedded down"; "you'd go through a whole song that way"; " 'Bury Me Not on the Lone Prairie'" was a great song for awhile, but . . . they sung it to death"; "It was a saying on the range"; "nickered"; "it got so they'd throw you in the creek if you sang it."

p. 204 Reading Skill

Fact: "The number of cattle on the move was sometimes staggering." Opinion: "All the cattle in the world . . . seemed to be coming up from Texas."

p. 204 Reading Check

Students should circle "they'd throw you in the creek if you sang it."

p. 204 Reader's Response

Sample response: Students may say that they learned that cowboys sang songs not just for entertainment but to keep the cattle peaceful.

p. 205 Apply the Skills

1. Sample response: Teddy Blue participated in several cattle drives.
2. Sample response: Successful cowboys are disciplined. They can entertain themselves. They love the open trail.
3. Sample response: The facts show what happened on the trail. The opinions show how the cowboys felt about what was happening on the trail.
4. **Graphic Organizer**

Sample response:

Technical Vocabulary: quarantine lines, called "deadlines"

Formal Language: "Regardless of its ultimate destination . . ."

Informal Language: ". . . when they were still raising punkins in Illinois."; "I've monkeyed as long as I want to with you."

p. 207 Reading/Writing Connection

Sample response: One way to respond to something that frightens you is by turning away from it. It is difficult to acquire a deeper respect for what you fear. Facing something scary can benefit a person by making him or her get over the fear.

p. 207 Note-taking Guide

Box 3: She describes the snakes' behavior in an unemotional way.

Box 4: She heads off by herself to hunt a snake.

p. 208 Apply the Skills

1. Rawlings has won because she has conquered a fear.
2. Rawlings views herself as more courageous, and she views nature as less dangerous.
3. Rawling's opinions show how she felt about snakes show what she learned about snakes.
4. **Graphic Organizer**

Sample response:

Technical Vocabulary: coupe; arid

Formal Language: "I felt an upsurgence of spirit."

Informal Language: "I've got one"; "Well, pick it up."

Reading Informational Materials: Manuals

p. 210 Graphic Organizer:

Which details can be verified as facts? The copperhead has diamond shaped markings; Pit vipers puncture their victims with fangs; Coral snakes are red, yellow, and blue.

Which details are opinions? It is the most striking of the pit vipers; Pit vipers are the most frightening snakes; Coral snakes are beautiful.

p. 211 Reading Manuals

This snake is venomous. The snake has pits between its eyes and its nostrils, fangs, a triangular head, and eyes with narrow pupils.

p. 211 Stop to Reflect

Sample response: Students may say that they would use this manual if they went on a hike or a camping trip. They might use it if they had a job in the woods or fields. They could even see these kinds of snakes in their yard if they lived where these snakes are found.

It is important to know how to spot a poisonous snake in order to stay away from it. If a poisonous snake bites someone, it is important to know what to do because it could save someone's life.

p. 211 Reading Manuals

Sample response: Most manuals include pictures because manuals are meant to give information.

p. 211 Reading Check

Students should underline "the water moccasin."

p. 212 Reading Informational Materials

Sample response: What to do in a fire. How to treat a cut or a burn.

p. 212 Reading Manuals

Students should circle any three of the following: "cut into a snake bite"; "apply cold compresses"; "apply a tourniquet"; "raise the site of the bite above the level of the victim's heart"; give the victim aspirin, stimulants, or pain medication"; "allow the person to exercise"

p. 212 Reading Skill

Sample response: No, it is not a fact that all victims become anxious after being bitten by a snake. There is no way to prove that all victims will have the same emotional reaction to being bit by a snake.

p. 213 Reading Check

Students should underline two of the following: "lay the victim flat," "raise his or her feet 8 to 12 inches," or "cover the victim with a coat or blanket." Students should circle one of the following: "elevate the bitten area above the person's heart," or "place the victim in this position if you suspect any head, neck, back, or leg injury or if the position makes the victim uncomfortable."

p. 214 Apply the Skills
Thinking About the Manual

1. Anxiety can aggravate his or her reaction to the bite. This can make the bite more painful and more difficult to treat. It can also make recovery harder.

2. In North America, all venomous snakes—except the coral snake—are pit vipers. Pit vipers have triangular heads, fangs, narrow vertical pupils and pits between their nostrils and eyes. Nonvenomous snakes do not have these characteristics.

Reading Skill

3. You could use encyclopedias, other manuals, reliable Internet sources, or reference books from the library to check facts about venomous snakes.

4. Manuals are reference materials. Reference materials must have facts to provide reliable information.

"Maestro"

"The Desert Is My Mother"

"Bailando"
Pat Mora

p. 217 Note-taking Guide
Sample response:
"The Desert Is My Mother"
Speaker: A woman who loves the desert.
Memories or Commands: She commands the desert to feed, tease, frighten, hold, heal, caress, sing, and teach her, and to make her beautiful.

"Bailando"
Speaker: A grown adult remembering her aunt.
Memories or Commands: She remembers her aunt dancing as a young woman, dancing with her, dancing with her children, and dancing on her ninetieth birthday.

p. 218 Activate Prior Knowledge
Some students may say that baking cookies reminds them of a time when a grandmother taught them how to make cookies. Other students may say that a day at the lake reminds them of a time when their father taught them how to fish.

p. 218 Poetry
Students should write "singing" and "songs."

p. 218 Poetry
Students should circle "smile" and "slid."

p. 218 Reading Check
Students should underline "when he bows."

p. 219 Poetry
"She" is the desert. Students may underline "serves," "sprinkles," and "shouts."

p. 219 Poetry
Students should list "silence" and "driest."

p. 219 Stop to Reflect
Sample response: The speaker loves the desert as a child loves his or her mother.

p. 220 Poetry
Students could underline "Le digo" or "Me."

p. 220 Poetry
Students may notice "susurra" in the fourth stanza. It is an example of onomatopoeia because it sounds like "whisper," which is what it means in English.

p. 220 Stop to Reflect
Students may say that they associate the words *dune* and *mirage* with the desert.

p. 221 Poetry
Sample response: This poem is free verse because the lines do not rhyme. There are no stanzas. The lines have different numbers of syllables.

p. 221 Poetry
Students should circle "spinning round and round."

p. 221 Reading Check
Students should underline "my dear aunt."

p. 221 Reader's Response
Students may say they think she will be lively and energetic. They may say that she might seem younger than she is.

p. 222 Apply the Skills
1. Sample response: The musician feels gratitude and comfort when he thinks about his parents. They inspired him to become a musician.
2. The poem is about the speaker's aunt.
3. In "Maestro," "again and again," "bit by bit," and "note to note" are repeated. In "The Desert Is My Mother," "I say" and "Le digo" are repeated. In "Bailando," "spinning round and round" is repeated.
4. **Graphic Organizer**
Sample response:
. . . a woman: serves, shouts, whispers, gives, strokes, offers, chants
. . . a hot and dry region: spiked cactus, sunny day, thunder and lightening, pink blossoms, windy, sun's glare, driest sand
both: "She gives me chamomile and other spices" and "warm breath."

Poetry Collection 1

Poetry Collection 2

p. 224 Graphic Organizer:
Sample response:
Poetry Collection 1:
"Haiku"
Detail 1: The pond is watched by a weasel.
Detail 2: The moon sets.
Detail 3: Shadows drift.

How are the details related? They all take place in a woodsy area.

Conclusion: The poet is concerned with nature.

Poetry Collection 2:
"Winter"

Detail 1: Frogs burrow in the mud.

Detail 2: "Snails bury themselves."

Detail 3: The speaker airs quilts.

How are the details related? All of the details describe how animals and people prepare for winter.

Conclusion: Animals and people want to stay warm, cozy, fed, and healthy during the winter.

p. 225 Reading/Writing Connection

Sample response: People write poems because poetry helps communicate feelings, ideas, and action in few words. The images in poetry can generate feelings of love, curiosity, anger, or longing. Poetry reinforces a love of words and wordplay.

p. 225 Note-taking Guide
"The Rider"

Topic of Poem: The topic is a person riding a bicycle.

Actions in Poem: Action in the poem includes pedaling hard, leaving loneliness, panting, and floating free.

"Seal"

Topic of Poem: The topic is a seal swimming through the water.

Actions in Poem: Action in the poem includes dives, darts, a swerve, a twist, a flip, a flick, plunges, and plops.

"Haiku"

Topic of Poem: The topics are ducklings in pond, the woods, and shadows in the forest.

Actions in Poem: Action in the poem include pond is watched, not one leaf moves, moon sets, and shadows drift and disappear.

p. 226 Activate Prior Knowledge

Students may say that they have been inspired by the image of an actor performing in a Shakespearean play. The actor's talent and dedication to his art would be a good subject for a poem.

p. 226 Reading Skill

Students may underline "float free," "a cloud of sudden azaleas," and "luminous pink petals."

p. 226 Literary Analysis

Sample response: The poem is inspired by the idea of moving so fast that one might escape from loneliness.

p. 227 Literary Analysis

Students should say that a concrete poem focuses on a visual image. The poet arranges the letters and lines in a way that suggests that image. Some students may say the poet chose this form because the poem's lines resemble a seal. Others may say that the lines resemble the seal's movement as it swims and dives.

p. 227 Reading Skill

Sample response: The speaker admires the seal for its graceful movements in the water.

p. 227 Reading Check

Students should circle "A whoop, a bark."

p. 228 Reading Skill

Students should say the speaker is worried that if the ducklings swim in the pond, the weasel will catch and eat them. Students might underline: "ducklings," "old green pond," and "weasel."

p. 228 Stop to Reflect

Students may say that it seems as if the woods themselves are afraid. The wind does not blow, and the leaves do not dare to move. Some students may say a predator is hunting in the woods. Other students may say that the woods are afraid of people who might do harm.

p. 228 Literary Analysis

Students should circle the syllables as follows: "Af-," "-ter," "the," "moon," "sets"; "slow," "through," "the," "for-," "-est," "sha-," "-dows"; "drift," "and," "dis-," "-ap-," and "-pear."

p. 228 Reader's Response

Students who like "The Rider" may say they like its colorful language. They may also say that they like how the poet describes his or her feelings.

p. 229 Apply the Skills

1. Sample response: The two sports have wheels, movement, and speed in common.
2. Sample response: These words create a playful, lively mood.

3. Sample response: What do the details about speed and movement mean all together?

4. **Graphic Organizer**

"The Rider" checkmarks under Musical language, Single image or idea, and Thoughts of one speaker

"Seal" checkmarks under Lines shaped like subject

"Haiku" checkmarks under Thoughts of one speaker; Three-lines; 17 syllables

p. 231 Reading/Writing Connection

Sample response: People might write a poem to capture their feelings about the desert. They could concentrate on details about animals, plants, and the climate of the desert. The poem would emphasize the variety and beauty of living things in the desert.

p. 231 Note-taking Guide

Sample response:

"Winter"

Supporting Details: "Chipmunks gather nuts." The speaker collects books.

"Forsythia"

Main Idea: Forsythia is a messenger of spring.

Supporting Details: "FORSYTHIA OUT" and "SPRING'S YELLOW TELEGRAM"

"Haiku"

Main Idea: Flowers are a sign of spring on a mountain.

Supporting Details: "sweet plum blossoms," "fragrant blossoms," and "Has spring come indeed?"

p. 232 Apply the Skills

1. Sample response: The words suggest that forsythia plants burst out in early spring to let everyone know that spring is on its way.

2. Sample response: He is respectful and awe-inspired by nature.

3. Sample response: How are the words about forsythia related?

4. **Graphic Organizer**

"Winter" checkmarks under Musical language, Single image or idea, and Thoughts of one speaker

"Forsythia" checkmarks under Lines shaped like subject

"Haiku" checkmarks under Thoughts of one speaker, and Three lines; 17 syllables

Poetry Collection 1

Poetry Collection 2

p. 234 Graphic Organizer

Sample response:

Poetry Collection 1:

Simile (from "The Courage That My Mother Had"): She had "courage like a rock."

Personification (from "Loo-Wit"): "She sprinkles ashes on the snow."

Metaphor (from "Life"): "Life is but a toy."

Symbol (from "Life"): The watch is a symbol that stands for life.

Poetry Collection 2:

"The Village Blacksmith"

Simile: "the muscles of his brawny arms / Are strong as iron bands."

Personification: "the bellows roar"

Metaphor: Life is a "flaming forge" at which peoples' "fortunes must be wrought"

Symbol: The "tear" represents sorrow or grief.

p. 235 Reading/Writing Connection

Sample response: Though they occur rarely, volcanic eruptions are very dangerous and harmful. Smoke and ash indicate that a volcano is getting ready to erupt. It is not difficult for a volcano to impress most people.

p. 235 Note-taking Guide

Sample response:

Topic of the Poem:

"Life" The topic is life.

"The Courage That My Mother Had" The speaker's mother's courage is the topic.

Words Used to Describe Topic:

"Life" The poem uses the words "toy," "ticking," and "run down."

"The Courage That My Mother Had" The poem uses the words "granite" and "rock."

"Loo-Wit" The poem uses the words "old," "trembling," and "thin."

p. 236 Activate Prior Knowledge

Students may describe life as an exciting adventure that could lead them anywhere. They may describe courage as an attitude that can help them do things that would otherwise be impossible. They may describe a volcano as a sign of the power of nature.

p. 236 Reading Skill

Sample response: The poet seems to feel that life is like a toy that people play with until they get tired of it. Life does not seem very important to the speaker.

p. 236 Literary Analysis
Students should underline "That courage like a rock."

p. 236 Stop to Reflect
Sample response: Life comes to an end when the watch runs down.

p. 237 Reading Skill
Sample response: The most important details are the old woman spitting "black tobacco" and sprinkling "ashes / on the snow." Readers can conclude that the old woman is actually a volcano that is beginning to erupt.

p. 237 Literary Analysis
Sample response: The machinery is a symbol that stands for the harm that human beings do to nature.

p. 237 Reading Check
Students should circle "spits her black tobacco any which way."

p. 238 Literary Analysis
Sample response: The poet uses personification to compare the volcano to an old woman. Students may underline any of the following details: "her trembling / the source / of dawn," "stones dislodge," "she finds her weapons / and raises them high," "clearing the twigs from her throat," and "shaking the sky."

p. 238 Reading Skill
Sample response: Loo-wit's singing is the eruption of the volcano.

p. 238 Reading Check
Students should circle "but she heard the boot scrape, / the creaking floor, / felt the pull of the blanket / from her thin shoulder."

p. 238 Reader's Response
Students may find the image in "Life" as a watch the most striking. They may see the image of life as a watch as a powerful way to express mortality.

p. 239 Apply the Skills
1. Sample response: The image of the watch suggests that life does not last forever.
2. The scrape of a boot causes the eruption.
3. **Graphic Organizer**
Sample response:
Detail: A toy swings on a bright chain.

Detail: The ticking of the watch amuses a child.
Detail: The old man, once an infant, is tired and lets the watch wind down.
4. Sample response: The rock is a symbol for strength.

p. 241 Reading/Writing Connection
Sample response: My older sister displays many qualities to admire, including a concern for others. It is easy to appreciate how she really listens when I talk to her about something important to me. This person makes others aspire to better themselves.

p. 241 Note-taking Guide
Sample response:
Topic of the Poem:
"The Village Blacksmith" The topic is life.
"Fog" The topic is fog.

Words Used to Describe Topic:
"The Village Blacksmith" "Thus at the flaming forge of life / Our fortunes must be wrought; / Thus on its sounding anvil shaped / Each burning deed and thought."
"Fog" "The fog comes / on little cat feet"; "It sits . . . on silent haunches."

p. 242 Apply the Skills
1. Sample response: The mysterious atmosphere that fog creates makes it a good subject.
2. Sample response: She demonstrates the qualities of strength and determination.
3. **Graphic Organizer**
Sample response:
Detail 1: The staircase often had splinters, torn up boards, and bare places.
Detail 2: The mother continued to climb even in darkness.
Detail 3: The mother tells her son that even though life is hard, she keeps climbing, and so should he.
4. Sample response: The comparison of the blacksmith and the sexton is a simile.

Reading Informational Materials: Advertisements

p. 247 Apply the Skills
Thinking About the Advertisements
1. Sample response: Words such as "amazing," "miracle," and "astonishing" in the advertisements appeal to the reader's emotions.

2. Sample response: The prices are probably not mentioned so the reader will focus on how "great" the sole is instead of how much it might cost.

Reading Skill
3. Sample response: The claim, "Never before has scientific research come up with such a remarkable combination," cannot be proved.
4. Sample response: The goal of the Neolite ad is to convince readers to buy Neolite soles for their shoes.

Poetry Collection 1
Poetry Collection 2

p. 248 Graphic Organizer
Sample response:
Poetry Collection 1:
Onomatopoeia (from "Weather"): "Dot a dot dot dot a dot dot / Spotting the windowpane."
Alliteration (from "Sarah Cynthia Sylvia Stout Would Not Take the Garbage Out"): "Sarah Cynthia Sylvia Stout" is alliteration.
Repetition (from "Sarah Cynthia Sylvia Stout Would Not Take the Garbage Out"): She "*would not take the garbage out*" repeats throughout the poem.

Poetry Collection 2:
Onomatopoeia (from "Onomatopoeia"): "The rusty spigot *sputters*"
Alliteration (from "Full Fathom Five"): "*F*ull *f*athom *f*ive thy *f*ather lies"
Repetition (from "Train Tune"): *Back through* clouds / *Back through* clearing / *Back through* distance / *Back through* silence."

p. 249 Reading/Writing Connection
Sample response:
1. When people see how I dress, they <u>react</u> with shock and surprise.
2. To stand out from the crowd I <u>dedicate</u> myself to practicing very hard.
3. My <u>attitude</u> is that everyone should strive to be <u>unique</u>.

p. 249 Note-taking Guide:
Sample response:
Topic of the Poem:
"Sarah Cynthia Sylvia Stout Would Not Take the Garbage Out" a girl who refuses to take out the garbage
"One" individuality

Words Used to Describe the Topic:
"Sarah Cynthia Sylvia Stout Would Not Take the Garbage Out" "It filled the can, it covered the floor," "It raised the roof, it broke the wall"
"One" "Only one," "nobody can get a second one"

p. 250 Activate Knowledge
Students may recall words such as "carbuncle" or "squish," as in "Did you *squish* your *carbuncle* today?"

p. 250 Literary Analysis
The title uses alliteration. The poet creates alliteration by having each part of the main character's name—"Sarah Cynthia Sylvia Stout"—start with the same sound.

p. 250 Reading Skill
Students should circle the words "She'd," "out," "And," and "cheese." Students should also circle the commas after "pans," "hams," "shout," "grounds," "peelings," "bananas," and "peas"; the periods after "out" and "cheese"; and the colon after "ceilings."

p. 251 Literary Analysis
Students should circle the letters "s" and "c" at the beginning of "Sarah" "Cynthia" "Stout" and "said."

p. 251 Reading Skill
Sample response: Rain is falling on the window. The rain makes wet dots and little tapping sounds.

p. 251 Literary Analysis
The poet uses repetition and onomatopoeia in this stanza.

p. 251 Reading Check
Students should circle "the windowpane."

p. 252 Literary Analysis
Students should circle the two uses of "nobody," the three uses of "my," and the two uses of "or."

p. 252 Reading Skill
Sample response: The speaker shapes words; I am one person. No one else can talk for me.

p. 252 Reading Check
Students should underline "Only one of me."

p. 252 Reader's Response

Students may say that they like the sounds of "Sarah Cynthia Sylvia Stout" best. They may respond to the alliteration and the singsong rhyme scheme. They may also like the silly topic and the words used to describe it.

p. 253 Apply the Skills

1. Sample response: The poem is funny and not preachy. The poem was intended to entertain, not to teach a lesson.
2. Sample response: The poet feels bad about all three words. "Mimic" and "act" are especially bad actions that involve others making fun of the speaker.
3. **Graphic Organizer**
Sample response:
"Sarah Cynthia Sylvia Stout . . . "
Example from Poem: "It cracked the window and blocked the door / With bacon rinds and chicken bones."
Paraphrase: The garbage cracked the window. It also blocked the door.

"Weather"
Example from Poem: "Dot a dot dot dot a dot dot / Spotting the windowpane."
Paraphrase: Dots of rain are all over the windowpane.
4. Sample response: "Splatter" and "slosh" are two words that imitate the sound of water.

p. 255 Reading/Writing Connection

Sample response:
1. The sound of flowing water can affect how a person feels.
2. If it persists, the sound of a jackhammer can be very irritating.
3. The sound of birds singing generates a feeling of happiness in many people.

p. 255 Note-taking Guide:

Sample response:
"Onomatopoeia"
Visual Details: "rusty spigot," "smattering of drops"
Aural (sound) Descriptions: "splutter," "splatters," "scatters," "plash!"

"Train Tune"
Visual Details: "clouds," "groves," "lightning"
Aural (sound) Descriptions: "silence"

p. 256 Apply the Skills

1. Sample response: The father's bones have turned into coral. His eyes have turned into pearls. Coral and pearls are precious items, so the changes might be called special or "rich." The changes might be called unusual or "strange" because the human form of the father appears to have become a part of the sea.
2. Sample response: The poet may be remembering a love that has ended or a loved one who has died.
3. **Graphic Organizer**
Sample response:
"Full Fathom Five"
Example from Poem: "Nothing of him that doth fade / But doth suffer a sea change / Into something rich and strange"
Paraphrase: His whole body is transformed as it decays.

"Onomatopoeia"
Example from Poem: "The rusty spigot / sputters, / utters / a splutter, / spatters a smattering of drops, / gashes wider"
Paraphrase: The old faucet makes a hissing noise. It spits some drops of water, and the water spreads.

"Train Tune"
Example from Poem: The poem has no punctuation and is meant to be read without pausing.
Paraphrase: The train travels fast across time and place.
4. Students may suggest words such as "slosh," "glug," and "dribble."

Poetry Collection 1

Poetry Collection 2

p. 258 Graphic Organizer

Sample response:
Poetry Collection 1:
"Annabel Lee"
Original: "The angels, not half so happy in Heaven, / Went envying her and me."
Unfamiliar Words: "envying"
Dictionary Definitions: "Envying" means wanting to have something that someone else has.
Paraphrase: The angels were not as happy as the speaker and Annabel Lee. They wanted what the lovers had.

Poetry Collection 2:
"Father William"
Original: "'In my youth,' said the sage, as he shook his gray locks, / 'I kept all my limbs very supple'"
Unfamiliar Words: *sage, locks, supple*
Dictionary Definitions of Unfamiliar Words: *sage* = wise man, *locks* = hair, *limbs* = arms and legs, *supple* = flexible
Paraphrase: "When I was young," the wise man said as he shook his gray hair, "I kept my body very flexible."

p. 259 Reading/Writing Connection
Sample response: The president has dedicated his/her life to helping Americans. He/She represents the people of the United States. His/Her actions affect the entire world.

p. 259 Note-taking Guide
Sample response:
"Martin Luther King"
Topic of Poem: Martin Luther King
Feelings the Speaker Has for the Topic: admiration; hope

"I'm Nobody"
Topic of Poem: being an ordinary person instead of being famous
Feelings the Speaker Has for the Topic: likes being "nobody special"; finds fame boring

p. 260 Activate Prior Knowledge
A student may recall the words to "Pride (In the Name of Love)" by U2: "One man come in the name of love / One man come and go / One man come, he to justify / One man to overthrow."

p. 260 Literary Analysis
Students should circle the following syllables: "man-," "man-," "year," and "-go" in the first line; and "king-," "by," and "sea" in the second line.

p. 260 Reading Skill
"Highborn kinsmen" means "relatives born into noble families." "Bore" means "carried." The lines mean that Annabel Lee was from a noble family. Her relatives carried her away from the speaker and buried her in a tomb by the sea.

p. 261 Reading Skill
Students may find words and phrases such as "Heaven above," "demons," "dissever,"

and "my soul from the soul" confusing. Students may paraphrase with these words: "Nothing can separate my soul from Annabel Lee's soul."

p. 261 Literary Analysis
Students should circle and connect the following rhymed words: "beams" and "dreams"; "rise" and "eyes"; "nighttide," "side," and "bride"; and "Lee," "Lee," "sea," and "sea."

p. 261 Reading Check
Students should underline "I see the bright eyes / Of the beautiful Annabel Lee."

p. 262 Literary Analysis
Students should circle the following syllables: "came," "-on," and "age" in the first line; "-set," "grief," and "rage" in the second line.

p. 262 Reading Skill
Students may find the phrases "a suffering earth" and "the measure of man's worth" confusing. Students may paraphrase with these words: "He taught society to value people for their real worth."

p. 262 Reading Check
Students should underline the words "they'd banish us."

p. 262 Reader's Response
Students may say that "Annabel Lee" would make the best song. Its strong rhythm and regular rhyme scheme give it a musical quality. The repeated phrases could become choruses.

p. 263 Apply the Skills
1. Sample response: The poet means that King's passion was very strong and powerful.
2. Sample response: "I'm Nobody" talks about how celebrities are always in public. They never have private time. They have to keep their admirers happy. This lifestyle can become boring and annoying.
3. Sample response: Annabel Lee's relatives took her body from the speaker. They buried it in a tomb by the sea.
4. **Graphic Organizer**
Sample response:
"Annabel Lee" ago, know; sea, Lee, me; we, sea, Lee; beams, dreams; rise, eyes; nighttide, side, bride.
"Martin Luther King" age, rage; wide, aside; profound, around; earth, worth; slain, again.

p. 265 Reading/Writing Connection
Sample response:
1. A person's outlook on life can affect how well you remember him or her.
2. Someone with a positive attitude can enrich the lives of others.
3. He or she can teach others to appreciate simple pleasures.

p. 265 Note-taking Guide
Sample response:
Characters in poem:
"Father William" Father William, his son
"Stopping by Woods . . . " a traveler

Actions in poem:
"Jim" The sun shines on Jim. Jim brings his mother cocoa, broth, bread, and medicine. Jim tiptoes and tidies her room. He misses his baseball game.
"Father William" Father William and his son discuss the father's behavior. Father William stands on his head, turns a somersault, eats goose bones, and balances an eel on the end of his nose.
"Stopping by Woods . . . " A traveler stops to watch the woods fill up with snow. The person wonders at the beauty and quiet of the snow and then continues the journey.

p. 266 Apply the Skills
1. Sample response: Jim's decision to give up his baseball game to take care of his mother shows that he is not selfish.
2. Sample response: Father William seems too old and too large to stand on his head or do somersaults.
3. Sample response: The only other sound in the wood is the wind blowing gently and the snow falling softly.
4. **Graphic Organizer**
Rhyming Words:
"Jim" Jim, him; in, medicine; see, terribly
"Father William" said, head; white, right; son, none; brain, again; before, door; fat, that; locks, box; supple, couple; weak, beak; suet, do it; law, jaw; wife, life; suppose, nose; ever, clever; enough, stuff; airs, downstairs
"Stopping by Woods . . . " know, though, snow; here, queer, year; lake, shake, mistake, flake; sweep, deep, keep, sleep

Reading Informational Materials: Magazine Articles

p. 268 Graphic Organizer
Sample response:
Sentence or Passage: It could be the hammering lyrics of a rap artist.
Replacement Words: hammering = pounding; lyrics = words
Paraphrase: It could be the pounding words of the rap artist.

p. 269 Reading Magazine Articles
Sample response: The people dancing add visual interest.

p. 269 Reading Skill
Students should circle "*Odyssey Magazine*, March 2002."

p. 269 Reading Check
Students should underline "Rap as a popular music style started in the late 1970s."

p. 269 Reading Magazine Articles
Sample response: The title catches a reader's attention. The title uses alliteration to help the reader understand that rap music is like poetry.

p. 270 Stop to Reflect
Sample response: Reading a poem and reading Dr. Seuss are like rap music because they use strong rhythmic phrasing.

p. 270 Reading Magazine Articles
Sample response: The main idea is "Sampling serves up yet more rhythms in rap."

p. 270 Reading Check
Students should circle "'MC' is the same as 'emcee' and stands for 'master of ceremonies.'"

p. 271 Reading Skill
Sample response: Listeners need interesting rhythm patterns to enjoy music. Rap music uses a mix of rhythms. It also has unpredictable lyrics and syncopation. Rap music is fun because it pleases and amazes listeners.

p. 271 Reading Informational Materials
Sample response: The last paragraph ties together the ideas in the article. It also lets the reader know that this paragraph is the end of the article.

p. 271 Reading Check

Students should circle "Too fast, and the brain can't perceive individual sounds. The music becomes one big blur."

p. 272 Apply the Skills
Thinking About the Magazine Article

1. Sample response: Tempo sets the mood for music. Tempo must not be too fast or too slow, or the song will not sound right.

2. Sample response: The brain remembers groups or patterns of rhythms in music. Music must use patterns or the brain will not process the sounds.

Reading Skill

3. Sample response: Rap is about people, and some rap songs get noticed.

4. Sample response: Sampling is taking a small part of one song and using it over and over to add background to a new song.

from Dragonwings
Laurence Yep

p. 275 Note-taking Guide
Sample response:
Novel: The narrator gets out of bed to answer the door.
Drama: Moon Shadow writes to his mother. Windrider and others pull Dragonwings to the top of the hill. Windrider flies and then falls to the ground. Windrider tells Moon Shadow that he won't fly again.
Both: Moon Shadow learns that Hand Clap, Uncle, and many others have come to help Father get the flying machine up the hill. Uncle Bright Star and Miss Whitlaw arrive.

p. 276 Activate Prior Knowledge
Some students may describe a place on a mountain. It would be a flat area, and not high enough for snow to be present. Other students may describe an airport runway, long and flat and surrounded by grass.

p. 276 Fiction
Sample response: The actor playing Moon Shadow would have to show his surprise and happiness with facial expressions. He would smile and his eyes would grow wide with surprise. The actors playing the other characters would have to use body language to show that they are tired from coming up the hill. They would try to catch their breath, and their shoulders might be slumped.

p. 276 Reading Check
Students should circle "Hand Clap stood there as if he had appeared by magic."

p. 277 Stop to Reflect
Sample response: Uncle cares about his brother. He wants to make up for his son's actions.

p. 277 Drama
Students should underline "later that day." Students should circle "Piedmont" and "outside the stable."

p. 277 Reading Check
Students should underline "Black Dog stole all we have, and the landlord will not give us an extension on our rent."

p. 278 Drama
Sample response: Windrider enters from upstage. He is wearing a cap.

p. 278 Drama
Sample response: Uncle cares about his brother. He is helping even though he doesn't believe in flying machines. He notices how thin and ragged his brother has become.

p. 278 Stop to Reflect
Sample response: It is very difficult to move the flying machine. Moon Shadow stumbles and then gives up. It appears that Uncle Bright Star and the others must use all their might to move the flying machine.

p. 279 Drama
Sample response: The characters are believable because they begin to speak their native dialect, Cantonese. They remember another challenging physical experience from their past, when they worked on the railroad.

p. 279 Drama
Sample response: Windrider is facing upstage with his back to the audience. He is in the center of the plane, with Miss Whitlaw to his right and Moon Shadow to his left.

p. 279 Reading Check
Students should underline "We made it."

p. 280 Drama
Sample response: Uncle Bright Star should turn slowly and look at the aeroplane. Miss Whitlaw should cross her fingers and look at the aeroplane. Windrider should do his flight ballet. Moon Shadow should be watching and pointing.

p. 280 Drama
Sample response: Moon Shadow is not talking with any other characters. Students should underline "steps forward and addresses the audience."

p. 280 Reading Check
Students should underline "He's up!"; "He's really flying."; "You did it."

p. 281 Stop to Reflect
Sample response: He will not fly Dragonwings again. Windrider feels that his son is more important to him than flying.

p. 281 Reader's Response
Some students may say that this is a good ending for the story because it shows that

Windrider is able to accept his not being able to fly and because Moon Shadow's mother will come to live with them. Other students may say no, pointing out that Windrider will never fly again.

p. 282 Apply the Skills

1. Sample response: The audience knows that the actors move Dragonwings up the hill because the actors pantomime putting the ropes over their shoulders and pulling.

2. Sample response: Moon Shadow is saying that he and his father never forgot about building another aeroplane. Even though they did not, they still dreamed of doing so.

3. Sample response: The drama enhances the emotion of the situation because actors add tone, facial expressions, and body language to the scene, and these enhance the emotion of a situation. Drama also enhances emotion because the audience can see the scene unfold before them, not just read about it.

4. **Graphic Organizer**
Sample response:
To Show Action: "Take that propeller."; "We need to pull Dragonwings to the very top."
To Reveal Thoughts and Feelings: "When I was up in the air, I tried to find you. . . . Like you were disappearing from my life"; "But you haven't broken your neck, which was more than I ever expected."
To Describe Setting: "That hill is a very steep hill"; "Tramp the grass down in front."

A Christmas Carol: Scrooge and Marley, Act I Israel Horovitz *from* A Christmas Carol by Charles Dickens

p. 284 Graphic Organizer
Sample response:
What Is Suggested About the Work?
Picture: It will be set in the past.
Organization, Structure, Literary Form: It will be a play with many characters, acts, and scenes, and a story told through dialogue.
Beginnings of Passages: There will be ghosts and supernatural events.

p. 285 Reading/Writing Connection
Sample response:
1. A scrooge is someone who cares only about himself or herself.

2. Being a scrooge does not involve being generous to others.
3. A scrooge does not appreciate family and friends.

p. 285 Note-taking Guide
Sample response:
Evidence 1: He refuses to spend Christmas Eve with his nephew's family; he will not give money to help the poor.
Evidence 2: As a boy, he loved his sister; as a young apprentice, he was happy with his friends and his boss.
Evidence 3: He wishes he had treated Cratchit more kindly; he wishes he had not chosen greed over the woman he loved.

p. 286 Activate Prior Knowledge
Some students may say that ghosts appear in stories to frighten readers. Other students may say that the role of a ghost is to give a warning to the living. Some may also say that ghosts act as observers in stories. Students may say that they remember the story of the Headless Horseman or a cartoon ghost.

p. 286 Stop to Reflect
Sample response: For a play that has many characters, as *A Christmas Carol* does, a list of characters helps readers identify and recall the characters. For example, a reader can review the list to see that Fred is Scrooge's nephew.

p. 286 Reading Skill
Students may circle "Ebenezer Scrooge," "Scrooge's lost love," "A Corpse," "The Ghost of Christmas Past," "The Ghost of Christmas Present," or "The Ghost of Christmas Future."

p. 287 Reading Skill
Some students may say that their purpose is to be entertained. Other students may say that their purpose is to be inspired because the play takes place on a day that is an important spiritual holiday for some people.

p. 287 Literary Analysis
Students should circle "He speaks straight out to auditorium" and "Marley."

p. 287 Reading Check
Students should underline "The entire action of the play takes place on Christmas Eve, Christmas Day, and the morning after Christmas, 1843."

p. 288 Reading Skill

Most students may say that their purpose for reading is to learn a lesson about generosity and the Christmas spirit. Some students may say that their purpose is to be entertained by a scary story. Other students may say that they want to find out what will happen to Scrooge.

p. 288 Stop to Reflect

Sample response: Readers cannot see lighting effects as an audience can. Readers need to be told what they would see if they were actually watching the play.

p. 288 Reading Check

Students should underline "It's all the same to him. And it's cheaper than painting in a new sign, isn't it?"

p. 289 Stop to Reflect

Sample response: Explosions accompanied by puffs of smoke would make Marley's entrances and exits more mysterious and ghostly.

p. 289 Literary Analysis

Some students may say the lines show that Scrooge is selfish and mean. He bullies Cratchit, apparently his only employee, by threatening to fire him. Students may also say that Scrooge is needlessly stingy.

p. 289 Reading Check

Students should circle "a fire so tiny as to barely cast a light: perhaps it is one pitifully glowing coal?"

p. 290 Literary Analysis

Students should recognize that the dialogue shows that the nephew values the ideas behind Christmas, such as love and unselfishness towards others. He has a cheerful attitude towards life. Students should note that Scrooge is grumpy and values neither Christmas nor love and unselfishness.

p. 290 Stop to Reflect

Sample response: People's personalities are shaped by their experiences. Scrooge and his nephew may have had very different experiences in life.

p. 290 Reading Skill

Students may underline "And therefore, Uncle, though it has never put a scrap of gold or silver in my pocket, I believe that it has done me good; and I say, God bless it!"

p. 291 Literary Analysis

Students may say that the nephew is kind and forgiving. Even though his uncle insults him, he invites Scrooge to Christmas dinner. However, Scrooge is rude and thoughtless.

p. 291 Stop to Reflect

Sample response: Scrooge thinks love is ridiculous. He may feel this way about love because has had an unhappy experience with it.

p. 291 Reading Check

Students should circle "Because I fell in love."

p. 292 Reading Skill

Some students may say that their purpose is to see what happens to someone like Scrooge, who is so against the Christmas spirit. Sample response: What happened in Scrooge's past to make him so mean?

p. 292 Literary Analysis

Sample response: Cratchit's words reveal a spirit so generous that he thinks the best of Scrooge, even though Scrooge is cruel to him.

p. 292 Reading Check

Students should circle "Mr. Marley has been dead these seven years. He died seven years ago this very night."

p. 293 Literary Analysis

Sample response: Scrooge has no compassion for the poor and believes that the current workhouses and prisons are enough for them.

p. 293 Stop to Reflect

Sample response: Life was extremely hard for the poor. They were often hungry and did not have enough education or housing. They were imprisoned or forced into labor because they were poor.

p. 293 Reading Skill

Sample response: He will learn that giving and kindness are more rewarding than being miserly. Students may underline "We choose this time, because it is a time, of all others, when Want is keenly felt, and Abundance rejoices."

p. 294 Stop to Reflect

Students may say that Cratchit gives the man money, a contribution for the poor. Students may say that Cratchit, although poor, is also generous and does not want to be put in the same category as Scrooge.

p. 294 Literary Analysis
Students should circle eleven ellipses on the page. Sample response: Everyone on the page pauses at least once. Cratchit might want to say "Merry Christmas" to Scrooge.

p. 294 Reading Check
Students should underline "It's not my business. It is enough for a man to understand his own business, and not to interfere with other people's."

p. 295 Literary Analysis
Some students may say that the dialogue does not teach them anything new about Scrooge. It reaffirms his miserliness and lack of generosity towards people. Students may also note that it underlines how little Scrooge thinks of Christmas.

p. 295 Stop to Reflect
Students should underline "Suddenly;" and "he runs out the door, shutting same behind him."

p. 295 Reading Check
Students should underline "Be here all the earlier the next morning!"

p. 296 Stop to Reflect
Sample response: Scrooge's behavior is exaggerated, which may seem comical. But although Scrooge is funny on some levels, he is much more pathetic and even sad. Students may describe Scrooge as cold, mean, miserly, and cruel.

p. 296 Reading Skill
Students may say that their purpose for reading is to be frightened and entertained by a spooky ghost story. Some students may look forward to seeing Scrooge receive what he deserves.

p. 296 Reading Check
Students should underline "A musical sound; quickly: ghostly."

p. 297 Literary Analysis
Sample response: Scrooge's words suggest that he is neither impressed nor frightened by the strange visions and sounds at the beginning of the scene. His "Bah! Humbug!" suggests that he does not want to believe that any of it is real. Students may underline "He checks each room," "He looks under the sofa, under the table," "Scrooge blinks his eyes," "Scrooge is stunned by the phenomenon," and "the stricken Scrooge."

p. 297 Stop to Reflect
Sample response: Scrooge does not like being weak or emotional, so he will not admit to being scared of strange noises.

p. 297 Reading Check
Students should underline "He fixes his evening gruel on the hob, changes his jacket."

p. 298 Literary Analysis
Students may say that Scrooge probably does not believe in ghosts because he believes everything can be explained by physical causes.

p. 298 Reading Skill
Students may say that the questions make them want to read more to learn what Marley's answers will be. Some students may say that although their main purpose for reading this play is to be entertained, they also expect Marley's answers to teach Scrooge a lesson.

p. 298 Reading Check
Students should underline "Because every little thing affects them. A slight disorder of the stomach makes them cheat."

p. 299 Literary Analysis
Sample response: Marley shows his anger by shouting. Marley's dialogue makes the point that people should care about the well-being of others, not about money and "business."

p. 299 Reading Skill
Sample response: Marley comes to say that Scrooge need not share Marley's fate. Students may say that their purpose is to find out how Scrooge can turn his life around.

p. 300 Stop to Reflect
Sample response: The ghosts suggest that many people made the same mistakes that Marley made and that Scrooge is making—valuing money more than the welfare of others.

p. 300 Literary Analysis
Students may circle "Don't leave me! I'm frightened!"

p. 300 Reading Skill

Students' questions may include the following: Will any ghosts visit Scrooge? Why will they visit? What will they do with Scrooge? Will their visits change him?

p. 301 Literary Analysis

Sample response: Marley says that he will remain visible to the audience but not to Scrooge. Marley also says that the audience will witness a change in Scrooge as the plot develops.

p. 301 Stop to Reflect

Students may underline "I cannot in any way afford to lose my days. Securities come due, promissory notes, interest on investments: these are things that happen in the daylight!"

p. 301 Reading Check

Students should circle "From this point forth . . . I shall be quite visible to you, but invisible to him."

p. 302 Reading Skill

Some students may say that their purpose is to find out what the Ghost of Christmas Past will show or tell Scrooge. Some students may say they expect to be frightened and impressed by the ghost.

p. 302 Literary Analysis

Sample response: Scrooge is very polite to the ghost. Scrooge was rude and nasty to everyone at the beginning of the play. His new manners show that he realizes that he is no longer an important or powerful person.

p. 303 Reading Skill

Students may say that Marley is telling the audience that Scrooge is awakening to life and feelings. He is beginning to change. Students may say that they expect Scrooge to begin to see the error of his ways in this scene. Some students may say that Scrooge will be forced to revisit poor choices he made in the past.

p. 303 Literary Analysis

Students should circle "nothing." Sample response: Scrooge wants to see the places from his past; but at the same time, he doesn't want to spend much time there because it is painful for him.

p. 303 Reading Check

Students should underline "In the background, we see a field that is open; covered by a soft, downy snow: a country road" and "I was bred in this place. I was a boy here!"

p. 304 Stop to Reflect

Students may say that they would feel happy because they would be able to see how their home and family once looked.

p. 304 Literary Analysis

Sample response: Remembering his own lonely experience as a boy allows Scrooge to relate to the singing boy. Scrooge was stingy before, but the dialogue shows that he now wishes that he had given something to the boy he heard singing earlier in the play. Scrooge is becoming more generous.

p. 304 Reading Check

Students should circle "a small boy, the young Scrooge, sitting and weeping, bravely, alone at his desk: alone in a vast space, a void."

p. 305 Reading Skill

Students may ask: Why was Scrooge left at school until his sister asked to have him come home? Is Scrooge's nephew Fan's son? Where is Fan now?

p. 305 Stop to Reflect

Students should underline "O! Quiet, Fan. It is the Schoolmaster, himself!"

p. 305 Reading Check

Students should circle "six."

p. 306 Literary Analysis

Sample response: The passage shows that Scrooge has a gentle side and that he once had love in his heart.

p. 306 Stop to Reflect

Students may say that they are surprised by how much Scrooge loved his sister. Students may say that it is surprising that Scrooge does not treat his nephew better, considering how much Scrooge loved Fan.

p. 306 Reading Check

Students could circle "Wasn't I apprenticed there?" and "Dick and Ebenezer are Fezziwig's apprentices."

p. 307 Stop to Reflect
Students may underline "dancing to the music" and "She dances with Ebenezer, lifting him and throwing him about."

p. 307 Literary Analysis
Sample response: The dialogue reveals that Young Scrooge greatly admired and respected Fezziwig. Scrooge's words are surprising because as an adult, he became the exact opposite of Fezziwig, treating his employees with disrespect and disdain.

p. 307 Reading Check
Students should circle "Small!"

p. 308 Literary Analysis
Sample response: Scrooge feels shame for failing to live up to Fezziwig's example as an employer. He seems to be thinking about apologizing to Cratchit and perhaps promising to treat his employee more kindly in the future.

p. 308 Reading Skill
Students should underline "a mourning dress," "She is crying," and "with hostility." Students may say that their purpose for continuing to read is to find out why the young girl is so upset.

p. 308 Literary Analysis
Sample response: The woman reveals that the man has changed from loving her to loving money. She says that once they were both poor and very much alike, but that now money has become important to him and they have become too different to be happy together.

p. 309 Literary Analysis
Sample response: Scrooge's love left him because she believed that he had become obsessed with money and considered her "unprofitable."

p. 309 Stop to Reflect
Some students may say that Scrooge no longer loved her and did not feel compelled to urge her to stay. Others may say that although he loved her, he had begun to value money more than love.

p. 309 Reading Check
Students should underline "Don't release me, madam. . . ." and "Ah, yes!"

p. 310 Literary Analysis
Students should recognize that Scrooge has come to regret letting the woman go. Scrooge's

shouts of "No!" show how he has changed. Students should also notice that while the younger Scrooge calls the woman a "fool" and a "mindless loon," the older Scrooge uses the same words to describe his younger self.

p. 310 Reading Skill
Students may underline "May you be happy in the life that you have chosen for yourself . . ."; "They are what they are. Do not blame me, Mr. Scrooge"; and "the recognition of what was."

p. 311 Reading Skill
Students may say their purpose for reading Act II is to be entertained, to be frightened, or to learn a lesson about the meaning of Christmas. Some students may say that they also want to find out what will happen to Scrooge and whether he will embrace the spirit of Christmas.

p. 311 Reading Check
Students should circle "The play house tells me there's hot cider," and "hurry back to your seats."

p. 311 Reader's Response
Students may say that recalling those sad memories would have upset them. They may also say that they would be afraid of the visits of the other specters.

p. 312 Apply the Skills
1. Sample response: No, Scrooge is a lonely and bitter man because he has forsaken humanity for greed.
2. Sample response: Scrooge currently treats people harshly. He might in the future make an effort to build friendly relationships with the people around him.
3. Some students may expect to be entertained, some may expect to be inspired, and some may expect both.
4. **Graphic Organizer**
Sample response:
What Does It Say? "Let me hear another sound from you and you'll keep your Christmas by losing your situation."
What Does It Mean? Scrooge threatens Cratchit with the loss of his job for agreeing with Scrooge's nephew.
Why Is It Important? It shows what a bully Scrooge is.

A Christmas Carol:
Scrooge and Marley, Act II
Israel Horovitz
from A Christmas Carol
by Charles Dickens

p. 314 Graphic Organizer
Sample response:
Types of Reading Material: Dialogue
Purpose for Reading: To be entertained
Reading Rate: Read quickly to mimic
conversation.

p. 315 Note-taking Guide
Sample response:
Details That Support These Statements:
Row 2: "A nervous giggle here"; "Oh, Ghost of
the Future, I fear you more than any Specter I
have seen!"
Row 3: "I am as happy as a schoolboy"; "An
act of kindness is like the first green grape of
summer: it leads to another and another and
another."

p. 316 Apply the Skills
1. Sample response: Scrooge feels drawn to
the caring young boy.
2. Sample response: Scrooge's actions suggest
that he has taken the lessons to heart. His
Christmas generosity shows that he is considering others and that he now enjoys giving.
3. Students may say that they read long
speeches with difficult vocabulary slowly and
carefully to improve their understanding of
the text.
4. **Graphic Organizer**
Sample response:
Characters on Stage: Scrooge, Marley
Movement of Characters: Marley moves
close to the sleeping Scrooge.
Description of Lighting: a spotlight on
Scrooge and one on Marley, lightning flashes,
candle, colors change
Description of Sound: singing, thunder,
ghostly music; Marley laughs and speaks.
Other Special Effects: A flame shoots from
Marley's hand.

Reading Informational Materials:
Literary Criticism

p. 318 Graphic Organizer
Sample response:
TNT:
Critic's summary: none
Positive comments: "But TNT's *Carol*
would be worth watching if only for the lead
performance of Patrick Stewart."
Negative comments: "gratuitous special
effects"
Critic's overall opinion: "Old story well told."

Meadow Brook Theater:
Critic's summary: none
Positive comments: "Wicks has infused the
show with new energy," "a more palatable
holiday treat for adults and children"
Negative comments: "paying only passing
attention to his English accent"
Critic's overall opinion: "A well-produced,
grand-scale event that is as much pageant
as play."

p. 319 Reading Check
Students should underline "But TNT's *Carol*
would be worth watching if only for the lead
performance of Patrick Stewart."

p. 319 Reading Literary Criticism
Students should underline: "TNT" and "Sun.,
Dec. 5, 8 p.m., ET." Sample response: The
audience for this review is people who have
televisions and who might want to watch *A
Christmas Carol.*

p. 319 Reading Skill
Students should circle "Bottom line: Old story
well told." Sample response: The critic would
recommend that people watch this show. The
critic thinks it is refreshingly different from
other versions of *A Christmas Carol* and therefore worth watching.

p. 320 Reading Skill
Sample response: The writer is positive about
the change made by the director and will
probably write a good review. Students may
underline "make the old holiday fruitcake
seem fresh."

p. 320 Reading Literary Criticism
Students may underline "The audience is still
serenaded by a band of merry carolers in the

lobby before the show," "the set and costumes are unchanged from these many Christmases past," and "set design for the show is, as always, enormous and gorgeous." Sample response: Kelleher discusses the actors more than the scenery and the atmosphere of the production because people will probably watch the show on television to see famous actors. For the local production, audiences want to know about the actors, but the set and atmosphere are also important.

p. 320 Stop to Reflect

Sample response: The sets for this play had to show many different locations and some of these had to show both past and future events. It might have been difficult for the stage crew to change the scenes without interrupting the actors' performances. It would also have been difficult for the technical crew to perfect the timing of the ghosts' appearances and disappearances and to make the scary voices sound real.

p. 321 Reading Check

Students should circle "pageant" and "beautifully wrapped gift under a well-decorated tree."

p. 321 Reading Informational Materials

Some students may say that hearing about the wonderful lights and staging of the play makes them want to see the production in the theater. Other students may say that the description of Patrick Stewart's performance makes them want to watch the TNT version.

p. 321 Reading Literary Criticism

Sample response: Sousanis is comparing one Ebenezer Scrooge to another. Both actors have strengths, but the new Scrooge fits with the new production and is quite intriguing to watch.

p. 321 Reading Skill

Students should underline "All in all, *A Christmas Carol* is what it always has been: A well-produced, grand-scale event that is as much pageant as a play. And like a beautifully wrapped gift under a well-decorated tree, it suits the season to a tee." Sample response: The production is large and impressive, showing that it was done with care.

p. 322 Apply the Skills
Thinking About the Literary Criticism

1. Sample response: *People Weekly*: "So you muttered 'humbug' when you spied yet another version of *A Christmas Carol* on the TV schedule." *Oakland Press*: "Director Debra Wicks has tinkered with Meadow Brook's recipe for *A Christmas Carol* just enough to make the old holiday fruitcake seem fresh."
2. Sample response: Kelleher believes that people should watch the production if only to see Patrick Stewart's portrayal of Scrooge.

Reading Skill

3. Sample response: The phrase "like a beautifully wrapped gift under a well-decorated tree, it suits the season to a tee," summarizes Sousanis's opinion.
4. Sample response: Kelleher thinks that the story has been done too many times.

The Monsters Are Due on Maple Street
Rod Serling

p. 323 Graphic Organizer

Sample response:
Character: Charlie
Action 1: says Les needs to be watched
Motive 1: thinks Les may be dangerous
Action 2: takes gun from Steve
Motive 2: wants to protect neighborhood
Action 3: shoots Pete
Motive 3: is afraid that Pete is an alien

p. 324 Reading/Writing Connection

Sample response:
1. It is easy to arouse suspicions by being different.
2. Too often, we contribute to rumors by repeating them without thinking.
3. Sadly, if you try to dispute a rumor, you will often become the object of another rumor.

p. 324 Note-taking Guide

Sample response:
Box 1: The neighbors turn on Charlie.
Box 2: People get scared.
Box 3: The people start destroying one another's possessions.
Box 4: Figure 1 explains to Figure 2 how to take over the world.

p. 325 Activate Prior Knowledge

Some students may have noticed that people in groups can get out of control quickly. Other students may have noticed that people sometimes do not express their opinions freely in large groups.

p. 325 Reading Skill

Sample response: Two men are watching a house. Sally says that she feels uncomfortable because Ethel Goodman is her friend. Charlie responds that there is something strange about the Goodmans and that in this scary time, the others need to be cautious.

p. 325 Reading Check

Students should underline: "From the various houses we can see candlelight but no electricity. . . ." Sample response: There is no electricity on the street.

p. 326 Stop to Reflect

Students should underline "Goodman stands there, his wife behind him, very frightened." Sample response: They would look around nervously, shout their lines, and stand with slumped shoulders.

p. 326 Literary Analysis

Sample response: Steve shouldn't associate with the Goodmans because he might cast suspicion on himself.

p. 326 Reading Skill

Sample response: Steve calls Charlie a "hanging judge" because the judgmental Charlie is quick to stir up trouble and accuse people.

p. 327 Reading Skill

Sample response: Steve is sarcastically saying that they should talk about anything that is odd about any of them. Then they should have trials and get rid of whoever is different.

p. 327 Reading Check

Students should underline "some kind of radio or something."

p. 327 Literary Analysis

Students should underline: "I talk to monsters from outer space. I talk to three-headed green men who fly over here in what look like meteors." Sample response: His answer should not be taken seriously. Steve becomes

sarcastic because he thinks Charlie is not making sense.

p. 328 Literary Analysis

Sample response: Steve is feeling frustrated, angry, and perhaps a bit fearful. He feels that he is losing a battle.

p. 328 Reading Skill

Students should circle: "carrying a shotgun." Sample response: It is mentioned in the stage directions because it is an important detail in the play.

p. 328 Reading Check

Students should underline "He pulls it out of Don's hand."

p. 329 Reading Skill

Sample response: Pete Van Horn is shot.

p. 329 Reading Check

Students should underline "a monster or something."

p. 329 Literary Analysis

Sample response: Charlie is motivated by fear and a desire to protect himself and his home.

p. 330 Stop to Reflect

They are probably starting to think that Charlie is the one to blame for everything and that he may be a monster or an alien.

p. 330 Reading Skill

Sample response: Steve repeats himself because he can't believe that Pete is dead and that Charlie thinks the entire situation is some kind of joke. Steve is trying to instill in Charlie some of the seriousness of the situation.

p. 330 Literary Analysis

Sample response: People think Charlie is the monster because he stirred up most of the trouble. He is also the person who shot Pete Van Horn, and his house is the only one on the street with electricity.

p. 330 Reading Skill

Sample response: People turn on Charlie and start chasing and beating him. He gets onto his porch and hugs his wife.

p. 331 Literary Analysis

Sample response: The people have become physically violent because a rock is thrown at Charlie and his wife.

p. 331 Literary Analysis

Sample response: People suspect Tommy because Charlie accuses him. Tommy is also the person who brought up the aliens and monsters.

p. 331 Reading Check

Students should underline "Goodman," "Charlie," and "Tommy."

p. 332 Reading Skill

Sample response: These stage directions are important because they show how the hysteria and frenzy of the situation is spiraling out of control.

p. 332 Reading Check

Students should circle "the kid" and "Charlie."

p. 332 Literary Analysis

Sample response: The people are motivated by their fear, which has reached a fever pitch. Their behavior is almost totally determined by the mob mentality.

p. 333 Literary Analysis

Sample response: Figure One's motive is conquest; when the humans have destroyed themselves, the aliens can assume control of the planet.

p. 333 Reading Skill

Students should circle "thoughts, attitudes, prejudices" and "suspicion." Sample response: Yes, these would be important details because they summarize the ways that society can be harmed.

p. 333 Reading Check

Students should underline "thoughts, attitudes, prejudices." Students should circle "a thought-less frightened search for a scapegoat."

p. 333 Reader's Response

Some students may say that they would have responded reasonably to the strange events and that they would not have participated in the hunt for suspects. Others may say that they would have made everyone leave to go to another street, not just Pete. That way, no one would be left behind to get suspicious.

p. 334 Apply the Skills

1. Sample response: Prejudices and attitudes lead people to destroy themselves; these are the tools of conquest.

2. Sample response: The monsters are the residents themselves.

3. **Graphic Organizer**

Sample response:

Important Details from the Beginning: There is a flash across the sky; the electricity goes out; a boy suggests that aliens may be responsible.

Important Details from the Middle: Les Goodman is suspected of being an alien; it is revealed that Steve has a radio in his basement, and the crowd's suspicions turn to him; Charlie shoots a shadowy figure who turns out to be Pete Van Horn.

Important Details from the End: The crowd accuses Charlie; Charlie accuses Tommy; the street dissolves into chaos; two aliens review the "procedure" used to get humans to destroy one another.

4. Sample response: Charlie keeps saying, "It's the kid." to throw suspicion off himself. They remember that it was Tommy who knew about the aliens in the first place.

Reading Informational Materials: Application

p. 337 Reading Informational Materials

Sample response: The playhouse wants to demonstrate the type and quality of its productions.

p. 337 Reading Applications

Sample response: The last sentence of the first paragraph suggests that the playhouse is looking for people who want to be apprentices and interns because a major purpose of the playhouse is to train people to perform there.

p. 337 Stop to Reflect

Students may say that the company seems a good place for an actor to get started. They may say that they would like to be accepted there because the chances of becoming a working performer are high. Students may circle "professional networking," "70% of whom were formerly apprentices and interns," and "Do you know how to get call backs at cattle-call auditions?"

p. 338 Reading Applications

Sample response: This application requires an address and Social Security number.

p. 338 Stop to Reflect

Sample response: Most people who fill out this application are probably in high school or college because there is a space for "Parent/Guardian Name."

p. 338 Reading Skill

Sample response: They are part of the same group because the information at the top of the application indicates that people should contact the Flat Rock Playhouse for information about the Vagabond School.

p. 338 Reading Check

Students should circle "However, if one's schedule or geographic distance from the Playhouse makes a personal audition impossible, one may send a videotaped audition consisting of two monologues and is applicable examples of singing and dance work."

p. 340 Apply the Skills
Thinking About the Application

1. Sample response: Applicants do not need much space to write a name. More space is included for the applicants' previous instruction so that applicants can list complete information and because this information is important to the school.

2. Sample response: The Vagabond School of the Drama provides advantages for someone looking for a career in acting because it provides opportunities for networking with professionals and education for marketing oneself in the theater business.

Reading Skill

3. The school requires a headshot or snapshot.
4. The section titled "Instruction" is designed to determine the applicant's experience.

"Grasshopper Logic"

"The Other Frog Prince"

**"duckbilled platypus
vs. beefsnakstik®"**
Jon Scieszka

p. 343 Note-taking Guide
Sample response:
"Grasshopper Logic"
Characters: Grasshopper, Mom Grasshopper
Problem: Grasshopper has waited too long to do a big homework assignment.
Moral: "There are plenty of things to say to calm a hopping mad Grasshopper mom. 'I don't know' is not one."

"The Other Frog Prince"
Characters: a frog, a princess
Problem: A frog says he is really a prince.
Moral: You should not believe everything you hear.

"duckbilled platypus vs. beefsnakstik®"
Characters: Duckbilled Platypus, BeefSnakStik®
Problem: Each character thinks it is better than the other.
Moral: Just because you have a lot of stuff, do not think you are so special.

p. 344 Activate Prior Knowledge
Sample response: A child lies. A child disobeys. A child does not do his or her schoolwork.

p. 344 Oral Traditions
Students should underline "Grasshopper" and "Mom Grasshopper."

p. 344 Oral Traditions
The assignment is exaggerated. It asks for twelve musicals with designed and built sets. One student cannot be expected to do all of that work.

p. 344 Reading Check
Students should underline "Just one small thing for History."

p. 345 Oral Traditions
Students should circle "frog."

p. 345 Oral Traditions
Sample response: In this story, the opposite happens. The princess kisses the frog, but the frog does not turn into the prince. The frog lies to the princess to get a kiss.

p. 345 Reading Check
Students should underline "the spell can only be broken by the kiss of a beautiful princess."

p. 346 Activate Prior Knowledge
Students should circle "Duckbilled Platypus." Students should underline "BeefSnakStik®."

p. 346 Stop to Reflect
Sample response: The words in bold type imply that the speaker is shouting or speaking louder.

p. 346 Reading Check
Students should underline "a tail like a beaver."

p. 346 Reader's Response
Sample response: Character: the frog: I think you played a great joke on the princess.

p. 347 Apply the Skills
1. Some students may prefer "Grasshopper Logic" because they can relate to Grasshopper procrastinating about his homework. Other students may prefer "The Other Frog Prince" because they are familiar with the original fairy tale and like the funny ending. Others may prefer the last story because it is very silly and different from the original version.
2. Grasshopper wants his mother to allow him to go out to play.
3. Sample response: "Grasshopper Logic": Do not put off doing something you have to do. "The Other Frog Prince": Do not trust everything you hear. "duckbilled platypus vs. beefsnakstik®": Do not brag.
4. **Graphic Organizer**
Sample response:
"Grasshopper Logic"
Hyperbole: the homework assignment
Personification: talking grasshoppers; a grasshopper that goes to school, carries a backpack, plays with friends, and has homework

"The Other Frog Prince"
Hyperbole: the princess kisses a frog so quickly
Personification: a frog talks

"duckbilled platypus vs. beefsnakstik®"
Hyperbole: BeefSnakStik argues with a duckbilled platypus
Personification: a beef stick wears a tie and talks with a duckbilled platypus

"Icarus and Daedalus"
Josephine Preston Peabody

"Demeter and Persephone"
Anne Terry White

p. 349 Graphic Organizer
Sample response:
"Icarus and Daedalus"
Cause: King Minos puts Daedalus and Icarus in prison on Crete.
Cause: Daedalus escapes his cell but cannot escape the island.
Cause: Daedalus sees seagulls flying.
Event: Daedalus builds wings to fly away.
Effect: Daedalus and Icarus fly away from Crete.
Effect: Icarus flies too close to the sun and crashes into the sea.
Effect: Daedalus names an island after his son and never flies again.

"Demeter and Persephone"
Sample response:
Cause: Aphrodite tells Eros to shoot an arrow at Pluto.
Cause: Eros shoots an arrow into Pluto's heart.
Cause: Pluto falls in love with Persephone.
Event: Pluto kidnaps Persephone.
Effect: Demeter makes Earth infertile.
Effect: Zeus sends Hermes to ask Pluto to release Persephone.
Effect: Pluto releases Persephone, but she must return during the winter months.

p. 350 Reading/Writing Connection
Sample response:
1. My dentist convinced me to eliminate candy before bedtime.
2. It was difficult to modify my free time so I could study and improve my grades.
3. It was easier to adapt to the new rules than it was to clean my room daily.

p. 350 Note-taking Guide
Sample response:
Second Box: Daedalus uses bird feathers, thread, and wax to make wings for himself and his son.
Third Box: Daedalus warns Icarus not to fly too close to the sun.
Fourth Box: Daedalus and Icarus fly away, but Icarus flies too close to the sun. His wings melt, and he falls into the sea.

p. 351 Activate Prior Knowledge
A student may describe a time when he or she tried to play a very difficult piece of music on an instrument or tried to read a book that was too difficult.

p. 351 Reading Skill
Daedalus watches the seagulls flying. He realizes that they are free because of their ability to fly. This realization causes Daedalus to make wings so that he and his son can fly away from the island.

p. 351 Literary Analysis
Students should underline "He held himself aloft, wavered this way and that with the wind, and at last, like a great fledgling, he learned to fly."

p. 351 Reading Check
Students should circle "never to fly very low or very high."

p. 352 Stop to Reflect
Sample response: No, the plan would not have worked. A person cannot fly merely by flapping his or her arms with wings made of feathers and wax attached.

p. 352 Reading Check
Students should circle "a vision of the gods—Apollo, perhaps, with Cupid after him."

p. 352 Reading Skill
The sun melts Icarus' wings. Without effective wings, Icarus falls into the ocean.

p. 353 Reading Skill
Daedalus searches for his son but finds only feathers from Icarus' wings on the water.

p. 353 Reading Check
Students should underline "in memory of the child."

p. 353 Reader's Response
Some students may say they would feel guilty for having made the wings. Other students

may say they would feel angry toward Icarus for not listening to the advice.

p. 354 Apply the Skills

1. Sample response: He designs a labyrinth for King Minos. He makes wings from bird feathers, thread, and wax.
2. Sample response: Icarus shows that he is irresponsible. To him, having fun is more important than being careful in a dangerous situation.
3. Daedalus names an island after his son. In his grief, he offers his wings to the temple of Apollo and never flies again.
4. **Graphic Organizer**
Sample response:
Icarus: Lesson: You should take warnings of danger seriously. **How Taught:** through Icarus' death
Daedalus: Lesson: It is dangerous to outwit fate using the secrets of the gods. **How Taught:** through Icarus' death

p. 356 Reading/Writing Connection

Sample response: I appreciate my favorite season because I love to watch the leaves change color. It serves to unify the summer and the winter. It is hard to specify how beautiful the trees look.

p. 356 Note-taking Guide

Sample response:
Pluto: Falls in love with Persephone; kidnaps her
Demeter: Makes it so that the earth will not produce food
Persephone: Misses the flowers of the earth; eats a pomegranate from the underworld
Zeus: Sends Hermes to ask Pluto to release Persephone

p. 357 Apply the Skills

1. Sample response: Some students may say that Demeter's actions are justifiable because she has lost someone she loves. Others may say that her actions are not justifiable because innocent people will suffer as a result.
2. Sample response: When Persephone returns to the underworld, Demeter grieves and vegetation dies. When Persephone returns to her mother, Demeter's joy brings life back to the fields.
3. Zeus intervenes, forcing Pluto to release Persephone.

4. **Graphic Organizer**
Sample response:
Demeter: Lesson: You should show restraint. **How Taught:** through Zeus' mercy toward humankind and Persephone's return
Persephone: Lesson: Appearances may be deceiving. **How Taught:** through Pluto's love for Persephone and his grief at her departure
Pluto: Lesson: Love is a powerful emotion. **How Taught:** through his feelings for Persephone

Reading Informational Materials: Textbooks

p. 360 Reading Textbooks

Students should underline "The Seasons on Earth," "How Sunlight Hits Earth," and "Earth's Tilted Axis." Students should recognize that the headings tell them that they will learn how sunlight and the Earth's axis affect the seasons on Earth.

p. 360 Reading Skill

The Earth's tilted axis causes it to have seasons.

p. 360 Reading Informational Materials

Sample response: The headings tell me what I am reading about and help me understand the main idea of each section. The figure and its caption illustrate the ideas in the text.

p. 360 Reading Check

Students should circle "Notice that sunlight hits Earth's surface most directly near the equator. Near the poles, sunlight arrives at a steep angle. As a result, it is spread out over a greater area. That is why it is warmer near the equator than near the poles."

p. 362 Apply the Skills
Thinking About the Textbook

1. As it is the beginning of summer at that time, one would expect warm weather in the Northern Hemisphere.
2. Because they receive the most direct sunlight all year, people living near the equator experience warmer temperatures.

Reading Skill

3. The tilt of Earth's axis causes the yearly cycle of seasons.
4. The season is summer.

"Tenochtitlan: Inside the Aztec Capital"
Jacqueline Dineen

"Popocatepetl and Ixtlaccihuatl"
Juliet Piggott Wood

p. 363 Graphic Organizer
Sample response:

"Tenochtitlan: Inside the Aztec Capital"
Cause/Effect: *Because* Tenochtitlan was built in a swamp, the city needed land to grow food.
Effect/Cause: The people built chinampas, or small islands, where they could grow food.
Cause/Effect: *Because* the chinampas were built on the swamp, the huts on them had to be light so that they would not sink.

p. 363 Graphic Organizer
Sample Response:

"Popocatepetl and Ixtlaccihuatl"
Cause/Effect: *Because* some warriors were jealous of Popo's strength and success, they told the emperor that Popo had had been killed in battle.
Effect/Cause: The emperor told Ixtla that Popo had died, and Ixtla died of a broken heart.
Cause/Effect: *As a result of* Ixtla's death, Popo refused to become emperor and had two pyramids built, one for Ixtla and one for himself to watch over her.

p. 364 Reading/Writing Connection
Sample response: City planners should adapt old city centers for the needs of current residents. City roads need to maximize ways to travel through downtown. One can modify a city plan by reworking public transportation.

p. 364 Note-taking Guide
Sample response:
The Floating Gardens: made of piles of earth in the shallow parts of the lakes; called chinampas; supplied with fresh water by ditches and canals
The Homes: nobles' houses: large homes like palaces, one story high around a courtyard, built from adobe and whitewashed; poor people's houses: built on chinampas with lighter material such as wattle-and-daub, grouped with other houses in walled compounds, had outdoor patio and gardens

The Furniture and Decoration: plain, dirt floor, mats of reeds for sleeping, clay cooking pots and utensils, reed baskets, grinding stones, household shrines with statues of the gods, no windows, no chimneys, no doors, open doorways

p. 365 Activate Prior Knowledge
Students may comment that ancient people lived more simply than people do today. They did not have electricity or toilets or cars. They had to grow their own food.

p. 365 Reading Skill
Three causeways linked the city to the mainland. Parts of the bridges on these causeways could be removed to protect the city against invaders. Stone aqueducts brought fresh water to the city.

p. 365 Literary Analysis
Sample response: The Spaniards' first account of Tenochtitlan refers to it as "an enchanted vision." It talks about the city "rising from the water." The Spaniards were impressed with the city, and their account of it likely inspired many stories.

p. 365 Reading Check
Students should circle "There the Aztecs built their first temple to Huitzilopochtli. The place was given the name Tenochtitlan. . . . "

p. 366 Stop to Reflect
Sample response: The city was built on a swamp in a lake. It was probably easier to use the water to travel than to try to build roads.

p. 366 Literary Analysis
Students should circle "but the northern lakes contained salt water, which was no good for irrigation."

p. 366 Reading Skill
The residents had to drain more land for farming and building.

p. 367 Stop to Reflect
Sample response: Many of the buildings were probably made from materials that did not last over time. Few ruins probably exist today.

p. 367 Literary Analysis
Certain historical records have provided the facts about the homes. For example, documents have been found that record the sales of building sites on chinampa gardens.

p. 367 Reading Check
Students should circle "Some houses on the island in the center of the city were built of adobe—bricks made from mud and dried in the sun."

p. 368 Stop to Reflect
Students most likely will say that it would have been difficult to live in a house with no windows or chimneys. It would have been dark and hard for a person to breathe. Also, it would have been difficult without doors for privacy and security.

p. 368 Reading Check
Students should circle "The houses had no windows or chimneys, so they must have been dark and smoky from the cooking fire."

p. 368 Reader's Response
Sample response: People could have used the city's location, large size, and unique design to write a legend. These features are interesting within themselves and would make for an interesting legend.

p. 369 Apply the Skills
1. **Graphic Organizer**
Sample response:
Questions: How did the Aztecs keep their cities safe? Why is there so little evidence about poor people's houses in Tenochtitlan?
Details: They built bridges that could be removed. What we know has been pieced together from scattered documents.
Understanding the Article: Their enemies could not get across the lake to attack them. No remains of poor people's houses survived to be studied.
2. Sample response: The Aztecs built chinampas, which allowed the people of Tenochtitlan to produce more of their own food. Each chinampa produced enough food to feed one family. The Aztecs also dug ditches and built canals to bring fresh water to the city.
3. Sample response: The Aztecs had water for irrigation.
4. Sample response: Facts: The Aztecs built three causeways over the swamp; Tenochtitlan was built in a huge valley; water flowed along stone aqueducts from the mainland to Tenochtitlan. Predictions or assumptions: About one million people lived in the Valley of Mexico when Tenochtitlan was at its height; between one third and one half of people in Tenochtitlan were farmers.

p. 371 Reading/Writing Connection
Sample response: My favorite family stories illustrate what life was like for my ancestors. I hope my children appreciate how difficult life was for our ancestors. These stories reinforce my belief in the strength of family.

p. 371 Note-taking Guide
Sample response:
What Popo Does: He buries Ixtla under a heap of stones on one pyramid. He refuses to become emperor and climbs to the top of his own pyramid. He lights a torch and stays there to watch over Ixtla's body.
What Happens: Over the years, the pyramids become high, white-capped mountains.

p. 372 Apply the Skills
1. Graphic Organizer
Sample response:
Questions: Why does the Emperor care whether, after he dies, Ixtla rules alone or with a husband? Why does the Emperor offer his daughter to whoever defeats his enemies?
Details: The Emperor does not think anyone but his daughter will rule as he wants the city to be ruled. Enemies surround the city, and the Emperor is too weak to lead the fight against them.
Understanding the Legend: The Emperor is so proud that he wants to control what happens even after his death. The Emperor does not think that his daughter can defend the city without help.
2. Sample response: The Aztecs admired wisdom, honesty, bravery, and loyalty.
3. Popo's torch, still burning in memory of Ixtla, causes the volcano to smoke.
4. Sample response: Facts: Ixtlaccihuatl and Popocatepetl are volcanic mountains; Popocatepetl means "smoking mountain." The reader knows that they are facts because they can be proven true.

"Sun and Moon in a Box"
Richard Erdoes and Alfonso Ortiz

"How the Snake Got Poison"
Zora Neale Hurston

p. 374 Graphic Organizer
Sample response:

"Sun and Moon in a Box"
Story Title: "Sun and Moon in a Box"
Time: a long time ago, early in the history of Earth
Place: American Southwest, Kachina Pueblo
Customs: Native American dancing
Beliefs: A coyote released the sun and the moon into the sky. This action created winter.

"How the Snake Got Poison"
Story Title: "How the Snake Got Poison"
Time: probably a long time ago
Place: Earth and heaven
Customs: African American dialect
Beliefs: God gave snakes poison to protect themselves against other animals. He also gave snakes rattles to warn other animals of their approach.

p. 375 Reading/Writing Connection
Sample response: Some stories have a character who tries to exploit other characters. He will often convince others to trust him. He might interact with others in a normal way, but he is really trying to trick them.

p. 375 Note-taking Guide
Sample response:
Effect/Cause 1: They want to borrow the sun and moon, so Eagle grabs the box and flies off.
Effect/Cause 2: Coyote wants the box, so he pleads to carry it. He says his family will think badly of him for not helping. He promises not to open the box.
Effect/Cause 3: Eagle gives Coyote the box. Coyote cannot control his curiosity.
Effect/Cause 4: Coyote opens the box, and the sun and moon escape into the sky.

p. 376 Activate Prior Knowledge
Students may be familiar with the Greek legend of the god Apollo and his twin sister Artemis. When Apollo rode his golden chariot across the sky, he was the sun. When Artemis rode her silver chariot across the sky, she was the moon. Students also may be familiar with the Bible's account of God's creation of the sun, moon, and Earth.

p. 376 Literary Analysis
Sample response: Eagle and Coyote must cross canyons and rivers as they head west. The Kachinas are in charge of the sun and moon. The Kachinas are Native Americans who lived in the American Southwest.

p. 376 Reading Check
Students should circle "In it they kept the sun and the moon."

p. 377 Literary Analysis
Coyote addresses Eagle as "my chief." This title reflects the Native American culture.

p. 377 Stop to Reflect
Eagle does not trust Coyote and does not want him to carry the box. He thinks Coyote will open the box.

p. 377 Reading Skill
Students should underline the following: "I am ashamed to let you do all the carrying." "You might be curious and open the box and then we could lose the wonderful things we borrowed." "People will talk badly about me, letting you carry this burden"; "You won't be able to refrain from opening the box." "I am really embarrassed." "It is too precious to entrust to somebody like you." "My wife will scold me, and my children will no longer respect me." Sample response: Eagle wants to carry the box to keep it safe, so that they do not lose the things they borrowed. Coyote says he wants to carry the box because he is embarrassed to let Eagle take all of the responsibility for the box. Coyote is really curious and wants to open the box. Eagle's reasons are unselfish, and Coyote's reasons are selfish.

p. 378 Reading Skill
Students should underline "In a flash, Sun came out of the box and flew away, to the very edge of the sky . . ." and ". . . Moon jumped out and flew away to the outer rim of the sky. . . ." Sample response: Sun and Moon both flew out of the box and caused immediate changes to the climate.

p. 378 Literary Analysis
Sample response: Eagle says that if Coyote had acted responsibly, they could have always enjoyed summer. The story treats winter as a

bad and unpleasant season. Ancient people probably did not like winter as much as summer. They had a hard time finding food and staying warm in the winter.

p. 378 Reading Check
Students should circle "He could not curb his curiosity."

p. 378 Reader's Response
Some students may think that Eagle should have given Coyote the box. He was teaching Coyote responsibility and showing him trust. Other students may say that that Eagle should not have given Coyote the box because he knew Coyote could not be trusted.

p. 379 Apply the Skills
1. Sample response: Eagle may have decided that Coyote must be serious because of his constant begging to carry the box.
2. Sample response: Eagle shares responsibility. Eagle knew that he should not trust Coyote, but he let him carry the box anyway.
3. **Graphic Organizer**
Sample response:
Coyote: poor hunter, lazy, sneaky, irresponsible
Eagle: good hunter, strong, responsible, trusting
Both: Both want the box with the sun and the moon; both want to carry the box.
4. Sample response: The Kachinas were Native Americans who lived in the American Southwest. This detail shows that Native Americans from the Southwest told this story.

p. 381 Reading/Writing Connection
Sample response: Most people communicate by talking and writing. When people interact in different settings they behave in different ways. Language helps them comprehend what other people are doing and thinking.

p. 381 Note-taking Guide
Sample response:
Snake: complains to God because he has no protection; takes the poison and kills anything that tries to step on him; explains that he cannot tell who is an enemy and who is a friend
Varmints: tread on snakes and kill them; complain to God when snake gets poison because snake starts killing everything

p. 382 Apply the Skills
1. Sample response: The varmints and the snake are afraid of each other. They dislike

and misunderstand each other because of their past actions.
2. Sample response: This answer might reflect how people ignore each other unless there is a threat of harm. It might also show that two people sometimes need a third party to help them solve their differences.
3. **Graphic Organizer**
Sample response:
Snake: defenseless; living on the ground without protection from other animals; has no poison, rattle, legs, or claws; can see only feet
Varmints: can't see, smell, or hear the snake in the bushes; step on snake and kill its kind
Both: do not see enemies clearly; accidentally kill too many of the other's kind
4. The use of dialect helps readers understand that the folk tale comes from the African-American oral tradition.

Reading Informational Materials: Editorials

p. 384 Graphic Organizer
Sample response:
Animals in Zoos: do not learn the survival techniques needed to live in the wild; provide entertainment; are protected; educate visitors
Animals in the Wild: learn how to survive in their natural habitat; have better chances of success and reproduction; are free to behave naturally

p. 385 Reading Editorials
Sample response: The title suggests that there is a question to be answered. It shows that the author will be expressing an opinion.

p. 385 Reading Skill
The writer compares the zoo to a place of captivity where a person is deprived of his or her natural home and put on display.

p. 385 Reading Check
Students should underline "you're taken from your home," "people come from far and wide to ogle at you," and "your captors force you to perform for thousands of people."

p. 386 Reading Skill
The writer compares and contrasts how animals behave in zoos and how they behave in the wild. Students should underline "but" and "although."

p. 386 Stop to Reflect
Sample response: The writer tells readers that zoos have some good points because she wants readers to know that she has considered both sides of the issue.

p. 386 Reading Editorials
The writer supports this point by mentioning that the San Diego Zoo has four shows each day.

p. 387 Reading Editorials
Sample response: The paragraph says that zoos are supposed to be places to learn about and enjoy nature and animals, but that zoos do not live up to these ideals. The author explains that zoos take care of animals, but they do not treat animals with the respect they deserve.

p. 387 Reading Informational Materials
Some students may say that the editorial showed them that zoos are not as good as they thought they were. The article explains that it is not fair to keep animals in small pens and cages. It also explains how animals in zoos do not act as they would in their natural habitats. Therefore, people cannot go to the zoo and learn how animals act in their natural habitats. Other students may think zoos are good places to keep animals. The author admits that zoos take care of animals and protect them.

p. 387 Reading Check
Students should underline "look at the enclosure of the tigers and watch the seals balance a ball on their noses, and then think about what you are really learning from your day at the zoo."

p. 388 Apply the Skills
Thinking About the Editorial
1. The writer claims that zoos neither help endangered animals nor educate the public about animals' authentic behavior.
2. The writer would claim that a film showing lions in the wild is more educational because it shows how lions really behave in their natural environment.

Reading Skill
3. Animals learn survival techniques in the wild.
4. Animals are better off in the wild than in a zoo.

"The People Could Fly"
Virginia Hamilton

"All Stories Are Anansi's"
Harold Courlander

p. 389 Graphic Organizer
Sample response:
"The People Could Fly"
Character 1: Toby: has wings, is an old man, helps Sarah, teaches Sarah and other slaves to fly, says the magic words
Character 2: Sarah: sheds her wings; is a young woman, is a mother, is afraid, has no heart to comfort her baby, is whipped, is weak, is sad, is starving, appeals to Toby for help
Both: slaves, fly away

"All Stories Are Anansi's"
Character 1: Mmoboro: are hornets; fly into a gourd
Character 2: Onini: is a python; gets tied to a pole
Both: are caught by Anansi and taken to the Sky God

p. 390 Reading/Writing Connection
Sample response:
1. Children may not appreciate their stories until they grow older.
2. Families that share stories establish their history.
3. Stories from long ago help define the past for younger generations.

p. 390 Note-taking Guide
Sample response:
What Character Says: "I must go soon"; "Now, before it's too late. . . . Now, Father!"
What Character Does: works in the field; is not able to soothe baby; is whipped by driver; falls down; bleeds; appeals to Toby; flies away
What Character Thinks: She thinks that she does not have the heart to soothe her child.
What Others Say about Character: Driver: "Get up, you black cow." Toby: "Yes, Daughter, the time is come. . . . Go, as you know how to go!"

p. 391 Activate Prior Knowledge
Sample response: "Cinderella" is a tale portraying the enslavement of a young girl at the hands of her stepmother. The tale ends with the girl's freedom.

p. 391 Literary Analysis
Students should circle "standin."

p. 391 Reading Skill
Sample response: They both work for the Master and watch the slaves.

p. 391 Reading Check
Students should underline "They couldn't take their wings across the water on the slave ships."

p. 392 Stop to Reflect
Students may say that they would feel hopeless and depressed. They may think that the Driver is a cruel person who cares only about himself and does not care who he hurts.

p. 392 Reading Check
Students should underline "she rose just as free as a bird."

p. 392 Literary Analysis
Toby says magic words to help Sarah fly. Sarah feels the magic and flies away with her baby.

p. 393 Literary Analysis
Sample response: Toby's actions show his goodness in response to the evil actions of the Driver.

p. 393 Reading Skill
The Master pulls out his gun and prepares to kill Toby. Toby just laughs.

p. 393 Reading Check
Students should underline "I heard him say the magic words."

p. 394 Reading Skill
Sample response: The Master would not want other slaves to know it was possible to fly away and escape.

p. 394 Literary Analysis
Students should underline "The slaves who could not fly told about the people who could fly to their children" and "They say that the children of the ones who could not fly told their children."

p. 394 Stop to Reflect
Sample response: They gave future generations hope by telling them about the slaves who could fly.

p. 394 Reader's Response
1) Students may say that they would feel happy to be able to escape but would feel bad about leaving the others behind. 2) Students may say that they would feel happy for those who got away but would feel sad and angry that they could not fly away, too.

p. 395 Apply the Skills
1. Sample response: The author uses the African words to represent the free life to which the slaves hope to return. The words represent their history and heritage.
2. "Flying" is a metaphor for being free and living a free life in one's own culture.
3. Sample response: Toby is helpful, caring, and powerful in an unexpected way. The Overseer is brutal, violent, and mean. Both men are leaders, but Toby leads quietly and effectively. The Overseer has to use fear and pain to force people to do what he wants.
4. **Graphic Organizer**
Sample response:
Good: characters such as Toby and Sarah
Evil: the Master, the Overseer, the Driver, and their cruelty toward the slaves
Lesson: Remembering your past or your heritage will give you strength; hope and faith are powerful.
Theme: Freedom comes to those who remember how important it is.

p. 397 Reading/Writing Connection
Sample response:
1. Trickster tales require a clever trickster.
2. The trickster will demonstrate cunning and intelligence.
3. Good tricksters exhibit sneakiness.

p. 397 Note-taking Guide
Sample response:
What does Anansi do to the hornets?
Anansi pours water on himself and the hornets' nest. He then tells them to get out of the rain. He convinces them to fly into a gourd. He traps them in the gourd and takes them to the Sky God.
What does Anansi do to the python?
Anansi challenges the python to stretch alongside a bamboo pole. Anansi ties the python to the pole and takes him to the Sky God.
What does Anansi do to the leopard?
Anansi digs and covers a hole into which the leopard falls. Anansi says he will help the leopard and ties the leopard to a bent tree. Anansi cuts the rope holding the tree. The

leopard hangs from the tree. Anansi kills
him and takes him to the Sky God.

p. 398 Apply the Skills

1. Sample response: Students may infer that
all of the animals trust Anansi.

2. Sample response: Anansi acts out of self-
interest. He will do and say anything to get
what he wants.

3. The animals are different in that the
hornets are afraid of rain, the python is vain,
and the leopard is too trusting. They are
similar in that all of the animals are bigger
and stronger than Anansi, and yet all are
tricked by Anansi.

4. **Graphic Organizer**
Students may notice that elements of good
and evil are not very clear in this tale.
Sample response:
Good: The Sky God offers Anansi a fair price
for the stories.
Evil: All of the animals are motivated by
self-interest.
Lesson: Do not be too trusting; learn to
think for yourself.
Theme: Intelligence is more powerful than
physical strength or size.

ANSWERS TO UNIT 1

"The Three-Century Woman"
Richard Peck

"The Fall of the Hindenburg"
Michael Morrison

p. 4 Note-taking Guide
Sample response:
Setting: The setting is Whispering Oaks Elder Care Facility, New Year's Day 2001.
Narrator: The narrator is a young girl named Megan.
Events of the Plot: Media people want to interview Great-grandma Breckenridge; Great-grandma allows them to come into her room; she makes up stories about her life, including having lived through the San Francisco earthquake and the Hindenburg disaster; the news team leaves, and Great-grandma admits to having learned her facts by reading.
Ending: In the end, Megan feels new appreciation for her great-grandmother.

p. 5 Activate Prior Knowledge
Some students might say that the stories are boring and always the same. Other students might say that they enjoy the stories because they like to learn about life in the past.

p. 5 Fiction
Sample response: Facts about Great-grandmother Breckenridge include that she lives at Whispering Oaks, that she has lived there since the narrator was a little girl, and that she has lived in three centuries. Students should list two of these.

p. 5 Fiction
Megan is the narrator.

p. 6 Fiction
The interview takes place in Great-grandma's room at Whispering Oaks.

p. 6 Fiction
The TV anchor begins to interview Great-grandma.

p. 6 Reading Check
Students should circle "like a Barbie doll."

p. 7 Stop to Reflect
Sample response: The stories are made-up and didn't really happen. Great-grandma didn't really live through the events she retells.

p. 7 Read Fluently
Students should circle "hissed." Sample response: *Hissed* means to make a sound like that of the first *s* in the word *sash*.

p. 7 Fiction
Sample response: Great-grandma is moving on to another lie. She is telling about being on the Hindenburg when it blew up.

p. 7 Reading Check
Students should circle "I was on the Hindenburg when it blew up."

p. 8 Fiction
Sample response: The characters are made up.

p. 8 Read Fluently
Students should circle "little withered-up leaf of a lady."

p. 8 Fiction
Sample response: Older people should not be stereotyped, and they should be valued.

p. 9 Note-taking Guide
Sample response:
Where: The Hindenburg disaster took place in Lakehurst, New Jersey.
What Happened: Thirteen passengers and twenty-two crewmembers were killed; people have tried to learn what caused the disaster, but the cause is still uncertain.
Why: The cause may have been the varnish on the fabric on the outside of the vessel.

p. 10 Activate Prior Knowledge
Sample response: 1. It was a German-built airship for flying across the Atlantic. 2. It exploded just as it was landing in New Jersey.

p. 10 Nonfiction
Sample response: It is an article about the *Hindenburg* disaster in 1937. This article mentions Herb Morrison, a reporter from Chicago who was covering the event.

p. 10 Read Fluently
Students should circle "Oh, the Humanity!"

p. 10 Reading Check
Students should circle "Germany."

p. 11 Apply the Skills
1. Sample response: Yes, Great-grandma Breckenridge is very lively mentally. She has a sense of humor. She knows how to have fun. She also knows a lot of stories.
2. **Graphic Organizer**
Sample response:
Her Comments: "I was on the Hindenburg when it blew up, you know."
Her Character: She makes up stories.
Message/Theme: We should not stereotype older people. Some of them are like Great-grandma, with lively imaginations and a great sense of humor.
3. Sample response: It has made-up characters and some made-up events. It has a narrator who is a character inside the story. It has a series of events that make up a plot. It has a theme.
4. Sample response: The fictional account contains far fewer facts and details and has some made-up information. The nonfiction article consists only of details about what really happened and who was really there.

"Papa's Parrot"
Cynthia Rylant

"mk"
Jean Fritz

p. 13 Graphic Organizer
Sample response:
"Papa's Parrot"
Beginning: Harry and his friends stop going to Papa's store.
Middle: Papa buys a parrot.
End: Harry realizes that Papa missed seeing him at the store.

"mk"
Beginning: Jean finishes sixth grade at the British School in Wuhan.

Middle: Jean goes to the Shanghai American School.
End: Jean moves to America. She goes to a school in America for the first time.

p. 14 Reading/Writing Connection
Sample responses:
1. Age might help a teenager appreciate any extra time that he or she has.
2. He or she might learn to react more calmly to problems.
3. A more mature person might be more likely to act in a responsible way.

p. 14 Note-taking Guide
Sample response:
Before Harry Starts Junior High: Harry brings his friends to visit the store and to eat nuts and candy.
After Harry Starts Junior High: His father embarrasses Harry by talking to the parrot.
After Harry's Father Gets Sick: Because of his experience with the parrot, Harry realizes how much his father misses him; Harry decides to spend more time with his father.

p. 15 Activate Prior Knowledge
Students may say that their feelings for someone close to them changed after they had an argument with that person. They no longer felt as close to that person after the fight.

p. 15 Reading Skill
Sample response: The word *though* is a clue to the meaning of *merely*. The word *though* shows that Harry liked his Papa in spite of his papa's shortcomings: his Papa was fat, and owning a candy and nut store was not an exciting job.

p. 15 Read Fluently
Students should circle "on his way somewhere else," and "The more Mr. Tillian grew to like his parrot, and the more he talked to it instead of to people, the more embarrassed Harry became."

p. 16 Reading Skill
Sample response: Harry walks away when he sees his father talking to the bird. This helps readers understand that "embarrassed" is an uncomfortable feeling.

p. 16 Literary Analysis
Sample response: At the beginning of the
story, Harry liked being with his Papa in the
store. By the middle of the story, Harry was
older. He became interested in other things.
He was also embarrassed when his Papa
talked to the parrot.

p. 16 Reading Check
Students should circle: "Mr. Tillian asks him
to take care of the store and to feed Rocky."

p. 17 Literary Analysis
Sample response: Harry finally realizes that
his father misses him. The problem between
father and son is about to be resolved.

p. 17 Stop to Reflect
Some students might say that Harry should
tell his father what happened with Rocky so
that Harry can say he knows that his father
misses him.

p. 17 Reading Check
Students should circle, "he left to go visit
his papa."

p. 18 Apply the Skills
1. Sample response: Harry and his friends are
now interested in things such as video games.
They are no longer interested in candy.
2. Sample response: Mr. Tillian buys Rocky
because he is lonely; Harry and his friends no
longer visit at the store.
3. **Graphic Organizer**
Sample response:
Context Clues: on his way somewhere else;
walking.
Possible Meaning: *Stroll* might mean "to walk
slowly."
Context Clues: "so the bird wouldn't get cold."
Possible Meaning: A *furnace* might be a
machine that produces heat.
4. Sample response: A narrative is any type of
writing that tells a story. It can be fiction or
nonfiction, and it is often told in chronological
order. "Papa's Parrot" is fiction that tells a
story in chronological order. This makes it a
narrative.

p. 20 Reading/Writing Connection
Sample response:
1. Kids in other countries might imitate
American styles of clothing.
2. People overseas often observe things that
people in America do not see.

3. Living in another country would allow a
person to explore that country's natural
wonders.

p. 20 Note-taking Guide
Sample response:
What Character Says: Jean "talks" to
Priscilla about hardships. Jean says, "I always
felt a tingling when I saw the American flag
flying over the American consulate."
What Character Thinks: Jean thinks that
the Shanghai American school will help her
feel more American. Jean thinks that
American children are ignorant.
What Character Does: Jean is shy and
sensitive. She keeps the name of her home-
town a secret so that the other students won't
laugh at it.
What Others Say about Character:
Mrs. Barrett asks whether Jean is all grown
up. Fletcher says that Jean is pretty. Paula,
the American roommate, says that Jean looks
like an MK.

p. 21 Apply the Skills
1. Sample response: The school is not exactly
as Jean thinks it will be. She does not get a
tingling feeling from the flag when she walks
into the school. She does not feel more
American at the school. She does enjoy the
tea dances, though.
2. Sample response: Both Jean and Priscilla
look forward to a new life in America. They
are excited and interested in learning about
America.
3. **Graphic Organizer**
Sample response:
Context Clues: "more than a tingling"
Possible Meaning: *Overwhelm* might mean
"overpower."
4. Sample response: A narrative is any type of
writing that tells a story. It can be fiction or
nonfiction, and it is often told in chronological
order. "mk" is a nonfiction story told in
chronological order.

Reading Informational Materials:
Reference Materials

p. 26 Apply the Skills
Thinking About the Reference Material
1. Sample response: The climate, landscape,
and soil are better in the eastern area than in
the other parts of the country. That area is
also closer to the East China Sea.

2. Shanghai is located on the east coast of China. It touches the East China Sea. Jiaxing and Wuxi are near Shanghai.

Reading Skill

3. Sample response: A *booming* economy is one that is thriving. The context clue is that Taiwan "exports its products around the world."

4. The context clue is an example: Exporting is one reason that the economy is thriving.

from An American Childhood
Annie Dillard

"The Luckiest Time of All"
Lucille Clifton

p. 27 Graphic Organizer

Sample response:

from An American Childhood

Unfamiliar Word in Context: Any normal adult would have quit, having *sprung* us into flight and made his point.

Word's Function in Sentence: *Sprung* is a verb that describes what happens to Dillard and her friends.

Meaning of Word: *Sprung* probably means "thrown" or "hurled."

"The Luckiest Time of All"

Unfamiliar Word in Context: Her granddaughter brought her a big bunch of dogwood blooms.

Word's Function in Sentence: Dogwood is the name of the blossoms.

Meaning of Word: Dogwood is probably a type of tree, shrub, or plant.

p. 28 Reading/Writing Connection

Sample response:

1. I have always enjoyed the <u>challenge</u> of building something new.
2. It will be hard to win the game unless I <u>exert</u> all my energy.
3. Sometimes I <u>exceed</u> my own goals.

p. 28 Note-taking Guide

Sample response:

Conflict: The driver wants to teach the children a lesson. The children want to escape.

Climax: An angry driver chases Dillard and her friends.

Second Event: The driver catches Dillard and Mikey.

Third Event: The driver lectures Dillard and Mikey.

Resolution: Dillard is excited that she had to try so hard to get away.

p. 29 Activate Prior Knowledge

Students may describe a time when they played a certain sport or performed well in a play. Because they really enjoyed the activity, they wanted to perform to the best of their ability.

p. 29 Literary Analysis

"Some boys taught me to play football" shows that this story is told from the first-person point of view.

p. 29 Reading Check

Students should underline "Dillard also likes going out for a pass." "Her favorite part of the game is tackling." "Your fate, and your team's score, depended on your concentration and courage."

p. 30 Reading Skill

Sample response: The words "he was still after us" give clues to the meaning of the word *incredibly*. The words show Dillard's surprise that the man continues to chase her.

p. 30 Stop to Reflect

Students may circle "yes." They may suggest that the driver wanted to teach the children a lesson. To do so, he would have to catch them.

p. 30 Literary Analysis

Students should underline "You have to throw yourself into an activity with all your energy if you want to win."

p. 31 Read Fluently

Students should underline the words "our pursuer, our captor, our hero."

p. 31 Literary Analysis

Sample response: The narrative is told from the first-person point of view. Only the narrator's thoughts are known.

p. 31 Reading Skill

Students should circle the phrase "a mere formality, and beside the point."

p. 31 Reading Check

Students should draw a box around the words "in an obscure hilltop backyard."

p. 32 Reading Skill
Students should circle "more of her than anything else ever has." Sample response: Dillard says that you have to throw yourself completely into something if you want to win. Dillard had to try very hard not to let the man catch her. She tried harder than she had ever tried to do anything else. The word *required* means "needed" or "necessary."

p. 32 Reading Check
Students should underline "That's because the chase in the snow required more of her than anything else ever has."

p. 33 Apply the Skills
1. Sample response: Dillard admires his commitment to flinging himself into the chase and not giving up.
2. Sample response: The words "redundant, a mere formality, and beside the point" suggest the meaning of *perfunctorily.*
3. Sample response: It could mean "without excitement."
4. **Graphic Organizer**
Sample response:
Situation: The man from the Buick catches the narrator and Mikey.
Thoughts or Feelings: Dillard wants "the glory to last forever." She thinks that being pursued by a grown-up who throws himself into chasing her and Mikey is glorious.

p. 35 Reading/Writing Connection
Sample response: Many people define luck as good fortune. Many of us cannot interpret right away whether an event will bring good luck. We may need to wait for the outcome of an event to confirm whether or not the event was lucky.

p. 35 Note-taking Guide
Sample response:
Cause: Elzie goes to the show.
Effect/Cause: Elzie throws her lucky rock at the dancing dog.
Effect/Cause: The dog chases Elzie.
Effect/Cause: A young man chases the dog.
Effect/Cause: Elzie and the man meet.
Effect: The man later marries Elzie.

p. 36 Apply the Skills
1. Sample response: Elzie seems to be looking for adventure.

2. Sample response: Mr. Pickens saves Elzie from the dog and checks the dog to see whether it is hurt.
3. Sample response: *Lit out* may mean "to chase or run at top speed."
4. Sample response: Context clues are "I flew," "Round and round we run," and "a runnin dog."
5. **Graphic Organizer**
Sample response:
Situation: Elzie goes to the show.
Thoughts or Feelings: She feels adventurous.

"All Summer in a Day"
Ray Bradbury

"Suzy and Leah"
Jane Yolen

p. 38 Graphic Organizer
Sample response:
"All Summer in a Day"
Entertain: ". . . the gigantic sound of the rain . . . "
Teach: "A thousand forests had been crushed under the rain and grown up a thousand times to be crushed again."
Reflect: "The silence was so immense and unbelievable that you felt your ears had been stuffed. . . ."

"Suzy and Leah"
Entertain: The story is told entirely through diary entries.
Teach: It is wrong to judge others.
Reflect: Suzy's comments in her diary show how comfortable her life has been, compared with Leah's life.

p. 39 Reading/Writing Connection
Sample response: I don't know whether I could survive in a rainy climate. It would require that I adjust to losing many things that I love. I am sure that there is some benefit to living in a rainy climate, but I don't know what it is!

p. 39 Note-taking Guide
Sample response:
What Happens: 2. Margot writes a poem. 3. Margot refuses to play games with the other children. 4. The sun shines.
What Is the Result? 2. William says that Margot did not write the poem. 3. Margot does not have many friends. 4. The children laugh and play.

p. 40 Apply the Skills

1. Sample response: Thee children have never seen the sun. They cannot imagine how it feels or why Margot misses it.

2. Sample response: The children play the mean joke because they do not feel that Margot is one of them. They may feel less responsibility because the joke is William's idea.

3. Sample response: The author's main purpose is to show that people can be cruel and that we should think carefully about what we do.

4. Sample response: The rain on Venus makes the story sad and dark. The mood is happier when the sun comes out. If the story were set on Earth, the conflict would not be about the weather or the sun.

5. **Graphic Organizer**
Sample response:
Setting: 1. Venus is sunless.
Character's Mood: 1. Margot is sad.

p. 42 Reading/Writing Connection

Sample response: To communicate with others might be difficult in a new country. The person would have to adapt to a new language and a different culture. It might be hard to participate in activities and events in a strange country.

p. 42 Note-taking Guide

Sample response:
Leah Beginning: Leah says that Suzy has a "false smile," makes her feel terror, and treats her "like a pet." She says that Suzy laughed at Leah's friend, has a meaningless name, and "wants to feed [Leah] like an animal."
Leah End: Leah says that Suzy is friendly, honest, generous, and understanding.
Suzy Beginning: Suzy says that Leah is strange, "prickly as a porcupine," unfriendly, stuck-up, and mean. Suzy also says that Leah never smiles, has a permanent frown, doesn't eat enough, has a funny accent, and knows nothing about America.
Suzy End: Suzy says that Leah is strong, has been through a lot, and is scared rather than stuck-up. Suzy thinks that she and Leah might yet be able to become friends.

p. 43 Activate Prior Knowledge

Students may name themselves, friends, or family members as people who keep diaries.

One famous person who kept a diary was Anne Frank.

p. 43 Literary Analysis

Students should underline "A high fence with twisted, sharp-pointed wire at the top separates Americans from the refugees."

p. 43 Reading Check

Students should underline "A girl with yellow hair and a false smile."

p. 44 Stop to Reflect

Sample response: Avi stopped speaking when his grandmother hid him from the Nazis. He stayed in a cupboard for three days without food and water and without words to comfort him. He did not speak again.

p. 44 Read Fluently

Students should circle the three appearances of the word *safe* in the paragraph beginning "The adults of the Americans say we are safe now." Sample response: The author chose to repeat this word to show how important security is to Leah, especially because she had not been safe in Germany.

p. 44 Reading Check

Students should underline "And there you and baby Natan were killed."

p. 45 Literary Analysis

Students should underline "the blue skies over their farm."

p. 45 Reading Skill

Sample response: The author wants readers to think about Suzy's feelings. The details show that Suzy doesn't know what Leah has been through. She doesn't like Leah because she doesn't understand why Leah is "prickly as a porcupine."

p. 45 Stop to Reflect

Students may suggest that Suzy does not like Leah because she is grouchy and suspicious.

p. 45 Reading Check

Students should circle "She tears off her name tag and throws it behind a bush."

p. 46 Literary Analysis

Students should circle "Leah goes to Suzy's house for dinner, but her stomach hurts the whole time."

p. 46 Reading Skill

Students should underline these passages: "the Nazis killed people, including mothers and children in concentration camps" and "Jews had to wear yellow stars."

p. 46 Literary Analysis

Sample response: Where Leah was during the war is very important. It was a terrible place where Leah's mother and brother were killed. The setting is important because it is a secret that Suzy has not understood until now.

p. 46 Reading Check

Students should put a box around "She has had her appendix out. Leah almost died."

p. 47 Stop to Reflect

Sample response: Avi helps Leah by telling the guards that she is sick. His action is important because he saves Leah's life. It's also important because it's the first time that Avi speaks aloud to anyone but Leah.

p. 47 Read Fluently

Students should underline these incomplete sentences: "A new word," "A new land," and "And—it is just possible—a new friend."

p. 47 Reading Skill

Students may say that the author has young people tell the story because they can reach young readers. A young American like Suzy might not know what happened in Europe during World War II. A young refugee like Leah would not know about America. Readers learn along with the characters.

p. 48 Apply the Skills

1. Sample response: Suzy has lived a comfortable, sheltered life. She does not like Leah because Leah is strange to her.
2. Sample response: Leah has survived a terrible experience. She is afraid of strangers. She detects Suzy's "false smile." Leah is afraid to be Suzy's friend.
3. Sample response: The author's purpose was to teach people about what happened to the Jews in Germany when the Nazis were in control.
4. **Graphic Organizer**
Sample response:
Setting: Leah is in a refugee camp.
Character's Mood: Leah feels afraid and suspicious.

Setting: Suzy visits Leah in the hospital.
Character's Mood: Suzy is sorrowful and friendly.

"My First Free Summer"
Julia Alvarez

"My Furthest-Back Person"
(The Inspiration for *Roots*)
Alex Haley

p. 50 Graphic Organizer

Sample response:
"My First Free Summer"
What I Know About the Author: She spent her early life in the Dominican Republic. Words make her feel "complete."
What I Know About the Topic: The Dominican Republic was ruled by a dictator for thirty-one years. Many families fled the country during a rebellion.
Author's Purpose: The author writes to describe a personal experience.

"My Furthest-Back Person"
What I Know About the Author: He grew up hearing stories about his family's history. He later wrote a book about his family's past.
What I Know About the Topic: Slavery is part of the history of the United States and of parts of Africa.
Author's Purpose: The author writes to describe a personal experience.

p. 51 Reading/Writing Connection

Sample response: Most people would respond to this news with complaints or grumbling. A person might react by feeling sad or upset. It would take time and effort to adjust.

p. 51 Note-taking Guide

Sample response:
Conflict: Julia does not want to learn English.
Event: Julia goes to summer school.
Event: Julia decides to try harder to learn English.
Event: Julia and her family try to leave the country.

p. 52 Activate Prior Knowledge

Students should describe at least one positive experience. Positive experiences could include taking trips with their families, making new friends, or learning a new sport or hobby. Students who have been to summer school may describe it as a positive experience.

p. 52 Literary Analysis

Students should underline this sentence: "For thirty years, the Dominican Republic had endured a bloody and repressive dictatorship."

p. 52 Reading Skill

Sample response: Julia's family left the Dominican Republic to live in the United States.

p. 53 Stop to Reflect

Students should recognize that Julia is different because she goes to school with Americans, not with other Dominicans. She does not get days off, march in parades, or see the palace. Many students will still say she is lucky, though. She gets to learn English and may have a chance to escape to the United States.

p. 53 Literary Analysis

Sample response: All of the children Julia knew were leaving for the United States. People were being arrested. Julia's family was frightened. All of this made Julia's summer boring because she had no one to play with her.

p. 53 Reading Check

Students should underline "It was because she wanted a summer free from school."

p. 54 Read Fluently

Students should circle the words "her" and "she." Students should draw arrows to "Julia's mother" and "Julia," respectively.

p. 54 Reading Skill

Sample response: By not telling what happens to these people, the author shows how much mystery and confusion there is. This helps the reader understand how frightening and dangerous Julia's situation is.

p. 54 Reading Check

Students should underline "I knew that ours was not a trip, but an escape. We had to get to the United States."

p. 55 Reading Skill

Sample response: Julia has learned to speak English and to be an eager student, so she says "Yes, sir!" to the American official. She is also eager to answer the official because she is afraid of being sent back. The scene shows that the author's purpose is to show that Julia's family is afraid of being sent back to

the Dominican Republic. They escape to America in order to save their lives. The author also wants to show that learning and school are part of being free.

p. 55 Reading Check

Students should underline "'Welcome to the United States.'"

p. 56 Apply the Skills

1. Sample response: The American school teaches English and American history. The other schools on the island teach about the dictator and have many days off in honor of the dictator.
2. Sample response: Julia improves her English.
3. Sample response: The author is sharing information about the Dominican Republic as it was during the time when the author was growing up. The author's family left the country during this time.
4. **Graphic Organizer**
Sample response:
Author's Actions: 2. Packs her things and prepares to leave the country

p. 58 Reading/Writing Connection

Sample response:
1. Many people want to acquire information about their ancestors.
2. They want to identify their roots.
3. They are curious about the circumstances surrounding major events in their family history.

p. 58 Note-taking Guide

Sample response:
What: Haley found the names of his relatives in census records from just after the Civil War.
Whom: Haley told his cousin, Georgia Anderson, who used to tell him stories about his ancestors.
Why: Haley thought that Dr. Vansina might know where in Africa Haley's ancestors came from.
Where: Haley went to a village in Gambia to hear the *griot*.
How: Haley linked the *griot's* tale to his family history through certain details that were common to both stories.

p. 59 Apply the Skills

1. Sample response: Both the sounds and the writing had to be translated. The African sounds in Haley's family were spoken; the words on the Rosetta Stone were written.

2. Sample response: The *griot* tells what happened before Kunte Kinte left Africa. Haley's family stories begin after Kunta Kinte's arrival in America. Together, these stories complete the family history.

3. Sample response: The author's purpose is to tell the story of his ancestor, who was one of the many Africans brought to America as slaves.

4. Sample response: Haley searches for his family's African roots.

Reading Informational Materials: Web Sites

p. 64 Apply the Skills
Thinking About the Web Site

1. Sample response: The *About Us* link on the home page and the *Biography of John Carlin* link on the Welcome page should lead to more information about NARA and its director.

2. Sample response: Clicking on the links to related government Web sites should lead to sites with similar information.

Reading Skill

3. Sample response: The purpose of the NARA Welcome page is to persuade readers to make use of the documents that NARA provides.

4. Sample response: The purpose of this Web site might be to inform people about the history and development of airplanes.

"The Treasure of Lemon Brown"
Walter Dean Myers

p. 67 Note-taking Guide
Sample response:
Event: The bad men go after Lemon Brown.
Event: Lemon Brown tells Greg about his treasure.
Event: Greg understands a new meaning for treasure.
Climax: Lemon Brown and Greg scare off the men.
Resolution: Greg goes home with a better understanding of his father.
Conflict: Greg cannot accept what his father has to say.

p. 68 Activate Prior Knowledge
Students may write about a time when their parents were upset with them but were really just concerned about their safety.

p. 68 Short Story
Students should underline "Greg" and "his father." Greg is remembering a time when they talked about Greg's poor effort at school and why, as a result, he can't play basketball.

p. 68 Reading Check
Students should underline "Now Greg cannot bring himself to go inside to hear more of the same."

p. 69 Read Fluently
Students should underline the footnote at the bottom of the page. A neon sign is a brightly lit outdoor sign; a bodega is a Latino grocery store.

p. 69 Short Story
Sample response: Greg doesn't want to listen to what his father has to say.

p. 69 Short Story
Sample response: **Characters:** Greg and his father; **Time:** late evening or at night; **Place:** an old, empty building

p. 70 Short Story
Students should draw a box around the word "Ain't."

p. 70 Short Story
Sample response: Greg and Lemon Brown see three men breaking into the building. They

are carrying pieces of pipe. They say that they want Lemon Brown's treasure.

p. 70 Reading Check
Students should circle "You ain't one of them bad boys looking for my treasure, is you?"

p. 71 Read Fluently
Students should circle a comma.

p. 71 Short Story
Students should circle "Between the two of them, they scare the three men off."

p. 71 Reading Check
Students should underline "He unties the rags on one leg and removes a piece of plastic that contains yellowed newspaper clippings and a bent harmonica."

p. 72 Short Story
Sample response: They are a treasure to Brown because his son valued them. They link Brown to his son.

p. 72 Stop to Reflect
Sample response: Greg has learned something about fathers and sons from his time with Lemon Brown.

p. 72 Reading Check
Students should underline "he will be heading west in the morning."

p. 73 Apply the Skills
1. Some students may say that Greg should not tell his father. Greg's father might not understand why Greg was in an abandoned building. Other students may suggest that Greg should tell his father about the lesson he learned from Lemon Brown. Doing so might resolve the conflict between them.
2. **Graphic Organizer**
Sample response:
Column 1: Brown's treasures are his harmonica, his newspaper clippings, and his memories.
Column 2: These were Brown's legacy to his son.
Column 3: Greg realizes that his father's lectures are his legacy.
3. Sample response: Greg has a conflict with his father because Greg doesn't want to work hard or listen to his father.
4. Sample response: Details about the stormy weather and the inside of the tenement building could be real.

p. 75 Graphic Organizer
Sample response:

"The Bear Boy"

Exposition: Kuo-Haya's father mourns the death of his wife. He does not teach his son to wrestle or to run.

Event: Kuo-Haya follows bear tracks.

Event: Kuo-Haya plays with bear cubs.

Event: The villagers and Kuo-Haya's father find Kuo-Haya with the bears and try to get him back.

Climax: Kuo-Haya's father treats the bears with respect. He gives them honey.

Event: Kuo-Haya's father promises to be friendly with bears.

Event: Kuo-Haya agrees to go back with his father.

Resolution: Kuo-Haya becomes the best wrestler and greatest runner in the village.

"Rikki-tikki-tavi"

Exposition: A flood destroys Rikki's home.

Event: Teddy's family adopts Rikki.

Event: Rikki rescues Teddy by killing a small snake.

Event: Teddy's father and Rikki kill Nag.

Climax: Rikki chases Nagaina into a hole and kills her.

Event: The coppersmith announces that Rikki has killed Nagaina.

Event: Rikki eats a large meal.

Resolution: Teddy's family and Rikki are safe.

p. 76 Reading/Writing Connection
Sample response:

1. At the zoo, people appreciate seeing unusual animals.

2. Scientists observe wild animals to learn how these animals find food.

3. Lions might teach people how to survive when they are in danger.

p. 76 Note-taking Guide
Sample response:

Column 2, row 1: timid

Column 2, row 2: sad

Column 3, row 1: He learns to wrestle.

Column 3, row 2: He learns how to treat his son.

Column 4, row 1: He is confident.

Column 4, row 2: He is proud of his son.

p. 77 Activate Prior Knowledge
Sample response: They probably will not get along. Bears and people are usually enemies.

p. 77 Short Story
Sample response: A bear might find the boy. The boy could get hurt.

p. 77 Literary Analysis
Students should underline "As they played, however, a shadow came over them" or "Kuo-Haya looked up and saw the mother bear standing above him."

p. 78 Literary Analysis
Sample response: The paragraph shows that a conflict will arise between the bears and the humans.

p. 78 Read Fluently
Students should underline "realizes his responsibility. He began to realize that he had been blind to his son's needs because of his own sorrow. 'You are right,' he said. 'I will go and bring back my son.'" Sample response: *Change of heart* means that a person sees things in a new way.

p. 78 Reading Check
Students should circle "But as soon as the mother bear caught their scent, she growled and pushed her cubs and the boy back into the cave."

p. 79 Stop to Reflect
Sample response: The father wants to get Kuo-Haya back.

p. 79 Literary Analysis
Students should underline "Kuo-Haya's father prays for help. Then he gets an idea after a bee flies past his face. He goes to a beehive, makes a fire, and blows smoke into the hive. The smoke puts the bees to sleep. He then takes some honey from the hive." Sample response: A reader can now predict how the problem will be solved.

p. 79 Stop to Reflect
Sample response: The father was beginning to learn the importance of paying attention and being thankful.

p. 80 Literary Analysis
Sample Response: Kuo-Haya comes home. The father teaches Kuo-Haya and shows him love.

p. 80 Reading Check

Students should circle "It reminds parents how important it is to show their love for their children."

p. 81 Apply the Skills

1. Sample response: The mother bear encourages Kuo-Haya and teaches him to be strong. Kuo-Haya feels that he belongs with the bears. In Kuo-Haya's village, where he is neglected by his father, the boy feels that he is an outsider.
2. Sample response: He will distract the bears with honey.
3. **Graphic Organizer:**
Sample response:
Story Details: The father decides to get his son back.
My Prior Knowledge: Bears like honey.
Prediction: The father will use honey to get his son back.
4. Sample response: These two plot events make the story more exciting: the mother bear's anger and the father's hunt for weapons.

p. 83 Reading/Writing Connection

Sample response:
1. Firefighters demonstrate bravery when they put out fires.
2. Police officers exhibit courage when they protect people from harm.
3. Acrobats in the circus display courage when they jump from one bar to another.

p. 83 Note-taking Guide

Sample response:
Why does Rikki leave his home? Rikki leaves his home because it has been flooded.
Where does Rikki go to live? Rikki lives with Teddy's family in India.
What creatures does Rikki meet in his new home? Rikki meets a tailorbird named Darzee, Darzee's wife, a muskrat named Chuchundra, Karait the dusty brown snakeling, and Nag and Nagaina, the cobras.
How does Rikki protect his adopted family? Rikki fights the cobras.

p. 84 Apply the Skills

1. Sample response: Rikki and the cobras are alike because they want to protect their families. They are different because Rikki is brave and good. The cobras are greedy and evil.

2. Students may say that this story deserves to be popular because its plot is suspenseful and exciting. Also, its hero is likable and its villains are evil.
3. **Graphic Organizer**
Sample response:
Story Details: Rikki hears the cobras' plot.
My Prior Knowledge: Cobras kill people.
Prediction: Rikki will protect Teddy and his family against the cobras.
4. Sample response: These events create more conflict: Rikki bites Nagaina. He also kills Karait.

Reading Informational Materials: Magazine Articles

p. 86 Graphic Organizer

Sample response:
Clue: The title is "Mongoose on the Loose."
Clue: A subhead reads "Population Explodes."
Clue: Another subhead reads "Scientist Studies Problem."
Prediction: The article will be about mongoose overpopulation and what a scientist is doing to solve the problem.

p. 87 Reading Magazine Articles

Mongooses were imported to eat the rats that were feeding on the crops in Jamaica.

p. 87 Reading Informational Materials

Students should predict that the article will be about mongoose overpopulation.

p. 87 Reading Check

The huge mongoose population is now threatening other animals. Students should underline ". . . the mongoose population exploded, and within a few years, they were killing not just rats, but pigs, lambs, chickens, puppies, and kittens."

p. 88 Stop to Reflect

Students may be interested in the project. Volunteers can see mongooses while helping solve a problem.

p. 88 Read Fluently

Students might circle "five-year, $60,000 study," "sponsored by Earthwatch Incorporated, a non-profit group," "Volunteers," "set out mongoose traps, study the animals, and keep records," "perform surgery," "implant the electronic devices," and "track the animal's habits."

p. 88 Reading Skill
It tells readers that the article refers to a unique situation.

p. 88 Reading Check
Students should underline "'I want to know what happens when you take a small animal and put him in an area with no competition.'"

p. 89 Stop to Reflect
Sample response: Yes, it is a good idea. Implanting tracking devices in animals can help scientists learn more about animal behavior.

p. 89 Reading Informational Materials
Students should underline the caption "A mongoose is tagged."

p. 89 Reading Check
Students should underline "Among them: mongooses have a life expectancy of six to ten years, much longer than the previously accepted figure of three years."

p. 90 Apply the Skills
Thinking About the Magazine Article
1. Sample response: The title, subheads, and photos and captions help the reader predict what a magazine article is about.
2. Sample response: The information tells how and why mongooses were brought to the Caribbean. It also explains their value to farmers.

Reading Skill
3. The subhead tells the reader that a problem exists with the mongooses and that a scientist is studying this problem.

from Letters from Rifka
Karen Hesse

"Two Kinds" *from* The Joy Luck Club
Amy Tan

p. 91 Graphic Organizer
Sample response:
from **Letters from Rifka**
Prediction: Something bad will happen.
Details: There is talk of death, prison, and escape.
Revised or Confirmed Prediction: Rifka and her family will make it to Poland.
New Details: They work together, take precautions, and are determined.
Actual Outcome: Their fate is still undetermined by the end of the story.

"Two Kinds" *from* The Joy Luck Club
Prediction: Jing-mei will become a prodigy.
Details: Jing-mei is just as excited as her mother at the idea of being a prodigy. Jing-mei thinks that she will become perfect.
Revised or Confirmed Prediction: Jing-mei will not become a prodigy.
New Details: Jing-mei does not learn the capitals. She cannot pass her mother's tests. She begins to hate the tests.
Actual Outcome: Jing-mei does not become a prodigy. She and her mother argue about this fact.

p. 92 Reading/Writing Connection
Sample response:
Most people could adjust to life without television. They would adapt their lives without it by reading books. Some children might feel that their parents deprive them of their favorite television shows.

p. 92 Note-taking Guide
Sample response:
Beginning: Rifka's brother leaves the army.
Event: The family decides to leave the country.
Event: The family packs to leave.
Event: The family hides in a cellar.
Event: Rifka distracts the guards so that her family can hide.
Event: The guards search the train.

p. 93 Activate Prior Knowledge
Sample response: People write letters to relatives and friends to share family news. They also write to keep in touch with relatives and friends who live far away.

p. 93 Reading Skill
Sample response: The story will be about a family escaping from Ukraine or from a country near Ukraine.

p. 93 Literary Analysis
Sample response: She is twelve years old; she wants to help her family escape.

p. 93 Reading Check
Students should circle "My Dear Cousin Tovah."

p. 94 Literary Analysis
Sample response: She does not tell because no one must know that the escaping family is on the train.

p. 94 Reading Skill
Sample response: Nathan has committed a crime.

p. 94 Reading Check
Students should circle "I think the guards missed seeing me at first because they were so busy in their search of the train."

p. 95 Read Fluently
Students should circle "no matter how frightened I was."

p. 95 Literary Analysis
Sample response: They need a safe place to plan their escape.

p. 95 Reading Skill
Sample response: She will feel even more worried about her family. She will fear for her safety.

p. 96 Apply the Skills
1. Students may say that Nathan felt relieved when he saw his family because he could warn them about the soldiers.
2. Some students may say that because she is young, Rifka is more afraid of what might happen. Others may say that Rifka's youth helps her get caught up in the excitement of the journey.
3. Students probably determined that the family was leaving Russia when they read that the Russian army shoots deserters. Students should have made the connection between Rifka's brothers and the army.
4. Students may identify Rifka as young, brave, small, poor, and loving.

Graphic Organizer
Sample response:
Rifka is young: She is twelve years old in the story.
She is brave: She distracts the guards so her family can hide.
She is small: The guards do not notice her at first.
She is poor: She does not have many things.
She loves her family: She wants everyone to be safe, even the brother she says she dislikes.

p. 98 Reading/Writing Connection
Sample response:
1. One day, I would like to achieve success as a great Olympic diver.

2. To pursue a Nobel Prize is another day-dream I have.
3. Sometimes I dream that I can attain the status of a legendary actor.

p. 98 Note-taking Guide
Sample response:
Mother's Plans: [row 2] She wants her daughter to be remarkable and smart.
[row 3] She wants her daughter to play the piano well.
Daughter's Response: [row 1] Jing-mei looks forward to her future fame. [row 2] Jing-mei begins to hate the tests her mother gives her. [row 3] Jing-mei does not put in the effort necessary for playing the piano well.

p. 99 Apply the Skills
1. Sample response: The daughter believes she can never meet her mother's expectations, and the mother is angry because her daughter refuses to try.
2. Students may suggest that the mother pushed her daughter too hard. The mother's efforts backfired. Her daughter believed that she would never be good enough to meet her mother's expectations and stopped trying.
3. **Graphic Organizer**
Sample response:
sad, angry, powerful, willful, bored, lazy
She is sad and angry when she cries in the bathroom. She becomes powerful and willful after she realizes that she does not have to do as her mother says. She is bored and lazy when practicing the piano.
4. Sample response: The daughter will perform poorly because she is not interested in playing, and her teacher is not a good one. The prediction was accurate.

"The Third Wish"
Joan Aiken

"Amigo Brothers"
Piri Thomas

p. 101 Graphic Organizer
Sample response:
"The Third Wish"
Details: Mr. Peters offers to turn Leita's sister into a human. Mr. Peters uses his second wish to turn Leita back into a swan.
Inference: Mr. Peters loves his wife and wants her to be happy.

"Amigo Brothers"

Details: Antonio waves to Felix from the dressing room. The boys stop in mid-punch as the bell rings.

Inference: Antonio still thinks of Felix as a friend. The two respect the match and play by the rules.

p. 102 Reading/Writing Connection

Sample response:

1. A person would be wise to <u>maximize</u> three wishes by asking for more wishes.
2. Some students might want teachers to <u>grant</u> them freedom from homework.
3. Some people might want money, but I want to <u>obtain</u> happiness.

p. 102 Note-taking Guide

Sample response:

1. Wish: Mr. Peters wishes for a wife. **Result:** His wife loves him, but she misses her swan sister.

2. Wish: Mr. Peters uses his second wish to turn his wife back into a swan. **Result:** The swans keep Mr. Peters company when he grows old.

3. Wish: Mr. Peters does not make a third wish. **Result:** The unexpected effects of another wish do not disappoint him.

p. 103 Activate Prior Knowledge

Students may wish for money, good friends, happiness, or other things of value.

p. 103 Literary Analysis

Sample response: A swan has become tangled in thorns and cannot get free.

p. 103 Reading Skill

Sample response: Mr. Peters is curious, brave, and kind. He is curious when he hears a strange noise. He is brave and kind enough to try to free the trapped swan.

p. 103 Reading Check

Students should circle "And, in a moment, instead of the great white bird, there was a little man all in green with a golden crown and long beard, standing by the water."

p. 104 Read Fluently

Students should put a box around each of the three dashes.

p. 104 Literary Analysis

Sample response: Mr. Peters feels lonely. He has no one to be with in old age. This is an internal conflict because it concerns what Mr. Peters wants.

p. 104 Reading Check

Students should underline "The only thing that troubled him was that he was a little lonely, and had no companion for his old age."

p. 105 Reading Skill

Sample response: Leita is glad to see the river because she enjoys the company of swans.

p. 105 Literary Analysis

Sample response: Leita wants to make Mr. Peters happy; however, she misses her swan sister.

p. 105 Stop to Reflect

Sample response: Someone is unhappy when he or she cries or cannot enjoy fun things.

p. 105 Reading Skill

Sample response: The marriage will not work out because both people cannot be happy.

p. 106 Reading Skill

Sample response: Leita wants to stay near the river. She wants to be close to her sister.

p. 106 Literary Analysis

Sample response: Mr. Peters loves his wife and wants her to be with him always, yet he knows that she longs to be a swan again. He struggles with loving her but letting her go.

p. 106 Reading Check

Students should number as follows: 1. "taking her for drives in the car"; 2. "finding beautiful music for her to listen to on the radio"; 3. "buying clothes for her"; 4. "suggesting a trip round the world." Some students may label the sentence stating that Mr. Peters builds his wife a special seat by the river.

p. 107 Stop to Reflect

Sample response: Mr. Peters spent all of his time with the swans, which is not something people usually do.

p. 107 Literary Analysis

Sample response: He uses his second wish to turn Leita back into a swan. He decides not to use his third wish. Instead, he lives near the swans for the rest of his life.

p. 107 Reading Skill

Sample response: The feather is probably one of Leita's feathers that Mr. Peters kept.

p. 108 Apply the Skills

1. He is already content with the material things he has.

2. Sample response: Mr. Peters uses his second wish for Leita instead of for himself.

3. Sample response: She spends a great deal of time with him.

4. **Graphic Organizer**

Sample response:

Smaller Conflict: Mr. Peters suffers from loneliness. Leita is unhappy as a human.

Resolution: Mr. Peters wishes for and receives a wife. He wishes that his wife be turned back into a swan.

Main Conflict: Mr. Peters has to decide whether to use a wish to turn Leita back into a swan (to make her happy) or keep her to alleviate his loneliness.

p. 110 Reading/Writing Connection

Sample response:

1. Fighting against a friend for the same prize involves being determined to win.

2. You must isolate yourself from troublesome people.

3. To accomplish your goal, you may have to make difficult decisions.

p. 110 Note-taking Guide

Sample response:

Physical traits/ Felix: dark, short, and husky

Fighting style/ Felix: short, muscular frame (better slugger)

Fighting gear/ Felix: sky-blue trunks, red socks, white shoes

Physical traits/ Antonio: fair, lean, and lanky

Fighting style/ Antonio: lean form, long reach (better boxer)

Fighting gear/ Antonio: white trunks, black socks, black shoes

p. 111 Apply the Skills

1. Sample response: It is a good idea. Training apart helps them focus on their training, rather than on fighting each other.

2. Some students may say that the solution was a good one because the boys remained friends. Other students may believe that the solution was not good because the boys did not really want to fight.

3. Graphic Organizer

Sample response:

Smaller Conflict: The boys need to focus on their fight; the boys want to remain friends.

Resolution: They decide to train apart; they agree to fight as hard as they can. Each accepts that the other will fight hard but still remain a friend.

Main Conflict: Both Antonio and Felix want to win, but only one can win.

4. Sample response: Each boy is bothered by the thought of hurting the other. The boys leave the fight together, arm in arm, without caring to learn who won.

Reading Informational Materials: Government Publications

p. 113 Graphic Organizer

Sample response:

Evidence: Walking is a popular form of exercise.

Evidence: Walking is popular with older people.

Evidence: Walking has been popular for a long time.

Generalization: Many older people walking, an exercise that has never lost popularity.

p. 114 Reading Government Publications

Students should circle "The President's Council on Physical Fitness and Sports."

p. 114 Reading Informational Materials

Students should underline "Walking: An Exercise for All Ages."

p. 114 Read Fluently

Students should put an asterisk next to " (18 years of age and older)" or "(39.4%)."

p. 114 Reading Check

Students should draw an arrow next to 39.4%. Men who are 65 and older make up the highest percentage of regular walkers.

p. 115 Reading Skill

Sample response: People who walk are almost always healthier than people who do not walk. Walking can improve the body's ability to use oxygen during exertion, lower the resting heart rate, lower blood pressure, and increase the efficiency of the heart and lungs.

p. 115 Reading Informational Materials

Students may circle "It also helps burn excess calories."

p. 115 Reading Check

Students may underline "improve the body's ability to consume oxygen during exertion," "lower the resting heart rate," "reduce blood pressure," and "increase the efficiency of the heart and lungs." Students may also underline "burn excess calories." Some students may underline "Almost everyone can do it," "You can do it almost anywhere," "You can do it almost anytime," and "It doesn't cost anything."

p. 116 Reading Skill

Students should underline "You can do it almost anywhere."

p. 116 Reading Informational Materials

Sample response: Pay attention to your body when you walk.

p. 116 Reading Check

Students should underline "The variety of settings available is one of the things that makes walking such a practical and pleasurable activity."

p. 117 Apply the Skills
Thinking About the Government Publication

1. Sample response: When done briskly on a regular schedule, walking can improve the body's ability to consume oxygen during exertion.
2. You should slow down if you develop dizziness, pain, nausea, or any other symptoms. These symptoms tell you that your body is working too hard.

Reading Skill

3. You can make the generalization that most people walk because it is good for them.
4. Sample response: It is possible to develop dizziness, pain, nausea, or other symptoms when walking.

"Zoo"
Edward D. Hoch

"Ribbons"
Laurence Yep

p. 118 Graphic Organizer

Sample response:

"Zoo"

Why Does the Writer tell the ticket price and the number of people who see the zoo?
Answer (inference): to suggest that Professor Hugo makes a lot of money from the zoo

Why Does the Writer describe the behavior of the horse-spider people of Kaan?
Answer (inference): to compare it with the behavior of the humans at the zoo

"Ribbons"

Why Does the Writer keep what happened to the grandmother's feet a secret?
Answer (inference): to make the reader wonder what happened to her feet

Why Does the Writer have the grandmother show affection to Ian but not to Stacy?
Answer (inference): to develop a conflict for the story

p. 119 Reading/Writing Connection

Sample response:
1. The border around my elephant habitat minimizes outside contact.
2. One benefit of being in the zoo is that animals cannot attack one another.
3. Overall, the people who run my zoo like to emphasize animal safety.

p. 119 Note-taking Guide

Sample response:
The Earth People: They walk on two legs. They walk on the ground. They wear clothes.
The Horse-Spider People: They walk on many legs. They walk in any direction. They wear no clothes.
Same: They have families. They like to see new things. They think that other ways of living are strange.

p. 120 Activate Prior Knowledge

Sample response: Zoos have animals from far-off places. People visit zoos to see these animals.

p. 120 Reading Skill

Sample response: The children know that the special zoo is coming, and they want to go and see it.

p. 120 Reading Check

Students should underline "move around quickly and make a high-pitched chattering noise" and/or "looked like horses but ran up the walls of their cages like spiders."

p. 121 Read Fluently

Students may circle *announces*, which means to say something publicly.

p. 121 Reading Skill

Sample response: The people of Kaan are part of the traveling zoo because the zoo is an opportunity for them to see the creatures of other worlds.

p. 121 Literary Analysis

Sample response: The creatures are telling what is unusual about Earth creatures. This description shows the theme that people are often afraid of something that seems different.

p. 122 Apply the Skills

1. Sample response: The crowd views the creatures as a nightmare because the creatures are totally unfamiliar.
2. Sample response: This quotation indicates that humans fail to accept and be open-minded when faced with live creatures that look different from themselves.
3. Sample response: The children behave themselves so that their parents will let them go to the Interplanetary Zoo.

4. Graphic Organizer

Sample response:

Theme: People view foreign creatures as strange or weird.

Setting: People in Chicago see the spaceship as a zoo, and the creatures on the spaceship see Chicago as a zoo.

Character: People on Earth are frightened of and curious about the horse-spider people. Horse-spider people are wary of and curious about Earth people.

p. 124 Reading/Writing Connection

Sample response:

1. A way to <u>maximize</u> your learning is to study other <u>cultures</u>.
2. <u>Ignore</u> your differences and pay attention to your <u>similarities</u>.
3. <u>Rely</u> on good manners to break down cultural barriers.

p. 124 Note-taking Guide

Sample response:

What does . . . Ian? She teaches him to speak Chinese.

What does . . . Stacy? She takes away Stacy's ribbons. She tells Stacy that she (Stacy) can dance.

p. 125 Apply the Skills

1. Students may suggest that the hardest changes for Stacy come when she has to change her behavior and give up her ballet lessons.
2. Sample response: Stacy's mother explains Grandmother's behavior to Stacy, and Stacy is finally able to explain her love of dancing to Grandmother.
3. Sample response: Why does the author include the detail about Grandmother's carrying her daughter on her back? Why does he include the detail about Grandmother's walking such a great distance?

4. Graphic Organizer

Sample response:

Theme: The theme might be understanding and overcoming differences.

Traits: Stacy tries hard and is loving and dedicated.

Motives: Stacy wants to dance and wants her grandmother to like her.

"What Makes a Rembrandt a Rembrandt?"
Richard Mühlberger

p. 129 Note-taking Guide
Sample response:
Circle 1: shows commotion in the scene
Circle 2: highlights person's rank
Circle 3: leads viewers to center of painting

p. 130 Activate Prior Knowledge
Students may say that they would make the scene more interesting by painting different expressions on people's faces, rather than all smiles.

p. 130 Nonfiction
Students should underline "In all of these group portraits, the men were evenly lined up so that each face got equal attention, just as they had been in traditional anatomy lesson paintings." Rembrandt's solution was to show the scene before a parade. He added people who were not in the military to add realism to the scene. He showed the excitement and activity before a military parade began.

p. 130 Reading Check
Students should underline "his militia company."

p. 131 Nonfiction
The officers are illuminated, or in the light. Everything else is in shadow.

p. 131 Nonfiction
Sample response: The captain is dressed in black. He wears a red sash. The captain is giving orders to his lieutenant.

p. 131 Nonfiction
Students should underline "Soldiers load and clean their weapons," "two girls carry a symbol of the company," and "the girls wear the colors of the company."

p. 132 Read Fluently
Students should circle "and" and "and." Students should place a box around "drummer" and "dog," and "Rembrandt" and "he."

p. 132 Stop to Reflect
Sample response: Students may think that "Washington Crossing the Delaware" is a great painting because it shows the bravery of General Washington and the difficult conditions of crossing the icy river.

p. 132 Reading Check
Students should underline "there are shadows that show daylight" and "No one seems to be on watch."

p. 133 Stop to Reflect
Sample response: Students may say that the way Rembrandt highlights figures in the background and his attention to individuals shows his greatness.

p. 133 Reading Check
Students should circle "red."

p. 134 Apply the Skills
1. Sample response: Students may name the painting *The Militia Parade*, or *Citizen Soldiers*.
2. Rembrandt wanted to make his painting more realistic. He wanted to show the excitement before a parade. He included people moving and doing things.
3. The two highest-ranking men are at the front of the portrait. One officer's face is illuminated against a dark background. The other's entire figure is painted in bright colors.
4. **Graphic Organizer**
Sample response:
Examples of Description: describing Banning Cocq; describing the other officer; describing the girls.
Examples of Exposition: explaining the use of color to create contrasts between light and dark; explaining how Rembrandt included activity and excitement to make the scene seem real.

"Life Without Gravity"
Robert Zimmerman

"Conversational Ballgames"
Nancy Masterson Sakamoto

p. 137 Graphic Organizer
Sample response:
"Life Without Gravity"
Column 3, row 1: weightlessness
Column 3, row 2: "In space, bodies change."
Column 3, row 3: spines

"Conversational Ballgames"
Column 3, row 1: "A western-style conversation between two people is like a game of tennis."

Column 3, row 2: "If I introduce a topic, a conversational ball, I expect you to hit it back."
Column 3, row 3: elaboration

p. 137 Reading/Writing Connection
Sample response: Gravity will require you to be careful when you are jumping on a trampoline. Gravity forces you to react if you were to fall off your bicycle. Can you predict what would happen without gravity?

p. 137 Note-taking Guide
Sample response:
Effects on Blood: Blood flows to head and not to legs.
Effects on Stomach: The stomach gets upset.
Effects on Eating: Astronauts must drink out of a special straw.

p. 138 Activate Prior Knowledge
Students may say that they would like to be an astronaut. They may think it would be exciting to go places where few people have been before.

p. 138 Literary Analysis
The words "being weightless in space," "Zero gravity," and "Living in space" tell the topic of this essay.

p. 138 Reading Skill
Students should underline "the Red Planet."

p. 138 Reading Check
Students should circle "Blood flows from the feet to the head," "legs to become thin," "the head to swell," "Bones and muscles weaken," "upset stomachs," and "disks between the bones in the spine spread."

p. 139 Stop to Reflect
Sample response: An unhealthy person could not be an astronaut. A person should be active and in very good shape to be an astronaut. An astronaut has to exercise in space or their muscles become so weak that they cannot walk when they come back to Earth.

p. 139 Reading Skill
Students should underline "In space, you cannot pour milk into a bowl of cornflakes."

p. 139 Read Fluently
Students should draw a box around "in space" and "in orbit."

p. 140 Apply the Skills
1. Sample response: People get dizzy and feel sick to their stomachs because they lose their sense of balance without gravity.
2. Sample response: An astronaut can choose to move up or down, or left or right, just by moving his or her head. He or she must also choose to store away tools or let them float way and possibly get lost.
3. The main idea is that weightlessness has negative effects, but these effects can be overcome.
4. **Graphic Organizer**
Sample response:
Column 2: It is fun to float around. A person can use every inch of space to work. A person can change direction just by moving his or her head.
Column 3: Weightlessness can make a person feel dizzy and sick to his or her stomach. It causes the head to swell and the muscles to weaken.
Column 4: Weightlessness can be fun, and its effects are quickly reversed on Earth. It is important to know about the effects of weightlessness if astronauts are going to explore outer space.

p. 142 Reading/Writing Connection
Sample response: Newcomers to American culture may not comprehend that *cool* means "cold" or "very good." They may try to communicate using formal language. Americans may respond to them with confusion.

p. 142 Note-taking Guide
Sample response:
Column 2, row 3: Players take their own turn to hit the ball; the game does not stop for them to take their turn.
Column 3, row 3: People speak one at a time.
Column 4, row 1: bowling ball
Column 4, row 2: A player bowls and his or her turn ends.

p. 143 Apply the Skills
1. The author did not understand that she should wait her turn to speak, and that she should not respond to other people's comments.
2. Sample response: The newcomer should respect the rules of the other culture; the native speakers should be tolerant of the newcomer's style.

3. The main idea is that Western and Japanese-style conversations are very different.

4. Graphic Organizer

Sample response:

Describe Polite Conversation in Japan: It allows only one speaker at a time, according to his or her social standing. While the speaker talks, the others listen quietly. When it is time for a new speaker, he or she starts with a new topic.

"I Am a Native of North America"
Chief Dan George

from In Search of
Our Mothers' Gardens
Alice Walker

p. 145 Graphic Organizer

Sample response:

"I Am a Native of North America"

Main Idea: People of Chief Dan George's culture and people of white culture must love one another.

Left Key Point: Love is necessary for human life.

Detail 1: George's culture taught him to love and respect people.

Detail 2: George's father taught him to love and respect animals and nature.

Right Key Point: George wonders whether people from white culture know how to love.

Detail 1: The white man loves the things he owns rather than each other.

Detail 2: White culture abuses Earth.

***from* In Search of Our Mothers' Gardens**

Main Idea: Throughout history, women have often been forced to express their creativity in modest ways, such as storytelling, gardening, and quilting, but they have passed down the creative spirit to the next generation of women.

Left Key Point: The stories people tell are often the ones they heard and absorbed from their parents.

Detail 1: Many of the stories Walker has written are her mother's stories.

Detail 2: Through the years of listening to her mother's stories, Walker absorbed her mother's manner of storytelling.

Right Key Point: Gardening was an important means of self-expression for Walker's mother.

Detail 1: Whatever Walker's mother planted grew as if by magic.

Detail 2: In searching for her mother's garden, Walker found her own.

p. 146 Reading/Writing Connection

Sample response:

1. My cultural background has helped enrich my ability to respect others' opinions.

2. Many cultures stress that it is important to cooperate with one another.

3. People should evaluate how their cultural backgrounds influence their lives.

p. 146 Note-taking Guide

Sample response:

Native American Culture: values community; has learned much from white American culture

White American Culture: overtaking Native American culture; has not learned from Native American culture

[overlapping circle] Both groups must forgive each other.

p. 147 Activate Prior Knowledge

Students may suggest goals such as ending hunger, cleaning up the environment, or ending crime.

p. 147 Reading Skill

Students may circle "nature was considered a gift from the great spirit."

p. 147 Literary Analysis

The words are in the past tense.

p. 148 Reading Skill

Students should circle "they stripped the land and poisoned the water and air."

p. 148 Stop to Reflect

Students may say that the only thing separating humans from animals is humans' ability to love. Some students may agree with this statement and say that only humans have the mental ability to feel this emotion. Others may disagree and say that they believe animals can love as much as humans can. They may have pets that they believe love their human families.

p. 148 Literary Analysis

Sample response: The author says that without love, people lose strength, self-esteem suffers, and courage fails. People turn inward and destroy themselves.

p. 149 Literary Analysis

His culture believes that all things belong to nature and should be shared.

p. 149 Read Fluently

Students should circle each period, comma, dash, and ellipsis.

p. 150 Apply the Skills

1. Sample response: By "brotherhood," Chief Dan George means love, patience, trust, acceptance, peace, and forgiveness among all people.
2. Sample response: He means that his "white brothers" have been more successful in spreading their values than his culture has been.
3. Sample response: The author believes it is important for all Americans to love, respect, care for, and forgive one another and to live in peace.
4. **Graphic Organizer**
Sample response:
Chief George's Reflections: How his culture is fading
My Responses: Students' responses may include empathy or confusion.
After Rereading: Students may agree that the world would certainly benefit from people of different cultures showing more love, respect, and forgiveness to each other.

p. 152 Reading/Writing Connection

Sample response: I do not think that I can fully appreciate everything that my mother has done for me. She is the first person to contribute help when I need it. She has demonstrated love to me.

p. 152 Note-taking Guide

Sample response:
Anonymous Women: names unknown; lived hard lives; created beauty from everyday things: quilts, songs, and so on.
Alice Walker: very famous; lives much easier life; uses words and ideas to write

p. 153 Apply the Skills

1. Sample response: Walker's mother shares a creative spirit with all women and she has passed on the spirit of creativity to the next generation, just as other women before her have done.
2. Sample response: It is a tribute to all mothers, not just her own.

3. Sample response: The main idea is that throughout history, women have often been forced to express their creativity in modest ways. They garden, quilt, or tell stories. By doing so, they have passed down the creative spirit to the next generation of women.
4. **Graphic Organizer**
Sample response:
Walker's Reflections: The quilt by the "anonymous" black woman in Alabama is a work of art; Mother created beautiful gardens that were greatly admired.
My Responses: Students responses may include memories of quilts, stories, or gardens created by women in their families, or memories of other ways in which the women in their families have expressed creativity.
After Rereading: Students should identify ways their thinking has changed. For example, they may not have thought that quilts or gardens were creative outlets. After reading the essay, they may think otherwise.

Reading Informational Materials: Problem-and-Solution Essays

p. 156 Reading Problem-and-Solution Essays

Students should underline "As many as 9 million Americans have hearing loss caused by noise."

p. 156 Reading Skill

Students should circle "prevent hearing loss" and should number "using ear protectors," "buy quieter machines," "avoid using lawnmowers or power tools at quiet times of the day," and "turning down the volume on headphones for radios and CD players."

p. 156 Read Fluently

Students may write "motorbike."

p. 156 Reading Check

Students should draw a box around "120 decibels."

p. 157 Reading Skill

Students may choose "What Can Communities Do?" Students may number "locate airports away from dense populations," "prohibit late-night flights," "have laws against noise that exceeds a certain decibel level," and "give fines to people who use noisy equipment."

p. 157 Reading Problem-and-Solution Essays

Communities can locate airports away from dense population and prohibit late-night flights. Students may say that these solutions are not realistic because space for airports is limited and restricting flight times can cause problems that airline companies would not agree to.

p. 157 Reading Informational Materials

The last paragraph tells about things that the government can do that affect everyone. It says the federal government could bring back laws that set limits on noise. It says the best way to fix the problem of noise pollution is to have the government pay for research to make machines quieter.

p. 158 Apply the Skills
Thinking About the Problem-and-Solution Essay

1. Cars, trains, trucks, and planes are the largest source of noise pollution. About 15 million Americans live near an airport or under a flight path.
2. Noise that does not cause pain can still damage your hearing. Household appliances such as a kitchen blender can slowly damage the hair cells in your cochlea.

Reading Skill

3. The author uses facts to support each idea logically.
4. The effect is that the essay is logical and believable.

"The Eternal Frontier"
Louis L'Amour

"All Together Now"
Barbara Jordan

p. 159 Graphic Organizer

Sample response:
"The Eternal Frontier"
Appeals to Emotion: "And today is the past."
Appeals to Reason: "Computers, new medicines, and new ways of keeping healthy are results of space exploration."

"All Together Now"
Appeals to Authority: "President Lyndon B. Johnson pushed through the Civil Rights Act of 1964, which remains the fundamental piece of civil rights legislation in this century."

Appeals to Emotion: "I care about you because you are a fellow human being and I find it okay in my mind, in my heart, to simply say to you, I love you."
Appeals to Reason: "Each of us can decide to have one friend of a different race or background in our mix of friends."

p. 160 Reading/Writing Connection

Sample response:
1. People will have to invest too much time and money for space exploration.
2. The decision to undertake more space exploration could benefit the world.
3. Scientists will obtain new knowledge as a result of space exploration.

p. 160 Note-taking Guide

Sample response:
Circle 3: "The human mind has no limits. . . ."
Circle 4: ". . . if humans had not looked to new frontiers, we would still be hunters and food gatherers."
Circle 5: "It is our destiny to move out. . . ."

p. 161 Activate Prior Knowledge

Sample response: In the future people may live on other planets, travel in outer space on space shuttles, or spend time at space stations as a result of space exploration.

p. 161 Reading Skill

Students should circle "All space exploration in the past has been preparation for the future," and underline "People have already imagined and developed many things, from cars and paved roads to electricity and television."

p. 161 Reading Check

Students should circle "Outer space."

p. 162 Read Fluently

Students should underline "to move," "to accept," "to dare," "to achieve," and "to live." Students should underline "to move out," "to accept the challenge," "to dare the unknown," and "to live in the past."

p. 162 Literary Analysis

The author uses an appeal to emotion. Sample response: The author wants the audience to not settle. He is encouraging the audience to support space exploration.

p. 162 Reading Skill

The paragraph expresses an opinion. The phrase "we have no future" is the clue.

p. 163 Apply the Skills:

1. Sample response: These leaders may vote for legislation and funding that support space travel.

2. Sample response: The essay conveys the message that exploring outer space is our human destiny. It paints a noble picture of humankind. This is a positive message.

3. **Graphic Organizer**
Row 1: "all"
Row 2: "must"

4. Sample response: Students may write "Industries are growing because of our exploration of outer space."

p. 165 Reading/Writing Connection

Sample response: Many laws help integrate our society. However, it is impossible to legislate people's feelings. Each person must promote tolerance in the community. Then, people will begin to understand one another.

p. 165 Note-taking Guide

How can we achieve it? through laws and personal actions

Why is it important? It brings peace to the world and helps us appreciate differences among people.

p. 166 Apply the Skills

1. Sample response: Jordan means that a baby has not yet been influenced by society.

2. Sample response: Jordan's ideas could work if all people were as optimistic as Jordan.

3. **Graphic Organizer**
Sample response:
Clue 2: "need"
Clue 3: "best way"

4. Sample response: Appeal to reason: "Each of us can decide to have one friend of a different race or background in our mix of friends."

"The Real Story of a Cowboy's Life"
Geoffrey C. Ward

"Rattlesnake Hunt"
Marjorie Kinnan Rawlings

p. 168 Graphic Organizer

Sample response:
"The Real Story of a Cowboy's Life"
atlas or map: route of a typical cattle drive
dictionary: difficult words, such as *escorts*

encyclopedia: information about cattle drives
reliable Web site: information about the author, Geoffrey C. Ward

"Rattlesnake Hunt"
almanac: the burning of the countryside at that time of year in order to create cattle forage
atlas or map: the location of Big Prairie, the rattlesnake hunting ground
biographical dictionary: "Ross Allen, a young Florida herpetologist, invited me to join him on a hunt in the upper Everglades—for rattlesnakes."
dictionary: difficult words, such as *herpetologist*
encyclopedia: information about rattlesnakes
reliable Web site: information about the author, Marjorie Kinnan Rawlings

p. 169 Note-taking Guide

Sample response:
Inconveniences: dust; homesteaders
Dangers From Animals or Nature: stampede at night; prairie dog holes; deep cuts in the ground
Benefits: beautiful views

p. 170 Activate Prior Knowledge

Students may list herds of cattle, riding horses, dusty ground, cowboy hats and boots, etc.

p. 170 Reading Skill

Students should check "Encyclopedia" and "Reliable Web site."

p. 170 Literary Analysis

Students should underline "chair," "workbench," and "pillow at night."

p. 171 Read Fluently

Students should circle "–the Nueces, the Guadalupe, the Brazos, the Wichita, and the Red" and "—payable in money or beef." The words following the first dash explain which rivers the herd crossed. The words following the second dash explain how the cowboys paid tolls.

p. 171 Reading Skill

The sentence is an opinion. The clue is the word "pretty."

p. 171 Reading Check

Students should circle "the homesteaders set-tled near water and then charged the cowboys for the water," and "When the cattle got into their crops, they came with guns and demanded payment for the damage."

p. 172 Apply the Skills

1. Teddy Blue participated in several cattle drives.
2. Sample response: Successful cowboys worked as a team. They loved the open trail.
3. Sample response: If opinions were not included, the author would not give as color-ful a picture of cowboy life.
4. **Graphic Organizer**

Sample response:

Informal Language: ". . . it sure was a pretty sight to see them strung out for almost a mile, the sun shining on their horns."

p. 174 Reading/Writing Connection

Sample response: One way to respond to something that frightens you is by turning away from it. It is difficult to acquire a deeper respect for what you fear. Facing something scary can benefit a person by making him or her get over the fear.

p. 174 Note-taking Guide

Sample response:

Box 3: She describes the snakes' behavior in an unemotional way.

Box 4: She heads off by herself to hunt a snake.

p. 175 Apply the Skills

1. Rawlings has won because she has conquered a fear.
2. Rawlings views herself as more courageous, and she views nature as less dangerous.
3. The facts show what Rawlings learned about snakes.
4. **Graphic Organizer**

Sample response:

Technical Vocabulary: coupe; arid

Formal Language: "I felt an upsurgence of spirit." "As I had discovered with the insects and the varmints, it is difficult to be afraid of anything about which enough is known, and Ross' facts were fresh from the laboratory."

Informal Language: "I've got one"; "Well, pick it up."

Reading Informational Materials: Manuals

p. 177 Graphic Organizer:

Which details can be verified as facts?

The copperhead has diamond shaped markings; Pit vipers puncture their victims with fangs; Coral snakes are red, yellow, and blue.

Which details are opinions? It is the most striking of the pit vipers; Pit vipers are the most frightening snakes; Coral snakes are beautiful.

p. 178 Reading Manuals

This snake is venomous. The snake has pits between its eyes and its nostrils, fangs, a triangular head, and eyes with narrow pupils.

p. 178 Read Fluently

Students should underline "triangular," "narrow," "vertical," "round," "visible," "nonvenomous," and "round."

p. 178 Reading Manuals

Sample response: Most manuals include pictures because manuals are meant to give information.

p. 178 Reading Check

Students should underline "the water moccasin."

p. 179 Reading Informational Materials

Sample response: What to do in a fire. How to treat a cut or a burn.

p. 179 Reading Manuals

Students should circle any three of the following: "cut into a snake bite"; "apply cold compresses"; "apply a tourniquet"; "raise the site of the bite above the level of the victim's heart"; "give the victim aspirin, stimulants, or pain medication"; "allow the person to exercise"

p. 179 Reading Check

Students should circle "venomous snakes can bite reflexively even after they die."

p. 180 Reading Skill

Sample response: The statement is an opinion because it says that "the bitten area may swell." It is not certain that the bitten area *will* swell. Even so, it would be a good idea to com-plete step five when assisting a bite victim.

p. 180 Reading Check

Students should underline two of the following: "lay the victim flat," "raise his or her feet 8 to 12 inches," or "cover the victim with a coat or blanket." Students should circle one of the following: "elevate the bitten area above the person's heart," or "place the victim in this position if you suspect any head, neck, back, or leg injury or if the position makes the victim uncomfortable."

p. 181 Apply the Skills
Thinking About the Manual

1. Anxiety can aggravate his or her reaction to the bite. This can make the bite more painful and more difficult to treat. It can also make recovery harder.
2. In North America, all venomous snakes—except the coral snake—are pit vipers. Pit vipers have triangular heads, fangs, narrow vertical pupils and pits between their nostrils and eyes. Nonvenomous snakes do not have these characteristics.

Reading Skill

3. You could use encyclopedias, other manuals, reliable Internet sources, or reference books from the library to check facts about venomous snakes.
4. Manuals are reference materials. Reference materials must have facts to provide reliable information.

ANSWERS TO UNIT 4

"Maestro"
"The Desert Is My Mother"

"Bailando"
Pat Mora

p. 184 Note-taking Guide
Sample response:
"The Desert Is My Mother"
Speaker: A woman who loves the desert.
Memories or Commands: She commands the desert to feed, tease, frighten, hold, heal, caress, sing, and teach her, and to make her beautiful.

"Bailando"
Speaker: A grown adult remembering her aunt.
Memories or Commands: She remembers her aunt dancing as a young woman, dancing with her, dancing with her children, and dancing on her ninetieth birthday.

p. 185 Activate Prior Knowledge
Some students may say that baking cookies reminds them of a time when a grandmother taught them how to make cookies. Other students may say that a day at the lake reminds them of a time when their father taught them how to fish.

p. 185 Poetry
Students should write "singing" and "songs."

p. 185 Poetry
Students should circle "smile" and "slid."

p. 185 Reading Check
Students should underline "when he bows."

p. 186 Read Fluently
Students should underline "I say" and "She."

p. 186 Poetry
"She" is the desert. Students may circle "serves," "sprinkles," or "shouts."

p. 186 Poetry
Students should list "silence" and "driest."

p. 186 Stop to Reflect
Sample response: The speaker loves the desert as a child loves his or her mother.

p. 187 Poetry
Students could underline "Le digo," or "Me."

p. 187 Poetry
Students may notice "susurra" in the fourth stanza. It is an example of onomatopoeia because it sounds like "whisper," which is what it means in English.

p. 187 Stop to Reflect
Sample response: Spanish is often spoken in the American Southwest, where deserts are found. This might be another way to connect the speaker to the desert.

p. 188 Poetry
Sample response: This poem is free verse because the lines do not rhyme. There are no stanzas. The lines have different numbers of syllables.

p. 188 Poetry
Students should circle "spinning round and round."

p. 188 Reading Check
Students should underline "my dear aunt."

p. 189 Apply the Skills
1. Sample response: The musician feels grateful to his parents. He is comforted when he thinks about them. They inspired him to become a musician.
2. The poem is about the speaker's aunt.
3. In "Maestro," "again and again," "bit by bit," and "note to note" are repeated. In "The Desert Is My Mother," "I say" and "Le digo" are repeated. In "Bailando," "spinning round and round" is repeated.
4. **Graphic Organizer**
Sample response:
. . . a woman: serves, shouts, whispers, gives, strokes, offers, chants
. . . a hot and dry region: spiked cactus, sunny day, thunder and lightening, pink blossoms, windy, sun's glare, driest sand
both: "She gives me chamomile and other spices" and "warm breath."

Poetry Collection 1

Poetry Collection 2

p. 191 Graphic Organizer
Sample response:
Poetry Collection 1
"Haiku"
Detail 1: The pond is watched by a weasel.
Detail 2: The moon sets.
Detail 3: Shadows drift.

How are the details related? They all take place in a woodsy area.
Conclusion: The poet is concerned with nature.

Poetry Collection 2:
"Winter"
Detail 1: Frogs burrow in the mud.
Detail 2: "Snails bury themselves."
Detail 3: The speaker airs quilts.
How are the details related? All of the details describe how animals and people prepare for winter.
Conclusion: Animals and people want to stay warm, cozy, fed, and healthy during the winter.

p. 192 Reading/Writing Connection
Sample response: People write poems because poetry helps communicate feelings, ideas, and action in few words. The images in poetry can generate feelings of love, curiosity, anger, or longing. Poetry reinforces a love of words and wordplay.

p. 192 Note-taking Guide
"The Rider"
Topic of Poem: The topic is a person riding a bicycle.
Actions in Poem: Action in the poem includes pedaling hard, leaving loneliness, panting, and floating free.

"Seal"
Topic of Poem: The topic is a seal swimming through the water.
Actions in Poem: Action in the poem includes dives, darts, a swerve, a twist, a flip, a flick, plunges, and plops.

"Haiku"
Topic of Poem: The topics are ducklings in pond, the woods, and shadows in the forest.
Actions in Poem: Action in the poem include pond is watched, not one leaf moves, moon sets, and shadows drift and disappear.

p. 193 Activate Prior Knowledge
Students may say that they have been inspired by the image of an actor performing in a Shakespearean play. The actor's talent and dedication to his art would be a good subject for a poem.

p. 193 Reading Skill
Students may underline "float free," "a cloud of sudden azaleas," and "luminous pink petals."

p. 193 Literary Analysis
The two people in "The Rider" are the boy who rollerskates and the speaker in the poem.

p. 194 Literary Analysis
Students should say that a concrete poem focuses on a visual image. The poet places the letters and lines in a way that looks like that image. Some students will say the poet chose this form because the poem's lines look like a seal. Others may say that the lines resemble the seal's movement as it swims and dives.

p. 194 Read Fluently
Students should circle words such as "zoom," "dart," and "Quicksilver-quick."

p. 194 Reading Skill
Sample response: The speaker admires the seal for its graceful movements in the water.

p. 194 Reading Check
Students should draw a box around "A whoop, a bark."

p. 195 Reading Skill
Students should say the speaker is worried about the ducklings. If they swim in the pond, the weasel will catch and eat them.

p. 195 Stop to Reflect
Students may say that it seems as if the woods themselves are afraid. The wind does not blow, and the leaves do not dare to move. Some students may say a predator is hunting in the woods. Other students may say that the woods are afraid of people who might do harm.

p. 195 Read Fluently
Students should circle "shadows" and "drift." Some students may also circle "disappear."

p. 196 Apply the Skills
1. Sample response: Rollerskating and bicycle riding are discussed in "The Rider." The two sports have wheels, movement, and speed in common.
2. Sample response: These words create a playful mood.
3. Sample response: Why does the speaker in "The Rider" include such colorful details about speed and movement?

4. Graphic Organizer
"The Rider" checkmarks under Musical language, Single image or idea, and Thoughts of one speaker
"Seal" checkmarks under Lines shaped like subject
"Haiku" checkmarks under Thoughts of one speaker; Three-lines; 17 syllables

p. 198 Reading/Writing Connection
Sample response: People might write a poem to capture their feelings about the desert. They could concentrate on details about animals, plants, and the climate of the desert. The poem would emphasize the variety and beauty of living things in the desert.

p. 198 Note-taking Guide
Sample response:
"Winter"
Supporting Details: "Chipmunks gather nuts." The speaker collects books.

"Forsythia"
Main Idea: Forsythia is a messenger of spring.
Supporting Details: "FORSYTHIA OUT" and "SPRING'S YELLOW TELEGRAM"

"Haiku"
Main Idea: Flowers are a sign of spring on a mountain.
Supporting Details: "sweet plum blossoms," "fragrant blossoms," and "Has spring come indeed?"

p. 199 Apply the Skills
1. Sample response: The words suggest that forsythia plants burst out in early spring. They let everyone know that spring is on its way.
2. Sample response: He respects nature. Nature inspires and amazes him.
3. Sample response: How are the words about forsythia related?
4. **Graphic Organizer**
"Winter" checkmarks under Musical language, Single image or idea, and Thoughts of one speaker
"Forsythia" checkmarks under Lines shaped like subject
"Haiku" checkmarks under Thoughts of one speaker, and Three lines; 17 syllables

Poetry Collection 1
Poetry Collection 2

p. 201 Graphic Organizer
Sample response:
Poetry Collection 1
Simile (from "The Courage That My Mother Had"): She had "courage like a rock."
Personification (from "Loo-Wit"): "She sprinkles ashes on the snow."
Metaphor (from "Life"): "Life is but a toy."
Symbol (from "Life"): The watch is a symbol that stands for life.

Poetry Collection 2
"The Village Blacksmith"
Simile: "the muscles of his brawny arms / Are strong as iron bands."
Personification: "the bellows roar"
Metaphor: Life is a "flaming forge" at which peoples' "fortunes must be wrought"
Symbol: The "tear" represents sorrow or grief.

p. 202 Reading/Writing Connection
Sample response: Though they occur rarely, volcanic eruptions are very dangerous and harmful. Smoke and ash indicate that a volcano is getting ready to erupt. It is not difficult for a volcano to impress most people.

p. 202 Note-taking Guide
Sample response:
Topic of the Poem:
"Life" The topic is life.
"The Courage That My Mother Had" The speaker's mother's courage is the topic.

Words Used to Describe Topic:
"Life" The poem uses the words "toy," "ticking," and "run down."
"The Courage That My Mother Had" The poem uses the words "granite," and "rock."
"Loo-Wit" The poem uses the words "old," "trembling," and "thin."

p. 203 Activate Prior Knowledge
Students may describe life as an exciting adventure. Life could lead them anywhere. They may describe courage as an attitude that can help them do things that would be impossible without it. They may describe a volcano as a sign of the power of nature.

p. 203 Reading Skill
Students may underline "Life is but a toy" and "to amuse a fascinated infant."

p. 203 Literary Analysis
The poet is using a simile.

p. 203 Reading Check
Students should circle "lets the watch run down."

p. 204 Reading Skill
Sample response: The most important details are the old woman spitting "black tobacco" and sprinkling "ashes / on the snow."

p. 204 Read Fluently
Students should underline three prepositional phrases such as: "from her bumpy bed," "to earth," and "on her neck."

p. 204 Literary Analysis
Sample response: The machinery is a symbol that stands for the harm that human beings do to nature.

p. 205 Literary Analysis
The poet uses personification to give human qualities to a volcano.

p. 205 Stop to Reflect
Sample response: Loo-wit's singing is the eruption of the volcano.

p. 205 Reading Check
Students should circle "but she heard the boot scrape, / the creaking floor, / felt the pull of the blanket / from her thin shoulder."

p. 206 Apply the Skills
1. Sample response: Both life and the watch stop after a while.
2. The scrape of a boot causes the eruption.
3. **Graphic Organizer**
Sample response:
Detail 2: The ticking of the watch amuses a child.
Detail 3: The old man, once an infant, is tired and lets the watch wind down.
4. Sample response: The rock is a symbol for strength.

p. 208 Reading/Writing Connection
Sample response: My older sister displays many qualities to admire, including a concern for others. It is easy to appreciate how she really listens when I talk to her about something important to me. This person makes others aspire to better themselves.

p. 208 Note-taking Guide
Sample response:
Topic of the Poem:
"The Village Blacksmith" The topic is life.
"Fog" The topic is fog.

Words Used to Describe Topic:
"The Village Blacksmith" "Thus at the flaming forge of life / Our fortunes must be wrought; / Thus on its sounding anvil shaped / Each burning deed and thought."
"Fog" "The fog comes / on little cat feet"; "It sits . . . on silent haunches."

p. 209 Apply the Skills
1. Sample response: Fog makes the atmosphere seem mysterious. This quality makes it a good subject for a poem.
2. Sample response: The mother demonstrates the qualities of strength and determination.
3. **Graphic Organizer**
Sample response:
Detail 1: The staircase often had splinters, torn up boards, and bare places
Detail 3: The mother tells her son that even though life is hard, she keeps climbing, and so should he.
4. Sample response: The lines include a simile. The blacksmith's blows create a beat like a sexton ringing the village bell.

Reading Informational Materials: Advertisements

p. 214 Apply the Skills
Thinking About the Advertisements
1. Sample response: Words such as "amazing," "miracle," and "astonishing" in the advertisements appeal to the reader's emotions.
2. Sample response: The prices are probably not mentioned so the reader will focus on how "great" the sole is instead of how much it might cost.

Reading Skill
3. Sample response: The claim, "Never before has scientific research come up with such a remarkable combination," cannot be proved.
4. Sample response: The goal of the Neolite ad is to convince readers to buy Neolite soles for their shoes.

Poetry Collection 1

Poetry Collection 2

p. 215 Graphic Organizer
Sample response:
Poetry Collection 1:
Onomatopoeia (from "Weather"): "Dot a dot dot dot a dot dot / Spotting the windowpane."
Alliteration (from "Sarah Cynthia Sylvia Stout Would Not Take the Garbage Out"): "Sarah Cynthia Sylvia Stout" is alliteration.
Repetition (from "Sarah Cynthia Sylvia Stout Would Not Take the Garbage Out"): She "*would not take the garbage out*" repeats throughout the poem.

Poetry Collection 2:
Onomatopoeia (from "Onomatopoeia"): "The rusty spigot *sputters*"
Alliteration (from "Full Fathom Five"): "*Full fathom five thy father lies*"
Repetition (from "Train Tune"): "*Back through* clouds / *Back through* clearing / *Back through* distance / *Back through* silence.*"

p. 216 Reading/Writing Connection
Sample response:
1. People react with shock and surprise when people see how I dress.
2. I dedicate myself to practicing very hard to stand out from the crowd.
3. My attitude is that everyone should strive to be unique.

p. 216 Note-taking Guide
Sample response:
Topic of the Poem:
"Sarah Cynthia Sylvia Stout Would Not Take the Garbage Out" a girl who refuses to take out the garbage
"One" individuality

Words Used to Describe the Topic:
"Sarah Cynthia Sylvia Stout Would Not Take the Garbage Out" "It filled the can, it covered the floor," "It raised the roof, it broke the wall"
"One" "Only one," "nobody can get a second one"

p. 217 Activate Knowledge
Students may recall words such as "carbun-cle" or "squish," as in "Did you *squish* your *carbuncle* today?"

p. 217 Reading Skill
Students should circle the words "She'd," "out," "And," and "cheese." Students should also circle the commas after "pans," "hams," "shout," "grounds," "peelings," "bananas," and "peas"; periods after "out" and "cheese"; and the colon after "ceilings."

p. 217 Read Fluently
Students should circle: "With," "bacon rinds," "chicken bones," "ice cream cones," "prune pits," "peach pits," "orange peel," "oatmeal," "pizza crusts," "greens," "beans," "tangerines," "crusts," and "roasts."

p. 218 Literary Analysis
Students should circle the letters "s" and "c" at the beginning of "Sarah" "Cynthia" "Stout" and "said."

p. 218 Reading Skill
Sample response: The garbage piled up very high. Sarah's neighbors moved away and no one would come to play with her. Sarah finally agreed to take out the garbage.

p. 218 Reading Check
Students should underline "it touched the sky."

p. 219 Reading Skill
Sample response: Rain is falling on the window. The rain makes wet dots and little tapping sounds.

p. 219 Read Fluently
Students may underline "juddle," "luddle," and "puddmuddle."

p. 219 Literary Analysis
Students should circle the words "slosh," "galosh," "puddle" and "jump." Sample response: The poet might mean that people are sloshing through water in rubber boots.

p. 220 Literary Analysis
Students should circle the two uses of "nobody," the three uses of "my," and the two uses of "or."

p. 220 Reading Skill
Sample response: The speaker shapes words; I am one person. No one else can talk for me.

p. 220 Reading Check
Students should underline "Only one of me."

p. 221 Apply the Skills

1. Sample response: The poem is funny and not preachy. The poem was intended to entertain, not to teach a lesson.

2. Sample response: The poet feels bad about all three words. "Mimic" and "act" are especially bad actions that involve others making fun of the speaker.

3. **Graphic Organizer**

Sample response:

"Sarah Cynthia Sylvia Stout"

Example from Poem: "It cracked the window and blocked the door / With bacon rinds and chicken bones."

Paraphrase: The garbage cracked the window. It also blocked the door.

"Weather"

Example from Poem: "Dot a dot dot dot a dot dot / Spotting the windowpane."

Paraphrase: Dots of rain are all over the windowpane.

4. Sample response: "Splatter" and "slosh" are two words that imitate the sound of water.

p. 223 Reading/Writing Connection

Sample response:

1. The sound of flowing water can affect how a person feels.

2. If it persists, the sound of a jackhammer can be very irritating.

3. The sound of birds singing generates a feeling of happiness in many people.

p. 223 Note-taking Guide

Sample response:

"Onomatopoeia"

Visual Details: "rusty spigot," "smattering of drops"

Aural (sound) Descriptions: "splutter," "splatters," "scatters," "plash!"

"Train Tune"

Visual Details: "clouds," "groves," "lightning"

Aural (sound) Descriptions: "silence"

p. 224 Apply the Skills

1. Sample response: The father's bones have turned into coral. His eyes have turned into pearls. Coral and pearls are precious items, so the changes might be called special or "rich." The changes might be called unusual or "strange" because the human form of the father appears to have become part of the sea.

2. Sample response: The poet may be remembering a love that has ended or a loved one who has died.

3. **Graphic Organizer**

Sample response:

"Full Fathom Five"

Example from Poem: "Nothing of him that doth fade / But doth suffer a sea change / Into something rich and strange"

Paraphrase: His whole body is transformed as it decays.

"Onomatopoeia"

Example from Poem: "The rusty spigot / sputters, / utters / a splutter, / spatters a smattering of drops, / gashes wider"

Paraphrase: The old faucet makes a hissing noise. It spits some drops of water, and the water spreads.

"Train Tune"

Example from Poem: The poem has no punctuation and is meant to be read without pausing.

Paraphrase: The train travels fast across time and place.

4. Students may suggest words such as "slosh," "glug," and "dribble."

Poetry Collection 1

Poetry Collection 2

p. 226 Graphic Organizer

Sample response:

Poetry Collection 1:

"Annabel Lee"

Original: "The angels, not half so happy in Heaven, / Went envying her and me."

Unfamiliar Words: "envying"

Dictionary Definitions: "Envying" means wanting to have something that someone else has.

Paraphrase: The angels were not as happy as the speaker and Annabel Lee. They wanted what the lovers had.

Poetry Collection 2:

"Father William"

Original: "'In my youth,' said the sage, as he shook his gray locks, / 'I kept all my limbs very supple'"

Unfamiliar Words: sage, locks, supple

Dictionary Definitions of Unfamiliar Words: sage = wise man, locks = hair, limbs = arms and legs, supple = flexible

Paraphrase "When I was young," the wise man said as he shook his gray hair, "I kept my body very flexible."

p. 227 Reading/Writing Connection
Sample response: The president has dedicated his/her life to helping Americans. He/She represents the people of the United States. His/Her actions affect the entire world.

p. 227 Note-taking Guide
Sample response:
"Martin Luther King"
Topic of Poem: Martin Luther King
Feelings the Speaker Has for the Topic: admiration; hope

"I'm Nobody"
Topic of Poem: Being a normal person instead of famous.
Feelings the Speaker Has for the Topic: dislike; finds fame boring

p. 228 Activate Prior Knowledge
A student may recall the words to "Pride (In the Name of Love)" by U2: "One man come in the name of love / One man come and go / One man come, he to justify / One man to overthrow."

p. 228 Literary Analysis
Students should circle the following syllables: "man-," "year," and "-go" in the first line; and "king-," "by," and "sea" in the second line.

p. 228 Reading Skill
"Highborn kinsmen" means "relatives born into noble families." "Bore" means "carried." The lines mean that Annabel Lee was from a noble family. Her family carried her away from the speaker. They buried her in a tomb by the sea.

p. 229 Read Fluently
Students should circle "the wind."

p. 229 Reading Skill
Students may find words and phrases such as "Heaven above," "demons," "dissever," and "my soul from the soul" confusing. Students may paraphrase with these words: "Nothing can separate my soul from Annabel Lee's soul."

p. 229 Reading Check
Students should underline "I see the bright eyes / Of the beautiful Annabel Lee."

p. 230 Literary Analysis
Students should circle the following syllables: "came," "-on," and "age" in the first line; "-set," "grief," and "rage" in the second line.

p. 230 Reading Skill
Students may find the phrases "a suffering earth" and "the measure of man's worth" confusing. Students may paraphrase with these words: "He taught society to value people for their real worth."

p. 230 Reading Check
Students should underline "they'd banish us."

p. 231 Apply the Skills
1. Sample response: The poet means that King's passion was very strong and powerful.
2. Sample response: "I'm Nobody" talks about how celebrities are always in public. They never have private time. They have to keep their admirers happy. This lifestyle can become boring and annoying.
3. Sample response: Annabel Lee's relatives took her body from the speaker. They buried it in a tomb by the sea.
4. **Graphic Organizer**
Sample response:
"Annabel Lee" ago, know; sea, Lee, me; we, sea, Lee; beams, dreams; rise, eyes; nighttide, side, bride.

p. 233 Reading/Writing Connection
Sample response:
1. A person's outlook on life can affect how well you remember him or her.
2. Someone with a positive attitude can enrich the lives of others.
3. He or she can teach others to appreciate simple pleasures.

p. 233 Note-taking Guide
Sample response:
Characters in Poem:
"Father William" Father William, his son
"Stopping by Woods . . . " a traveler

Actions in Poem:
"Jim" The sun shines on Jim. Jim brings his mother cocoa, broth, bread, and medicine. Jim tiptoes and tidies her room. He misses his baseball game.
"Father William" Father William and his son discuss the father's behavior. Father William stands on his head, turns a somersault, eats goose bones, and balances an eel on the end of his nose.

"Stopping by Woods . . . " A traveler stops to watch the woods fill up with snow. The person wonders at the beauty and quiet of the snow and then continues the journey.

p. 234 Apply the Skills

1. Sample response: Jim's decision to give up his baseball game to take care of his mother shows that he is not selfish.
2. Students may say that they are surprised by Father William's actions. He seems too old and too large to stand on his head, or do somersaults.
3. Sample response: The only other sound in the wood is the wind blowing gently and the snow falling softly.
4. **Graphic Organizer**
Rhyming Words:
"Father William" said, head; white, right; son, none; brain, again; before, door; fat, that; locks, box; supple, couple; weak, beak; suet, do it; law, jaw; wife, life; suppose, nose; ever, clever; enough, stuff; airs, downstairs
"Stopping by Woods . . . " know, though, snow; here, queer, year; lake, shake, mistake, flake; sweep, deep, keep, sleep

Reading Informational Materials: Magazine Articles

p. 236 Graphic Organizer
Sample response:
Sentence or Passage: It could be the hammering lyrics of a rap artist.
Replacement Words: hammering = pounding; lyrics = words
Paraphrase: It could be the pounding words of the rap artist.

p. 237 Reading Magazine Articles
Sample response: The people dancing are interesting to look at.

p. 237 Reading Skill
Students should circle "*Odyssey Magazine*, March 2002."

p. 237 Reading Check
Students should underline "Rap as a popular music style started in the late 1970s."

p. 237 Reading Magazine Articles
Sample response: The title catches a reader's attention. The title uses alliteration to help the reader understand that rap music is like poetry.

p. 238 Stop to Reflect
Sample response: Reading a poem and reading Dr. Seuss are like rap music. They use strong rhythmic phrasing.

p. 238 Reading Magazine Articles
Sample response: The main idea is "Sampling serves up yet more rhythms in rap."

p. 238 Reading Check
Students should circle "'MC' is the same as 'emcee' and stands for 'master of ceremonies'"

p. 239 Read Fluently
Students should put a 1 next to "ONE" and a 2 next to "Three."

p. 239 Reading Skill
Sample response: Listeners need interesting rhythm patterns to enjoy music. Rap music uses a mix of rhythms. It also has unpredictable lyrics and syncopation. Rap music is fun because it pleases and amazes listeners.

p. 239 Reading Informational Materials
Sample response: The last paragraph ties together the ideas in the article. It also lets the reader know that this paragraph is the end of the article.

p. 239 Reading Check
Students should circle "Too fast, and the brain can't perceive individual sounds. The music becomes one big blur."

p. 240 Apply the Skills
Thinking About the Magazine Article
1. Sample response: Tempo sets the mood for music. Tempo must not be too fast or too slow, or the song will not sound right.
2. Sample response: The brain remembers groups or patterns of rhythms in music. Music must use patterns or the brain will not process the sounds.

Reading Skill
3. Sample response: Rap is about people. Some rap songs get noticed.
4. Sample response: Sampling is taking a small part of one song and using it over and over to add background to a new song.

from Dragonwings
Laurence Yep

p. 243 Note-taking Guide
Sample response:
Novel: The narrator gets out of bed to answer the door.
Drama: Moon Shadow writes to his mother. Windrider and others pull Dragonwings to the top of the hill. Windrider flies and then falls to the ground. Windrider tells Moon Shadow that he will not fly again.
Both: Moon Shadow learns that Uncle and others have come to help Father get the flying machine up the hill.

p. 244 Activate Prior Knowledge
Some students may describe a place on a mountain. It would be a flat area, and not high enough for snow to be present. Other students may describe an airport runway, long and flat and surrounded by grass.

p. 244 Fiction
Sample response: The actor playing Moon Shadow would have to show his surprise and happiness with facial expressions. He would smile and his eyes would grow wide with surprise. The actors playing the other characters would have to use body language to show that they are tired from coming up the hill. They would try to catch their breath, and their shoulders might be slumped.

p. 244 Stop to Reflect
Sample response: Uncle's actions show that he cares about his brother.

p. 245 Reading Check
Students should circle "he had come to help because he wanted to make up for the bad things his son had done to us."

p. 246 Drama
Students should circle "writing a letter to his mother" and "large wagon."

p. 246 Read Fluently
Students should underline "Windrider," "Uncle Bright Star," and "Moon Shadow." Students should write: Uncle: Uncle Bright Star; Narrator: Moon Shadow; Father: Windrider.

p. 246 Drama
Sample response: Uncle cares about his brother. He is helping even though he does not believe in flying machines. He notices how thin and ragged his brother has become.

p. 247 Stop to Reflect
Sample response: It is very difficult to move the flying machine. Moon Shadow stumbles and then gives up. It appears that Uncle Bright Star and the others must use all their might to move the flying machine.

p. 247 Drama
Students should underline "In pantomime, Windrider illustrates to the others how to put the heavy ropes over their shoulder to pull the airplane up the hill," "Windrider positions himself as if on board a plane, while Miss Whitlaw pantomimes turning the right propeller, and Moon Shadow pantomimes turning the left propeller. Through sound effects, we hear the roar of the plane's engine, and Windrider begins a ballet to simulate flying." Sample response: These lines would make good stage directions because no one is talking. The lines are just describing how people are moving and what the sound effects should be, which is what stage directions do.

p. 247 Reading Check
Students should underline "He's really flying" and "A human up in the sky. Off the ground."

p. 248 Drama
Students should underline "speaks directly to the audience." Students may say that they know it is a monologue because Moon Shadow is not talking with any other characters.

p. 248 Read Fluently
Students should circle "as an adult," "the adult Moon Shadow," "the scene shifts back to Moon Shadow's childhood," and "Then the scene shifts again."

p. 248 Reading Check
Students should underline "He wants to become a merchant so that he will be able to bring his wife, Moon Shadow's mother, here from China."

p. 249 Stop to Reflect
Sample response: He will not fly Dragonwings again. Windrider feels that his son is more important to him than flying.

p. 250 Apply the Skills

1. Sample response: The audience knows that the actors move Dragonwings up the hill because the actors pantomime putting the ropes over their shoulders and pulling.

2. Sample response: Moon Shadow is saying that he and his father never forgot about building another airplane. Even though they did not, they still dreamed of doing so.

3. Sample response: The drama enhances the emotion of the situation because actors add tone, facial expressions, and body language to the scene, and these enhance the emotion of a situation. Drama also enhances emotion because the audience can see the scene unfold before them, not just read about it.

4. **Graphic Organizer**

Sample response:

To Show Action: "He's really flying."

To Reveal Thoughts and Feelings: "I thought he'd fly forever and ever."

To Describe Setting: "And I'll haul that thing back down when it does not fly."

A Christmas Carol: Scrooge and Marley, Act I
Israel Horovitz

from A Christmas Carol by Charles Dickens

p. 252 Graphic Organizer

Sample response:

What Is Suggested About the Work?

Picture: It will be set in the past.

Organization, Structure, Literary Form: It will be a play with many characters, acts, and scenes, and a story told through dialogue.

Beginnings of Passages: There will be ghosts and supernatural events.

p. 253 Reading/Writing Connection

Sample response:

1. A scrooge is someone who cares only about himself or herself.

2. Being a scrooge does not involve being generous to others.

3. A scrooge does not appreciate family and friends.

p. 253 Note-taking Guide

Sample response:

Evidence 1: He refuses to spend Christmas Eve with his nephew's family; he will not give money to help the poor.

Evidence 2: As a boy, he loved his sister; as a young man, he was happy with his friends and his boss.

Evidence 3: He wishes he had treated Cratchit more kindly; he wishes he had not chosen greed over the woman he loved.

p. 254 Activate Prior Knowledge

Some students may say that ghosts appear in stories to frighten readers. Other students may say that the role of a ghost is to give a warning to the living. Some may also say that ghosts act as observers in stories. Students may say that they remember the story of the Headless Horseman or a cartoon ghost.

p. 254 Stop to Reflect

Sample response: For a play that has many characters, as *A Christmas Carol* does, a list of characters helps readers identify and recall the characters. For example, a reader can review the list to see that Fred is Scrooge's nephew.

p. 254 Reading Skill

Students may circle "Ebenezer Scrooge," "Scrooge's lost love," "A Corpse," "The Ghost of Christmas Past," "The Ghost of Christmas Present," or "The Ghost of Christmas Future."

p. 255 Reading Skill

Students may say that they looked at how long the play is and how many characters are in it. Some students may say that their purpose is to be entertained. Other students may say that their purpose is to be inspired because the play takes place on a day that is an important spiritual holiday for some people.

p. 255 Read Fluently

Students should underline "Ghostly music in the auditorium. A single spot light on Jacob Marley, D. C. He is ancient; awful, dead-eyed. He speaks straight out to auditorium," "Cackle-voiced," "He laughs" and "Pause; remembers."

p. 255 Reading Check

Students should underline "Scrooge was too stingy to remove Marley's name from the sign on their office."

p. 256 Literary Analysis

Some students may say the lines show that Scrooge is selfish and mean.

p. 256 Stop to Reflect

Sample response: The nephew means that Scrooge does not celebrate Christmas.

p. 256 Reading Check

Students should circle "A Merry Christmas to you, Uncle! God save you!" and "What reason have you to be morose? You're rich enough."

p. 257 Reading Skill

Sample response: Scrooge will probably learn a lesson about the true meaning of Christmas and how good it is to be kind and giving.

p. 257 Literary Analysis

Sample response: Some students may say the lines show that Scrooge is a bully. Students may also say that Scrooge is needlessly stingy.

p. 257 Stop to Reflect

Sample response: Cratchit is a good and giving man. He worries about other people's hardships more than he worries about his own.

p. 258 Literary Analysis

Sample response: The audience can tell that Scrooge is in a bad mood and that he does not feel the holiday spirit.

p. 258 Stop to Reflect

Sample response: Scrooge's behavior is exaggerated, which may seem comical. His actions might make the audience laugh, but he is really much more pathetic and even sad.

p. 258 Reading Skill

Students may underline "the door knocker changes into Marley's face," "the face disappears," "The pictures on the walls show Marley's face," "all the bells in the house begin to ring," and "hears a loud chain dragging across his basement floor and up the stairs. He hears doors fly open."

p. 259 Literary Analysis

Sample response: Scrooge's words suggest he is neither impressed nor frightened by the strange visions and sounds at the beginning of the scene.

p. 259 Stop to Reflect

Sample response: Marley is the first ghost to appear to Scrooge because he knew Scrooge when he was alive.

p. 259 Reading Check

Students should circle "Marley screams a ghostly scream and removes his head from his shoulders."

p. 260 Reading Skill

Sample response: Scrooge comes home and Marley's ghost appears to him. Scrooge is frightened but does not truly believe in Marley's ghost. Marley screams and Scrooge believes. Marley tells Scrooge that he will be visited by Three Spirits. Marley leaves and Scrooge begins to think that he might have imagined the whole thing. Students' questions may include: Will any ghosts visit Scrooge? Why will they visit? What will they do with Scrooge? Will it change him?

p. 260 Literary Analysis

Sample response: Marley talks directly to the audience because he has to inform them about the change they will see in Scrooge.

p. 261 Stop to Reflect

Some students may say they would be scared to meet a ghost. Other students may say that they would like to meet a ghost who could show them their past.

p. 261 Literary Analysis

Sample response: Remembering his own lonely experience as a boy allows Scrooge to relate to the singing boy. Scrooge was stingy before, but the dialogue description shows that he now wishes that he had given something to the boy he heard singing earlier in the play. Scrooge is becoming more generous.

p. 261 Reading Check

Students should circle "Bear just a touch of my hand here" and "touches the spirit's heart."

p. 262 Reading Skill

Students may ask: Why was Scrooge left at school until his sister asked to have him come home? Is Scrooge's nephew Fan's son? Where is Fan now?

p. 262 Stop to Reflect

Sample response: The golden idol the woman talks about is money.

p. 262 Literary Analysis

Sample response: This dialogue refers to a relationship Scrooge had in his past. However, he let money stand in the way of his love. Now he has come to regret it later in life.

p. 263 Read Fluently

Sample response: The woman shows that this conversation is very difficult for her because she loves Scrooge very much. The woman is both angry and sad.

p. 263 Reading Skill

Students may say they look forward to seeing where the Ghosts take Scrooge next and that their purpose is to be entertained. They may also want to see whether Scrooge's behavior will change. Students may say that their purpose for reading Act II is to be entertained and inspired. Sample response: Will Scrooge learn to be kind and giving to others? Will Scrooge be kinder toward his nephew and Bob Cratchit?

p. 263 Reading Check

Students should underline "Don't release me, madam . . ."

p. 264 Apply the Skills

1. Sample response: No, Scrooge is a lonely and bitter man because he has replaced kindness and a giving spirit with greed.
2. Sample response: Scrooge currently treats people harshly. In the future, he might try to build friendly relationships with the people around him.
3. Some students may say that they are reading this play in order to be entertained. Others may be reading to be inspired. Some students may expect both.
4. **Graphic Organizer**
Sample response:
What Does It Say? "If I could work my will, every idiot who goes around with 'Merry Christmas' on his lips, should be boiled with his own pudding, and buried with a stake of holly in his heart."
What Does It Mean? Scrooge wants all people who celebrate Christmas to be punished.
Why Is It Important? It shows how mean and heartless Scrooge is at the beginning of the play.

A Christmas Carol: Scrooge and Marley, Act II
Israel Horovitz

from A Christmas Carol by Charles Dickens

p. 266 Graphic Organizer

Sample response:
Types of Reading Material: Dialogue
Purpose for Reading: To be entertained
Reading Rate: Read quickly to imitate conversation.

p. 267 Note-taking Guide

Sample response:
Details That Support These Statements:
Row 1: Scrooge says, "Spirit, tell me if Tiny Tim will live."
Row 2: "A nervous giggle here," "Oh, Ghost of the Future, I fear you more than any Specter I have seen!"
Row 3: "I am as happy as a schoolboy," "An act of kindness is like the first green grape of summer: it leads to another and another and another."

p. 268 Apply the Skills

1. Sample response: Scrooge feels drawn to the caring young boy.
2. Sample response: Scrooge's actions suggest that he has taken the lessons to heart. His Christmas generosity shows that he thinks of others and that he now enjoys giving.
3. Students may say that they read long speeches with difficult vocabulary slowly and carefully to improve their understanding of the text.
4. **Graphic Organizer**
Sample response:
Characters on Stage: Scrooge, Marley
Movement of Characters: Marley moves close to the sleeping Scrooge.
Description of Lighting: a spotlight on Scrooge and one on Marley, lightning flashes, candle, colors change
Description of Sound: singing, thunder, ghostly music; Marley laughs and speaks.
Other Special Effects: A flame shoots from Marley's hand.

Reading Informational Materials: Literary Criticism

p. 270 Graphic Organizer

Sample response:
TNT
Critic's summary: none
Positive comments: "But TNT's *Carol* would be worth watching if only for the lead performance of Patrick Stewart."
Negative comments: "gratuitous special effects"
Critic's overall opinion: "Old story well told."

Meadow Brook Theater
Critic's summary: none

Positive comments: "Wicks has infused the show with new energy," "a more palatable holiday treat for adults and children"
Negative comments: "paying only passing attention to his English accent"
Critic's overall opinion: "A well-produced, grand-scale event that is as much pageant as play."

p. 271 Reading Check
Students should underline "But TNT's *Carol* would be worth watching if only for the lead performance of Patrick Stewart."

p. 271 Reading Literary Criticism
Students should underline: "TNT" and "Sun., Dec. 5, 8 p.m., ET." Sample response: The audience for this review is people who have televisions and who might want to watch *A Christmas Carol*.

p. 271 Reading Skill
Students should circle "Bottom line: Old story well told." Sample response: The critic would recommend that people watch this show. The critic thinks that this show is different from other versions of *A Christmas Carol* and therefore should be watched.

p. 272 Reading Skill
Sample response: The writer is positive about the change made by the director and will probably write a good review. Students may underline "make the old holiday fruitcake seem fresh."

p. 272 Reading Literary Criticism
Students may underline "The audience is still serenaded by a band of merry carolers in the lobby before the show," "the set and costumes are unchanged from these many Christmases past," and "set design for the show is, as always, enormous and gorgeous." Sample response: Kelleher discusses the actors more than the scenery and the atmosphere of the production because people will probably watch the show on television to see the famous actors. For the local production, audiences want to know about the actors, but the set and atmosphere are also important.

p. 272 Stop to Reflect
Sample response: The sets for this play had to show many different locations and some of these had to show both past and future events. It might have been difficult for the

stage crew to change the scenes without interrupting the actors' performances. It would also have been difficult for the technical crew to make sure that the ghosts' appearances, disappearances, and scary voices sound real and happen at the correct times.

p. 273 Reading Check
Students should circle "pageant" and "beautifully wrapped gift under a well-decorated tree."

p. 273 Reading Informational Materials
Some students may say that hearing about the wonderful lights and staging of the play makes them want to see the production in the theater. Other students may say that the description of Patrick Stewart's performance makes them want to watch the TNT version.

p. 273 Reading Skill
Students should underline "A well-produced, grand-scale event that is as much pageant as a play." Sample response: The production is large and impressive, which shows that it was done with care.

p. 274 Apply the Skills
Thinking About the Literary Criticism
1. Sample response: *People Weekly*: "So you muttered 'humbug' when you spied yet another version of *A Christmas Carol* on the TV schedule." *Oakland Press*: "Director Debra Wicks has tinkered with Meadow Brook's recipe for *A Christmas Carol* just enough to make the old holiday fruitcake seem fresh."
2. Sample response: Kelleher believes that people should watch the production if only to see Patrick Stewart's portrayal of Scrooge.

Reading Skill
3. Sample response: The phrase "like a beautifully wrapped gift under a well-decorated tree, it suits the season to a tee," summarizes Sousanis's opinion.
4. Sample response: Kelleher thinks that the story has been done too many times.

The Monsters Are Due on Maple Street
Rod Serling

p. 275 Graphic Organizer
Sample response:
Character: Charlie
Action 1: says Les needs to be watched
Motive 1: thinks Les may be dangerous

Action 2: takes gun from Steve
Motive 2: wants to protect neighborhood
Action 3: shoots Pete
Motive 3: is afraid that Pete is an alien

p. 276 Reading/Writing Connection
Sample response:
1. It is easy to <u>arouse</u> suspicions by being different.
2. Too often, we <u>contribute</u> to rumors by repeating them <u>without thinking.</u>
3. Sadly, if you try to <u>dispute</u> a rumor, you will often become the <u>object</u> of another rumor.

p. 276 Note-taking Guide
Sample response:
Box 1: The neighbors turn on Charlie.
Box 2: People get scared.
Box 3: The figures in the space craft wait for the people to destroy themselves.
Box 4: Figure 1 explains to Figure 2 how to take over the world.

p. 277 Activate Prior Knowledge
Some students may have noticed that people in groups can get out of control quickly. Other students may have noticed that people sometimes do not express their opinions freely in large groups.

p. 277 Literary Analysis
Sample response: Goodman's motive in telling Steve not to step on the porch is that Goodman does not want anything to happen to his house and family.

p. 277 Reading Check
Students should circle "the Goodman house."

p. 278 Literary Analysis
Sample response: Steve becomes anxious and sarcastic. This tells readers that Steve sees that things are getting out of control and that he thinks Charlie is not making sense.

p. 278 Reading Check
Students should underline "self-appointed hanging judge."

p. 279 Literary Analysis
Sample response: Charlie reacts this way because Pete's death is a very serious consequence of Charlie's behavior. Charlie realizes he has just committed murder in front of many people.

p. 279 Reading Skill
Sample response: Goodman accuses Charlie of killing Pete to stop Pete from telling the neighbors that Charlie is the one to blame for all of the trouble.

p. 279 Reading Check
Students should circle "You killed him, Charlie. You shot him dead!"

p. 280 Reading Skill
Students should underline: "cut their electric power and communication devices, throw them into darkness, and then sit back and wait for them to panic, grow suspicious, and then destroy themselves." Sample response: Yes, this is a good summary of what happened on Maple Street because there really was not anything wrong on Maple Street, but the people turned on one another anyways.

p. 280 Read Fluently
Students should circle the three ellipses following: "It's," "it's," and "It's." Sample response: The ellipses are used to show that Charlie is panicking. He is trying to figure out who he can blame so that people stop blaming him.

p. 280 Stop to Reflect
Sample response: The author repeats these lines because he wants to show how scared Charlie is. Also, he might want to show that the choosing of others to blame is random and not motivated by real information.

p. 281 Reading Skill
Sample response: Figure One plans to let humans destroy themselves. Then, the aliens can take control of the planet.

p. 281 Reading Check
Students should circle "a very successful procedure for conquering humans."

p. 282 Apply the Skills
1. Sample response: Prejudices and attitudes lead people to destroy themselves; these are the tools of conquest.
2. Sample response: The monsters are the residents themselves.
3. **Graphic Organizer**
Sample response:
Important Details from the Beginning:
There is a flash across the sky; the electricity goes out; a boy suggests that aliens may be responsible.

Important Details from the Middle: Les Goodman is suspected of being an alien; it is revealed that Steve has a radio in his basement, and the crowd's suspicions turn to him; Charlie shoots a shadowy figure who turns out to be Pete Van Horn.

Important Details from the End: The crowd accuses Charlie; neighbors begin throwing rocks and smashing windows; Charlie accuses Tommy; the neighbors argue and fight, accusing one another; two aliens review the "procedure" used to get humans to destroy one another.

4. Sample response: Charlie keeps saying, "It's the kid." to throw suspicion off himself. They remember that it was Tommy who knew about the aliens in the first place.

Reading Informational Materials: Application

p. 285 Reading Informational Materials
Sample response: The playhouse wants to show the type and quality of its productions.

p. 285 Read Fluently
Students should underline "it," "its," "its," and "its." Sample response: The "It" stands for the Flat Rock Playhouse.

p. 285 Reading Applications
Sample response: The last sentence of the first paragraph suggests that the playhouse is looking for people who want to be apprentices and interns because a major purpose of the playhouse is to train people to perform there.

p. 285 Stop to Reflect
Students may suggest "Career Preparation."

p. 286 Reading Applications
Sample response: This application requires an address and Social Security number.

p. 286 Stop to Reflect
Sample response: Most people who fill out this application are probably in high school or college because there is a space for "Parent/Guardian Name."

p. 286 Reading Skill
Sample response: They are part of the same group because at the top of the application it says that people should contact the Flat Rock Playhouse for information about the Vagabond School.

p. 286 Reading Check
Students should circle "However, if one's schedule or geographic distance from the Playhouse makes a personal audition impossible, one may send a videotaped audition consisting of two monologues and if applicable examples of singing and dance work."

p. 288 Apply the Skills
Thinking About the Application
1. Sample response: Applicants do not need much space to write a name. More space is included for the applicants' previous instruction so that applicants can list complete information and because this information is important to the school.
2. Sample response: The Vagabond School of the Drama provides advantages for someone looking for a career in acting because it provides opportunities for networking with professionals and education for marketing oneself in the theater business.

Reading Skill
3. The school requires a headshot or snapshot.
4. The section titled "Instruction" is designed to determine the applicant's experience.

"Grasshopper Logic"
"The Other Frog Prince"
"duckbilled platypus vs. beefsnakstik®"
Jon Scieszka and Lane Smith

p. 291 Note-taking Guide
Sample response:
"Grasshopper Logic"
Characters: Grasshopper, Mom Grasshopper
Problem: Grasshopper has waited too long to do a big homework assignment.
Moral: "There are plenty of things to say to calm a hopping mad Grasshopper mom. 'I don't know' is not one."

"The Other Frog Prince"
Characters: a frog, a princess
Problem: A frog says he is really a prince.
Moral: You should not believe everything you hear.

"duckbilled platypus vs. beefsnakstik®"
Characters: Duckbilled Platypus, BeefSnakStik®
Problem: Each character thinks it is better than the other.
Moral: Just because you have a lot of stuff, do not think you are so special.

p. 292 Activate Prior Knowledge
Sample response: A child lies. A child disobeys. A child does not do his or her schoolwork.

p. 292 Oral Tradition
Students should underline "Grasshopper" and "Mom Grasshopper."

p. 292 Oral Tradition
The assignment is exaggerated. It asks for twelve musicals with designed and built sets. One student cannot be expected to do all of that work.

p. 292 Reading Check
Students should underline "Just one small thing for History."

p. 293 Oral Tradition
Students should circle "frog."

p. 293 Oral Tradition
Sample response: In this story, the opposite happens. The princess kisses the frog, but the frog does not turn into the prince. The frog lies to the princess to get a kiss.

p. 293 Reading Check
Students should underline "the spell can only be broken by the kiss of a beautiful princess."

p. 294 Read Fluently
Sample response: I think the author uses the ® because it adds humor to the story.

p. 294 Oral Tradition
Students should circle "Duckbilled Platypus." Students should underline "BeefSnakStik®."

p. 294 Stop to Reflect
Sample response: The words in bold type imply that the speaker is shouting or speaking louder.

p. 295 Apply the Skills
1. Some students may prefer "Grasshopper Logic" because they can relate to Grasshopper procrastinating about his homework. Other students may prefer "The Other Frog Prince" because they are familiar with the original fairy tale and like the funny ending. Others may prefer the last story because it is very silly and different from the original version.
2. Grasshopper wants his mother to allow him to go out to play.
3. Sample response: Do not trust everything you hear.
4. **Graphic Organizer**
Sample response:
"Grasshopper Logic"
Personification: talking grasshoppers; a grasshopper that goes to school, carries a backpack, plays with friends, and has homework

"The Other Frog Prince"
Hyperbole: the princess kisses a frog so quickly
Personification: a frog talks

"duckbilled platypus vs. beefsnakstik®"
Hyperbole: BeefSnakStik argues with a duckbilled platypus

"Icarus and Daedalus"
Josephine Preston Peabody

"Demeter and Persephone"
Anne Terry White

p. 297 Graphic Organizer
Sample response:
"Icarus and Daedalus"
Cause: King Minos puts Daedalus and Icarus in prison on Crete.

Cause: Daedalus escapes his cell but cannot escape the island.
Cause: Daedalus sees seagulls flying.
Event: Daedalus builds wings to fly away.
Effect: Daedalus and Icarus fly away from Crete.
Effect: Icarus flies too close to the sun and crashes into the sea.
Effect: Daedalus names an island after his son and never flies again.

"Demeter and Persephone"
Sample response:
Cause: Aphrodite tells Eros to shoot an arrow at Pluto.
Cause: Eros shoots an arrow into Pluto's heart.
Cause: Pluto falls in love with Persephone.
Event: Pluto kidnaps Persephone.
Effect: Demeter makes Earth infertile.
Effect: Zeus sends Hermes to ask Pluto to release Persephone.
Effect: Pluto releases Persephone, but she must return during the winter months.

p. 298 Reading/Writing Connection
Sample response:
1. My dentist convinced me to eliminate candy before bedtime.
2. It was difficult to modify my free time so I could study and improve my grades.
3. It was easier to adapt to the new rules than it was to clean my room daily.

p. 298 Note-taking Guide
Sample response:
Second box: Daedalus uses bird feathers, thread, and wax to make wings for himself and his son.
Third box: Daedalus warns Icarus not to fly too close to the sun.
Fourth box: Daedalus and Icarus fly away, but Icarus flies too close to the sun. His wings melt, and he falls into the sea.

p. 299 Activate Prior Knowledge
A student may describe a time when he or she tried to play a very difficult piece of music on an instrument or tried to read a book that was too difficult.

p. 299 Reading Skill
Daedalus watches the seagulls flying. He realizes that they are free because of their ability to fly. This realization causes Daedalus

to make wings so that he and his son can fly away from the island.

p. 299 Reading Check
Students should circle "Labyrinth."

p. 300 Literary Analysis
He tries to teach Icarus how to use the wings safely.

p. 300 Reading Skill
Sample response: Icarus wants to feel joy and freedom when he flies.

p. 300 Read Fluently
Students should circle the -em dashes after "vainly" and "falling."

p. 300 Reading Check
Students should circle "the fogs about the earth would weigh you down."

p. 301 Stop to Reflect
Students may say that they would have listened to the advice of their father.

p. 301 Reading Check
Students should underline "in memory of the child."

p. 302 Apply the Skills
1. Sample response: He makes wings from bird feathers, thread, and wax.
2. Sample response: Icarus shows that he is irresponsible. Icarus would rather have fun than be careful in a dangerous situation.
3. Daedalus names an island after his son. In his grief, he offers his wings to the temple of Apollo and never flies again.
4. **Graphic Organizer**
Sample response:
Icarus: Lesson: You should take warnings of danger seriously.
Daedalus: How Taught: through Icarus' death

p. 304 Reading/Writing Connection
Sample response: I appreciate my favorite season because I love to watch the leaves change color. It serves to unify the summer and the winter. It is hard to specify how beautiful the trees look.

p. 304 Note-taking Guide
Sample response:
Pluto: Falls in love with Persephone; kidnaps her

Demeter: Makes it so that the earth will not produce food

Persephone: Misses the flowers of the earth; eats a pomegranate from the underworld

Zeus: Sends Hermes to ask Pluto to release Persephone

p. 305 Apply the Skills

1. Sample response: Some students may say that Demeter's actions are right because she has lost someone she loves. Others may say that her actions are wrong because her actions will hurt innocent people.
2. Sample response: When Persephone returns to the underworld, Demeter grieves and vegetation dies. When Persephone returns to her mother, Demeter's joy brings life back to the fields.
3. Zeus intervenes, forcing Pluto to release Persephone.
4. **Graphic Organizer**

Sample response:

Demeter: How Taught: through Demeter's search for and grief for her lost daughter, which caused her to change the earth

Persephone: Lesson: Appearances may be deceiving. **How Taught:** through Pluto's love for Persephone and grief at her departure

Pluto: How Taught: through the death of vegetation brought on by Demeter and through Persephone's departure

Reading Informational Materials: Textbooks

p. 308 Reading Textbooks

Students should underline "The Seasons on Earth," "How Sunlight Hits Earth," and "Earth's Tilted Axis." Students should recognize that the headings tell them that they will learn how sunlight and the Earth's axis affect the seasons on Earth.

p. 308 Reading Skill

The Earth's tilted axis causes it to have seasons.

p. 308 Read Fluently

A list of the seasons follows the colon in the first sentence.

p. 308 Reading Informational Materials

Sample response: The headings tell me what I am reading about and help me understand the main idea of each section. The figure and its caption illustrate the ideas in the text.

p. 310 Apply the Skills
Thinking About the Textbook

1. As it is the beginning of summer at that time, one would expect warm weather in the Northern Hemisphere.
2. Because they receive the most direct sunlight all year, people living near the equator experience warmer temperatures.

Reading Skill

3. The tilt of Earth's axis causes the yearly cycle.
4. Summer is the season.

"Tenochtitlan: Inside the Aztec Capital"
Jacqueline Dineen

"Popocatepetl and Ixtlaccihuatl"
Juliet Piggott Wood

p. 311 Graphic Organizer

Sample response:

"Tenochtitlan: Inside the Aztec Capital"

Cause/Effect: *Because* Tenochtitlan was built in a swamp, the city needed land to grow food.

Effect/Cause: The people built chinampas, or small islands, where they could grow food.

Cause/Effect: *Because* the chinampas were built on the swamp, the huts on them had to be light so that they would not sink.

p. 311 Graphic Organizer

Sample response:

"Popocatepetl and Ixtlaccihuatl"

Cause/Effect: *Because* some warriors were jealous of Popo's strength and success, they told the emperor that Popo had had been killed in battle.

Effect/Cause: The emperor told Ixtla that Popo had died, and Ixtla died of a broken heart.

Cause/Effect: *As a result of* Ixtla's death, Popo refused to become emperor and had two pyramids built, one for Ixtla and one for himself to watch over her.

p. 312 Reading/Writing Connection

Sample response: City planners should adapt old city centers for the needs of current residents. City roads need to maximize ways to travel through downtown. One can modify a city plan by reworking public transportation.

p. 312 Note-taking Guide

Sample response:

The Floating Gardens: made of piles of earth in the shallow parts of the lakes; called chinampas; supplied with fresh water by ditches and canals

The Homes: nobles' houses: large homes like palaces, one story high around a courtyard, built from adobe and whitewashed; poor people's houses: built on chinampas but not sturdy, grouped with other houses in compounds, had outdoor patio and gardens

The Furniture and Decoration: plain, dirt floor, mats of reeds for sleeping, clay cooking pots and utensils, household shrines with statues of the gods, no windows, no chimneys, no doors, open doorways

p. 313 Activate Prior Knowledge

Students may comment that ancient people lived more simply than people do today. They did not have electricity or toilets or cars. They had to grow their own food.

p. 313 Literary Analysis

Sample response: The Spaniards' first account of Tenochtitlan refers to it as "an enchanted vision." It talks about the city "rising from the water." The Spaniards were impressed with the city, and their account of it likely inspired many stories.

p. 313 Reading Check

Students should circle "Stone waterways brought fresh water to the city from the mainland."

p. 314 Reading Skill

Students should mark "The land around the lakes was dry because there was very little rain."

p. 314 Literary Analysis

The lakes to the north contained salt water.

p. 314 Reading Check

Students should circle "Some of the homes were built of adobe, or bricks of mud that had been dried in the sun."

p. 314 Read Fluently

Students should cross out "of flowers and vegetables," "in the courtyards," and "of rich Aztec homes." Students should circle "Gardens."

p. 315 Literary Analysis

Students should circle "What we do know has been pieced together from scattered historical records such as documents that record the sale of building sites on the chinampa gardens."

p. 315 Stop to Reflect

The houses of the rich people were like palaces, had courtyards, and were made from adobe. The houses of the poor people were smaller and built on chinampas. They were built in groups in walled compounds with gardens and patios.

p. 315 Reading Skill

The houses did not have windows or chimneys to vent smoke from cooking fires.

p. 316 Apply the Skills

1. **Graphic Organizer**
Sample response:
Questions: Why is there so little evidence about poor people's houses in Tenochtitlan?
Details: What we know has been pieced together from scattered documents.
Understanding the Article: No remains of poor people's houses survived to be studied.
2. Sample response: The Aztecs built chinampas, which allowed the people of Tenochtitlan to produce more of their own food. Each chinampa produced enough food to feed one family. The Aztecs also dug ditches and built canals to bring fresh water to the city.
3. Sample response: The Aztecs had water for irrigation.
4. Sample response: Two statements: Between one third and one half of people in Tenochtitlan were farmers; farmers' only tools were hoes and sticks. Facts: the Aztecs built three causeways over the swamp; Tenochtitlan was built in a huge valley; water flowed along stone aqueducts from the mainland to Tenochtitlan.

p. 318 Reading/Writing Connection

Sample response: My favorite family stories illustrate what life was like for my ancestors. I hope my children appreciate how difficult life was for our ancestors. These stories reinforce how much our family has struggled.

p. 318 Note-taking Guide

Sample response:
What Popo Does: He buries Ixtla under a heap of stones on one pyramid. He refuses to become emperor and climbs to the top of his own pyramid. He lights a torch and stays there to watch over Ixtla's body.
What Happens: Over the years, the pyramids become high, white-capped mountains.

p. 319 Apply the Skills

1. **Graphic Organizer**

Sample response:

Questions: Why does the Emperor care whether, after he dies, Ixtla rules alone or with a husband? Why does the Emperor offer his daughter to whoever defeats his enemies?

Details: The Emperor does not think anyone but his daughter will rule as he wants the city to be ruled. Enemies surround the city, and the Emperor is too weak to lead the fight against them.

Understanding the Legend: The Emperor is so proud that he wants to control what happens, even after his death. The Emperor does not think that his daughter can defend the city without help.

2. Sample response: The Aztecs admired people who displayed wisdom, honesty, bravery, and loyalty.

3. Popo's torch, still burning in memory of Ixtla, causes the volcano to smoke.

4. Sample response: Facts: Ixtlaccihuatl and Popocatepetl are volcanic mountains; Popocatepetl means "smoking mountain." The reader knows that they are facts because they can be proven true.

"Sun and Moon in a Box"
Richard Erdoes and Alfonso Ortiz

"How the Snake Got Poison"
Zora Neale Hurston

p. 321 Graphic Organizer

Sample response:

"Sun and Moon in a Box"

Story Title: "Sun and Moon in a Box"

Time: a long time ago, early in the history of Earth

Place: American Southwest, Kachina Pueblo

Customs: Native American dancing

Beliefs: A coyote released the sun and the moon into the sky. This action created winter.

"How the Snake Got Poison"

Story Title: "How the Snake Got Poison"

Time: probably a long time ago

Place: Earth and heaven

Customs: African American dialect

Beliefs: God gave snakes poison to protect themselves against other animals. He also gave snakes rattles to warn other animals of their approach.

p. 322 Reading/Writing Connection

Sample response: Some stories have a character who tries to exploit other characters. He will often convince others to trust him. He might interact with others in a normal way, but he is really trying to trick them.

p. 322 Note-taking Guide

Sample response:

Effect/Cause 1: They want to borrow the sun and moon, so Eagle grabs the box and flies off.

Effect/Cause 2: Coyote wants the box, so he pleads to carry it. He says his family will think badly of him for not helping. He promises not to open the box.

Effect/Cause 3: Eagle gives Coyote the box. Coyote cannot control his curiosity.

Effect/Cause 4: Coyote opens the box, and the sun and moon escape into the sky.

p. 323 Activate Prior Knowledge

Students may be familiar with the Greek legend of the god Apollo and his twin sister Artemis. When Apollo rode his golden chariot across the sky, he was the sun. When Artemis rode her silver chariot across the sky, she was the moon. Students also may be familiar with the Bible's account of God's creation of the sun, moon, and earth.

p. 323 Reading Skill

Sample response: Coyote does not do things well and expects Eagle to help him. Eagle is strong and helps Coyote.

p. 323 Read Fluently

Students should underline "they opened the box enough to let the sun peek out" and "they let the moon look out."

p. 324 Stop to Reflect

Sample response: Eagle thinks Coyote is too curious and will not be able to resist opening the box. He may not think Coyote can be trusted because Coyote wanted to steal the box.

p. 324 Reading Skill

Sample response: Sun and Moon both flew out of the box and caused immediate changes to the climate.

p. 324 Literary Analysis

Sample response: Eagle says that if Coyote had acted responsibly, they could have always enjoyed summer. The story treats winter as a bad and unpleasant season. Ancient people probably did not like winter as much as summer. They had a hard time finding food and staying warm in the winter.

p. 324 Reading Check

Students should circle "He could not curb his curiosity."

p. 325 Apply the Skills

1. Sample response: Eagle may have decided that Coyote must be serious because of his constant begging to carry the box.
2. Sample response: Eagle shares responsibility. Eagle knew that he should not trust Coyote, but he let him carry the box anyway.
3. **Graphic Organizer**

Sample response:

Coyote: lazy, sneaky, irresponsible
Eagle: strong, responsible, trusting
Both: Both want the box with the sun and the moon; both want to carry the box.
4. Sample response: The Kachinas were Native Americans who lived in the American Southwest. This detail shows that Native Americans from the Southwest told this story.

p. 327 Reading/Writing Connection

Sample response: Most people communicate by talking and writing. When people interact in different settings they behave in different ways. Language helps them comprehend what other people are doing and thinking.

p. 327 Note-taking Guide

Sample response:

Snake: complains to God because he has no protection; takes the poison and kills anything that tries to step on him; explains that he cannot tell who is an enemy and who is a friend
Varmints: tread on snakes and kill them; complain to God when snake gets poison because snake starts killing everything

p. 328 Apply the Skills

1. Sample response: The varmints and the snake are afraid of each other. They dislike and misunderstand each other because of their past actions.
2. Sample response: This answer might reflect how people ignore each other unless there is a threat of harm. It might also show that two people sometimes need a third party to help them solve their differences.

3. Graphic Organizer

Sample response:

Snake: living on the ground without protection from other animals; has no poison, rattle, legs, or claws; can see only feet
Varmints: can't see, smell, or hear the snake in the bushes; step on snake and kill its kind
Both: do not see enemies clearly; accidentally kill too many of the other's kind
4. The use of dialect helps readers understand that the folk tale comes from the African-American oral tradition.

Reading Informational Materials: Editorials

p. 330 Graphic Organizer

Sample response:

Animals in Zoos: do not learn the survival techniques needed to live in the wild; provide entertainment; are protected; educate visitors
Animals in the Wild: learn how to survive in their natural habitat; have better chances of success and reproduction; are free to behave naturally

p. 331 Reading Editorials

Sample response: The title suggests that there is a question to be answered. It shows that the author will be expressing an opinion.

p. 331 Reading Skill

The writer compares the zoo to a place of captivity where a person is deprived of his or her natural home and put on display.

p. 331 Read Fluently

Students should circle all instances of *your, you're, you,* and *they.* Sample response: Most of these pronouns are in second person. They connect the editorial to the reader. They make the discussion personal.

p. 332 Reading Skill

The writer compares and contrasts how animals behave in zoos and how they behave in the wild. Students should underline "but" and "although."

p. 332 Stop to Reflect

Sample response: The writer tells readers that zoos have some good points because she wants readers to know that she has considered both sides of the issue.

p. 332 Reading Editorials

The writer supports this point by mentioning that the San Diego Zoo has four shows each day.

p. 333 Reading Editorials

Sample response: The paragraph says that zoos are supposed to be places to learn about and enjoy nature and animals, but that zoos do not live up to these ideals. The author explains that zoos take care of animals, but they do not treat animals with the respect they deserve.

p. 333 Reading Informational Materials

Some students may say that the editorial showed them that zoos are not as good as they thought they were. The article explains that it is not fair to keep animals in small pens and cages. It also explains how animals in zoos do not act as they would in their natural habitats. Therefore, people cannot go to the zoo and learn how animals act in their natural habitats. Other students may think zoos are good places to keep animals. The author admits that zoos take care of animals and protect them.

p. 333 Reading Check

Students should underline "look at the enclosure of the tigers and watch the seals balance a ball on their noses, and then think about what you are really learning from your day at the zoo."

p. 334 Apply the Skills
Thinking About the Editorial

1. The writer claims that zoos neither help endangered animals nor educate the public about animals' authentic behavior.
2. The writer would claim that a film showing lions in the wild is more educational because it shows how lions really behave in their natural environment.

Reading Skill

3. They learn survival techniques in the wild.
4. Animals are better off in the wild than in a zoo.

"The People Could Fly"
Virginia Hamilton

"All Stories Are Anansi's"
Harold Courlander

p. 335 Graphic Organizer

Sample response:
"The People Could Fly"
Character 1: Toby: has wings, is an old man, helps Sarah, teaches Sarah and other slaves to fly, says the magic words
Character 2: Sarah: sheds her wings; is a young woman, is a mother, is afraid, has no heart to comfort her baby, is whipped, is weak, is sad, is starving, appeals to Toby for help
Both: slaves, fly away

p. 335 Graphic Organizer

Sample response:
"All Stories Are Anansi's"
Character 1: Mmoboro: are hornets; fly into a gourd
Character 2: Onini: is a python; gets tied to a pole
Both: are caught by Anansi and taken to the Sky God

p. 336 Reading/Writing Connection

Sample response:
1. Children may not appreciate their stories until they grow older.
2. Families that share stories establish their history.
3. Stories from long ago help define the past for younger generations.

p. 336 Note-taking Guide

Sample response:
What Character Says: "I must go soon"; "Now, before it's too late. . . . Now, Father!"
What Character Does: works in the field; is not able to soothe baby; is whipped by driver; falls down; bleeds; appeals to Toby; flies away
What Character Thinks: She thinks that she does not have the heart to soothe her child.
What Others Say about Character: Driver: "Get up, you black cow." Toby: "Yes, Daughter, the time is come. . . . Go, as you know how to go!"

p. 337 Activate Prior Knowledge

Sample response: "Cinderella" is a tale portraying the enslavement of a young girl at the hands of her stepmother. The tale ends with the girl's freedom.

p. 337 Reading Check
Students should underline "But they lost that ability when they were enslaved."

p. 338 Read Fluently
Students should circle "across the babe" and "to the earth."

p. 338 Stop to Reflect
Students may say that they would feel hopeless and depressed. They may think that the Driver is a cruel person who cares only about himself and doess not care who he hurts.

p. 338 Reading Skill
Sample response: Sarah is concerned about the welfare of her child; the Driver is not concerned about the welfare of Sarah's child.

p. 339 Reading Check
Students should underline ". . . *buba yali . . . buba tambe . . .*"

p. 339 Literary Analysis
Students should underline "The Overseer told it."

p. 339 Reading Skill
The Overseer told the story as the narrator tells it. The Master said the story was a lie. The Driver did not say anything.

p. 340 Literary Analysis
The slaves who could not fly away told their children the story. These children told their own children, and so on.

p. 340 Reading Check
Students should circle "The slaves who could not fly told about the people who could fly to their children."

p. 341 Apply the Skills
1. Sample response: The author uses the African words to represent the free life to which the slaves hope to return. The words represent their history and heritage.
2. "Flying" is a metaphor for being free and living a free life in one's own culture.
3. Sample response: Toby is helpful, caring, and powerful in an unexpected way. The Overseer is brutal, violent, and mean. Both men are leaders, but Toby leads quietly and effectively. The Overseer has to use fear and pain to force people to do what he wants.
4. **Graphic Organizer**
Sample response:
Evil: the Master, the Overseer, the Driver, and their cruelty toward the slaves

Lesson: Remembering your past or your heritage will give you strength; hope and faith are powerful.
Theme: Freedom comes to those who remember how important it is.

p. 343 Reading/Writing Connection
Sample response:
1. Trickster tales require a clever trickster.
2. The trickster will demonstrate cunning and intelligence.
3. Good tricksters exhibit sneakiness.

p. 343 Note-taking Guide
Sample response:
What does Anansi do to the hornets?
Anansi pours water on himself and the hornets' nest. He then tells them to get out of the rain. He convinces them to fly into a gourd. He traps them in the gourd and takes them to the Sky God.
What does Anansi do to the python?
Anansi challenges the python to stretch alongside a bamboo pole. Anansi ties the python to the pole and takes him to the Sky God.
What does Anansi do to the leopard?
Anansi digs and covers a hole into which the leopard falls. Anansi says he will help the leopard and ties the leopard to a bent tree. Anansi cuts the rope holding the tree. The leopard hangs from the tree. Anansi kills him and takes him to the Sky God.

p. 344 Apply the Skills
1. Sample response: Students may infer that all of the animals trust Anansi.
2. Sample response: Anansi is selfish. He will do and say anything to get what he wants.
3. The animals are different in that the hornets are afraid of rain, the python is vain, and the leopard is too trusting. They are similar in that all of the animals are bigger and stronger than Anansi, and yet all are tricked by Anansi.
4. **Graphic Organizer**
Students may notice that elements of good and evil are not very clear in this tale.
Sample response:
Evil: All of the animals are motivated by self-interest.
Lesson: Do not be too trusting; learn to think for yourself.
Theme: Intelligence is more powerful than physical strength or size.

ANSWERS TO UNIT 1

**"The Three-Century Woman"
Richard Peck**

**"The Fall of the Hindenburg"
Michael Morrison**

p. 4 Note-taking Guide
Sample response:
Setting: The setting is Whispering Oaks Elder Care Facility, New Year's Day 2001.
Narrator: The narrator is a young girl named Megan.
Events of the Plot: Media people want to interview Great-grandma Breckenridge; Great-grandma allows them to come into her room; she makes up stories about her life, including having lived through the San Francisco earthquake and the Hindenburg disaster; the news team leaves, and Great-grandma admits to having learned her facts by reading.
Ending: In the end, Megan feels new appreciation for her great-grandmother.

p. 5 Activate Prior Knowledge
Some students may say that the stories are boring and always the same. Other students may say that they enjoy the stories because they like to learn about life in the past.

p. 5 Fiction
Sample response: Facts about Great-grandmother Breckenridge include that she lives at Whispering Oaks, that she has lived there since the narrator was a little girl, and that she has lived in three centuries. Students should list two of these.

p. 5 Build English Skills
Students should underline "the mall is a place without homework."

p. 5 Fiction
Megan is the narrator.

p. 6 Fiction
The interview takes place in Great-grandma's room at Whispering Oaks.

p. 6 Fiction
The TV anchor begins to interview Great-grandma.

p. 6 Reading Check
Students should circle "like a Barbie doll."

p. 7 Stop to Reflect
Sample response: The stories are made-up and didn't really happen. Great-grandma didn't really live through the events she retells.

p. 7 Read Fluently
Students should circle "hissed." Sample response: *Hissed* means to make a sound like that of the first *s* in the word *sash.*

p. 7 Fiction
Sample response: Great-grandma is moving on to another lie. She is telling about being on the Hindenburg when it blew up.

p. 7 Reading Check
Students should circle "I was on the Hindenburg when it blew up."

p. 8 Fiction
Sample response: The characters are made up.

p. 8 Vocabulary and Pronunciation
Sample response: Another meaning for *rattle* is "to shake something to make several short knocking sounds."

p. 8 Read Fluently
Students should circle "little withered-up leaf of a lady."

p. 8 Fiction
Sample response: Older people should not be stereotyped, and they should be valued.

p. 9 Note-taking Guide
Sample response:
Where: The Hindenburg disaster took place in Lakehurst, New Jersey.
What Happened: Thirteen passengers and twenty-two crewmembers were killed; people have tried to learn what caused the disaster, but the cause is still uncertain.
Why: The cause may have been the varnish on the fabric on the outside of the vessel.

p. 10 Activate Prior Knowledge
Sample response: 1. It was a German-built airship for flying across the Atlantic. 2. It exploded just as it was landing in New Jersey.

p. 10 Read Fluently
Students should circle "Oh, the Humanity!"

p. 10 Reading Check
Students should circle "Germany."

p. 11 Apply the Skills
1. Sample response: Yes, Great-grandma Breckenridge is very lively mentally. She has a sense of humor. She knows how to have fun. She also knows a lot of stories.
2. **Graphic Organizer**
Sample response:
Her Comments: "I was on the Hindenburg when it blew up, you know."
Her Character: She makes up stories.
Message/Theme: We should not stereotype older people. Some of them are like Great-grandma, with lively imaginations and a great sense of humor.
3. Sample response: It has made-up characters and some made-up events. It has a narrator who is a character inside the story. It has a series of events that make up a plot. It has a theme.
4. Sample response: The fictional account contains far fewer facts and details and has some made-up information. The nonfiction article consists only of details about what really happened and who was really there.

"Papa's Parrot"
Cynthia Rylant

"mk"
Jean Fritz

p. 13 Graphic Organizer
Sample response:
"Papa's Parrot"
Beginning: Harry and his friends stop going to Papa's store.
Middle: Papa buys a parrot.
End: Harry realizes that Papa missed seeing him at the store.

"mk"
Beginning: Jean finishes sixth grade at the British School in Wuhan.
Middle: Jean goes to the Shanghai American School.

End: Jean moves to America. She goes to a school in America for the first time.

p. 14 Reading/Writing Connection
Sample response:
1. Age might help a teenager appreciate any extra time that he or she has.
2. He or she might learn to react more calmly to problems.
3. A more mature person might be more likely to act in a responsible way.

p. 14 Note-taking Guide
Sample response:
Before Harry Starts Junior High: Harry brings his friends to visit the store and to eat nuts and candy.
After Harry Starts Junior High: His father embarrasses Harry by talking to the parrot.
After Harry's Father Gets Sick: Through the parrot, Harry realizes how much his father misses him; Harry decides to spend more time with his father.

p. 15 Activate Prior Knowledge
Students may say that their feelings for someone close to them changed after they had an argument with that person. They no longer felt as close to that person after the fight.

p. 15 Reading Skill
Sample response: The word *though* is a clue to the meaning of *merely*. The word *though* shows that Harry liked his Papa in spite of his papa's shortcomings: his Papa was fat, and owning a candy and nut store was not an exciting job.

p. 15 Read Fluently
Students should circle "on his way somewhere else," and "The more Mr. Tillian grew to like his parrot, and the more he talked to it instead of to people, the more embarrassed Harry became."

p. 16 Reading Skill
Sample response: Harry walks away when he sees his father talking to the bird. This helps readers understand that "embarrassed" is an uncomfortable feeling.

p. 16 Literary Analysis
Sample response: At the beginning of the story, Harry liked being with his Papa in the store. By the middle of the story, Harry was older. He became interested in other

things. He was also embarrassed when his Papa talked to the parrot.

p. 16 Reading Check
Students should circle: "Mr. Tillian asks him to take care of the store and to feed Rocky."

p. 17 Literary Analysis
Sample response: Harry finally realizes that his father misses him. The problem between father and son is about to be resolved.

p. 17 Stop to Reflect
Some students may say that Harry should tell his father what happened with Rocky so that Harry can say he knows that his father misses him.

p. 17 Reading Check
Students should circle, "he left to go visit his papa."

p. 18 Apply the Skills
1. Sample response: Harry and his friends are now interested in things such as video games. They are no longer interested in candy.
2. Sample response: Mr. Tillian buys Rocky because he is lonely; Harry and his friends no longer visit at the store.
3. **Graphic Organizer**
Sample response:
Context Clues: on his way somewhere else; walking.
Possible Meaning: *Stroll* might mean "to walk slowly."
Context Clues: "so the bird wouldn't get cold."
Possible Meaning: A *furnace* might be a machine that produces heat.
4. Sample response: A narrative is any type of writing that tells a story. It can be fiction or nonfiction, and it is often told in chronological order. "Papa's Parrot" is fiction that tells a story in chronological order. This makes it a narrative.

p. 20 Reading/Writing Connection
Sample response:
1. Kids in other countries might <u>imitate</u> American styles of clothing.
2. People overseas often <u>observe</u> things that people in America do not see.
3. Living in another country would allow a person to <u>explore</u> that country's natural wonders.

p. 20 Note-taking Guide
Sample response:
What Character Says: Jean "talks" to Priscilla about hardships. Jean says, "I always felt a tingling when I saw the American flag flying over the American consulate."
What Character Thinks: Jean thinks that the Shanghai American school will help her feel more American. Jean thinks that American children are ignorant.
What Character Does: Jean is shy and sensitive. She keeps the name of her home-town a secret so that the other students won't laugh at it.
What Others Say about Character: Mrs. Barrett asks whether Jean is all grown up. Fletcher says that Jean is pretty. Paula, the American roommate, says that Jean looks like an MK.

p. 21 Apply the Skills
1. Sample response: The school is not exactly as Jean thinks it will be. She does not get a tingling feeling from the flag when she walks into the school. She does not feel more American at the school. She does enjoy the tea dances, though.
2. Sample response: Both Jean and Priscilla look forward to a new life in America. They are excited and interested in learning about America.
3. **Graphic Organizer**
Sample response:
Context Clues: "more than a tingling"
Possible Meaning: *Overwhelm* might mean "overpower."
4. Sample response: A narrative is any type of writing that tells a story. It can be fiction or nonfiction, and it is often told in chronological order. "mk" is a nonfiction story told in chronological order.

Reading Informational Materials: Reference Materials

p. 26 Apply the Skills
Thinking About the Reference Material
1. Sample response: The climate, landscape, and soil are better in the eastern area than in the other parts of the country. That area is also closer to the East China Sea.
2. Shanghai is located on the east coast of China. It touches the East China Sea. Jiaxing and Wuxi are near Shanghai.

Reading Skill

3. Sample response: A *booming* economy is one that is thriving. The context clue is that Taiwan "exports its products around the world."

4. The context clue is an example: Exporting is one reason that the economy is thriving.

from An American Childhood
Annie Dillard

"The Luckiest Time of All"
Lucille Clifton

p. 27 Graphic Organizer
Sample response:

from **An American Childhood**
Unfamiliar Word in Context: Any normal adult would have quit, having *sprung* us into flight and made his point.
Word's Function in Sentence: *Sprung* is a verb that describes what happens to Dillard and her friends.
Meaning of Word: *Sprung* probably means "thrown" or "hurled."

"The Luckiest Time of All"
Unfamiliar Word in Context: Her grand-daughter brought her a big bunch of dogwood blooms.
Word's Function in Sentence: Dogwood is the name of the blossoms.
Meaning of Word: Dogwood is probably a type of tree, shrub, or plant.

p. 28 Reading/Writing Connection
Sample response:
1. I have always enjoyed the challenge of building something new.
2. It will be hard to win the game unless I exert all my energy.
3. Sometimes I exceed my own goals.

p. 28 Note-taking Guide
Sample response:
Conflict: The driver wants to teach the children a lesson. The children want to escape.
Climax: An angry driver chases Dillard and her friends.
Second Event: The driver catches Dillard and Mikey.
Third Event: The driver lectures Dillard and Mikey.
Resolution: Dillard is excited that she had to try so hard to get away.

p. 29 Activate Prior Knowledge
Students may describe a time when they played a certain sport or performed well in a play. Because they really enjoyed the activity, they wanted to perform to the best of their ability.

p. 29 Literary Analysis
"Some boys taught me to play football" shows that this story is told from the first-person point of view.

p. 29 Reading Check
Students should underline "Dillard also likes going out for a pass." "Her favorite part of the game is tackling." "Your fate, and your team's score, depended on your concentration and courage."

p. 30 Reading Skill
Sample response: The words "he was still after us" give clues to the meaning of the word *incredibly*. The words show Dillard's surprise that the man continues to chase her. *Incredibly* is an adverb.

p. 30 Stop to Reflect
Students may say that the driver does the right thing in chasing the children. They may suggest that the driver wanted to teach the children a lesson. To do so, he would have to catch them.

p. 30 Build English Skills
Sample response: The colon shows that the sentence explains what Dillard realized.

p. 31 Read Fluently
Students should underline the words "our pursuer, our captor, our hero."

p. 31 Literary Analysis
Sample response: The narrative is told from the first-person point of view. Only the narrator's thoughts are known.

p. 31 Vocabulary and Pronunciation
The word *obscure* does not follow the normal accenting rule.

p. 31 Reading Check
Students should draw a box around the words "in an obscure hilltop backyard."

p. 32 Reading Skill
Students should circle "more of her than anything else ever has." Sample response: Dillard says that you have to throw yourself

completely into something if you want to win. Dillard had to try very hard not to let the man catch her. She tried harder than she had ever tried to do anything else. The word *required* means "needed" or "necessary."

p. 32 Reading Check
Students should underline "That's because the chase in the snow required more of her than anything else ever has."

p. 33 Apply the Skills
1. Sample response: Dillard admires his commitment to flinging himself into the chase and not giving up.
2. Sample response: The words "redundant, a mere formality, and beside the point" suggest the meaning of *perfunctorily.*
3. Sample response: It could mean "without excitement."
4. **Graphic Organizer**
Sample response:
Situation: The man from the Buick catches the narrator and Mikey.
Thoughts or Feelings: Dillard wants "the glory to last forever." She thinks that being pursued by a grown-up who throws himself into chasing her and Mikey is glorious.

p. 35 Reading/Writing Connection
Sample response: Many people define luck as good fortune. Many of us cannot interpret right away whether an event will bring good luck. We may need to wait for the outcome of an event to confirm whether or not the event was lucky.

p. 35 Note-taking Guide
Sample response:
Cause: Elzie goes to the show.
Effect/Cause: Elzie throws her lucky rock at the dancing dog.
Effect/Cause: The dog chases Elzie.
Effect/Cause: A young man chases the dog.
Effect/Cause: Elzie and the man meet.
Effect: The man later marries Elzie.

p. 36 Apply the Skills
1. Sample response: Elzie seems to be looking for adventure.
2. Sample response: Mr. Pickens saves Elzie from the dog and checks the dog to see whether it is hurt.
3. Sample response: *Lit out* may mean "to chase or run at top speed."

4. Sample response: Context clues are "I flew," "Round and round we run," and "a runnin dog."
5. **Graphic Organizer**
Sample response:
Situation: Elzie goes to the show.
Thoughts or Feelings: She feels adventurous.

"All Summer in a Day"
Ray Bradbury

"Suzy and Leah"
Jane Yolen

p. 38 Graphic Organizer
Sample response:
"All Summer in a Day"
Entertain: " . . . the gigantic sound of the rain . . . "
Teach: "A thousand forests had been crushed under the rain and grown up a thousand times to be crushed again."
Reflect: "The silence was so immense and unbelievable that you felt your ears had been stuffed. . . ."

"Suzy and Leah"
Entertain: The story is told entirely through diary entries.
Teach: It is wrong to judge others.
Reflect: Suzy's comments in her diary show how comfortable her life has been, compared with Leah's life.

p. 39 Reading/Writing Connection
Sample response: I don't know whether I could survive in a rainy climate. It would require that I adjust to losing many things that I love. I am sure that there is some benefit to living in a rainy climate, but I don't know what it is!

p. 39 Note-taking Guide
Sample response:
What Happens: 2. Margot writes a poem. 3. Margot refuses to play games with the other children. 4. The sun shines.
What Is the Result? 2. William says that Margot did not write the poem. 3. Margot does not have many friends. 4. The children laugh and play.

p. 40 Apply the Skills
1. Sample response: The children have never seen the sun. They cannot imagine how it feels or why Margot misses it.

2. Sample response: The children play the mean joke because they do not feel that Margot is one of them. They may feel less responsibility because the joke is William's idea.

3. Sample response: The author's main purpose is to show that people can be cruel and that we should think carefully about what we do.

4. Sample response: The rain on Venus makes the story sad and dark. The mood is happier when the sun comes out. If the story were set on Earth, the conflict would not be about the weather or the sun.

5. **Graphic Organizer**
Sample response:
Setting: 1. Venus is sunless.
Character's Mood: 1. Margot is sad.

p. 42 Reading/Writing Connection
Sample response: To communicate with others might be difficult in a new country. The person would have to adapt to a new language and a different culture. It might be hard to participate in activities and events in a strange country.

p. 42 Note-taking Guide
Sample response:
Leah Beginning: Leah says that Suzy has a "false smile," makes her feel terror, and treats her "like a pet." She says that Suzy laughed at Leah's friend, has a meaningless name, and "wants to feed [Leah] like an animal."
Leah End: Leah says that Suzy is friendly, honest, generous, and understanding.
Suzy Beginning: Suzy says that Leah is strange, "prickly as a porcupine," unfriendly, stuck-up, and mean. Suzy also says that Leah never smiles, has a permanent frown, doesn't eat enough, has a funny accent, and knows nothing about America.
Suzy End: Suzy says that Leah is strong, has been through a lot, and is scared rather than stuck-up. Suzy thinks that she and Leah might yet be able to become friends.

p. 43 Activate Prior Knowledge
Students may name themselves, friends, or family members as people who keep diaries.

p. 43 Literary Analysis
Students should underline "A high fence with twisted, sharp-pointed wire at the top separates Americans from the refugees."

p. 43 Reading Check
Students should underline "A girl with yellow hair and a false smile."

p. 44 Stop to Reflect
Sample response: Avi stopped speaking when his grandmother hid him from the Nazis. He stayed in a cupboard for three days without food and water and without words to comfort him. He did not speak again.

p. 44 Read Fluently
Students should circle the three appearances of the word *safe* in the paragraph beginning "The adults of the Americans say we are safe now." Sample response: The author chose to repeat this word to show how important security is to Leah, especially because she had not been safe in Germany.

p. 44 Build English Skills
Students should circle "wouldn't."

p. 45 Literary Analysis
Students should underline "the blue skies over their farm."

p. 45 Reading Skill
Sample response: The author wants readers to think about Suzy's feelings. The details show that Suzy doesn't know what Leah has been through. She doesn't like Leah because she doesn't understand why Leah is "prickly as a porcupine."

p. 45 Stop to Reflect
Students may suggest that Suzy does not like Leah because she is grouchy and suspicious.

p. 45 Reading Check
Students should circle "She tears off her name tag and throws it behind a bush."

p. 46 Literary Analysis
Students should circle "Leah goes to Suzy's house for dinner, but her stomach hurts the whole time."

p. 46 Reading Skill
Students should underline these passages: "the Nazis killed people, including mothers and children in concentration camps" and "Jews had to wear yellow stars."

p. 46 Literary Analysis
Sample response: Where Leah was during the war is very important. It was a terrible place where Leah's mother and brother were killed.

The setting is important because it is a secret that Suzy has not understood until now.

p. 46 Reading Check
Students should put a box around "She has had her appendix out. Leah almost died."

p. 47 Stop to Reflect
Sample response: Avi helps Leah by telling the guards that she is sick. His action is important because he saves Leah's life. It's also important because it's the first time that Avi speaks aloud to anyone but Leah.

p. 47 Read Fluently
Students should underline these incomplete sentences: "A new word," "A new land," and "And—it is just possible—a new friend."

p. 47 Reading Skill
Students may say that the author has young people tell the story because they can reach young readers. A young American like Suzy might not know what happened in Europe during World War II. A young refugee like Leah would not know about America. Readers learn along with the characters.

p. 47 Vocabulary and Pronunciation
Students should underline "diary." Sample response: A diary is a book in which people write down the thoughts and feelings that they do not always want to share.

p. 48 Apply the Skills
1. Sample response: Suzy has lived a comfortable, sheltered life. She does not like Leah because Leah is strange to her.
2. Sample response: Leah has survived a terrible experience. She is afraid of strangers. She detects Suzy's "false smile." Leah is afraid to be Suzy's friend.
3. Sample response: The author's purpose was to teach people about what happened to the Jews in Germany when the Nazis were in control.
4. **Graphic Organizer**
Sample response:
Setting: Leah is in a refugee camp.
Character's Mood: Leah feels afraid and suspicious.
Setting: Suzy visits Leah in the hospital.
Character's Mood: Suzy is sorrowful and friendly.

"My First Free Summer"
Julia Alvarez

"My Furthest-Back Person"
(The Inspiration for *Roots*)
Alex Haley

p. 50 Graphic Organizer
Sample response:
"My First Free Summer"
What I Know About the Author: She spent her early life in the Dominican Republic. Words make her feel "complete."
What I Know About the Topic: The Dominican Republic was ruled by a dictator for thirty-one years. Many families fled the country during a rebellion.
Author's Purpose: The author writes to describe a personal experience.

"My Furthest-Back Person"
What I Know About the Author: He grew up hearing stories about his family's history. He later wrote a book about his family's past.
What I Know About the Topic: Slavery is part of the history of the United States and of parts of Africa.
Author's Purpose: The author writes to describe a personal experience.

p. 51 Reading/Writing Connection
Sample response: Most people would respond to this news with complaints or grumbling. A person might react by feeling sad or upset. It would take time and effort to adjust.

p. 51 Note-taking Guide
Sample response:
Conflict: Julia does not want to learn English.
Event: Julia goes to summer school.
Event: Julia decides to try harder to learn English.
Event: Julia and her family try to leave the country.

p. 52 Activate Prior Knowledge
Students should describe at least one positive experience. Positive experiences could include taking trips with their families, making new friends, or learning a new sport or hobby. Students who have been to summer school may describe it as a positive experience.

p. 52 Literary Analysis
Students should underline this sentence:
"For thirty years, the Dominican Republic had
endured a bloody and repressive dictatorship."

p. 52 Reading Skill
Sample response: Julia's family left the
Dominican Republic to live in the
United States.

p. 53 Stop to Reflect
Students should recognize that Julia is
different because she goes to school with
Americans, not with other Dominicans. She
does not get days off, march in parades, or
see the palace.

p. 53 Vocabulary and Pronunciation
Students should circle "Mami." They
should also list words for mother in their
first language.

p. 53 Literary Analysis
Sample response: All of the children Julia
knew were leaving for the United States. People
were being arrested. Julia's family was frightened. All of this made Julia's summer boring
because she had no one to play with her.

p. 53 Reading Check
Students should underline "It was because
she wanted a summer free from school."

p. 54 Read Fluently
Students should circle the words: "her"
and "she." Students should draw arrows to
"Julia's mother" and "Julia," respectively.

p. 54 Reading Skill
Sample response: By not telling what happens to these people, the author shows how
much mystery and confusion there is. This
helps the reader understand how frightening
and dangerous Julia's situation is.

p. 54 Reading Check
Students should underline "I knew that ours
was not a trip, but an escape. We had to get
to the United States."

p. 55 Reading Skill
Sample response: Julia has learned to speak
English and to be an eager student, so she
says "Yes, sir!" to the American official. She is
also eager to answer the official because she
is afraid of being sent back. The scene shows
that the author's purpose is to show that

Julia's family is afraid of being sent back to
the Dominican Republic. They escape to
America in order to save their lives. The
author also wants to show that learning and
school are part of being free.

p. 55 Reading Check
Students should underline "'Welcome to the
United States.'"

p. 56 Apply the Skills
1. Sample response: The American school
teaches English and American history. The
other schools on the island teach about the
dictator and have many days off in honor of
the dictator.
2. Sample response: Julia improves
her English.
3. Sample response: The author is sharing
information about the Dominican Republic as
it was during the time when the author was
growing up. The author's family left the country during this time.
4. **Graphic Organizer**
Sample response:
Author's Actions: 2. Packs her things and
prepares to leave the country

p. 58 Reading/Writing Connection
Sample response:
1. Many people want to acquire information
about their ancestors.
2. They want to identify their roots.
3. They are curious about the circumstances
surrounding major events in their
family history.

p. 58 Note-taking Guide
Sample response:
What: Haley found the names of his relatives
in census records from just after the Civil War.
Whom: Haley told his cousin, Georgia
Anderson, who used to tell him stories about
his ancestors.
Why: Haley thought that Dr. Vansina might
know where in Africa Haley's ancestors
came from.
Where: Haley went to a village in Gambia to
hear the *griot*.
How: Haley linked the *griot's* tale to his family
history through certain details that were
common to both stories.

p. 59 Apply the Skills

1. Sample response: Both the sounds and the writing had to be translated. The African sounds in Haley's family were spoken; the words on the Rosetta Stone were written.

2. Sample response: The *griot* tells what happened before Kunte Kinte left Africa. Haley's family stories begin after Kunta Kinte's arrival in America. Together, these stories complete the family history.

3. Sample response: The author's purpose is to tell the story of his ancestor, who was one of the many Africans brought to America as slaves.

4. Sample response: Haley searches for his family's African roots.

Reading Informational Materials: Web Sites

p. 64 Apply the Skills

Thinking About the Web Site

1. Sample response: The *About Us* link on the home page and the *Biography of John Carlin* link on the Welcome page should lead to more information about NARA and its director.

2. Sample response: Clicking on the links to related government Web sites should lead to sites with similar information.

Reading Skill

3. Sample response: The purpose of the NARA Welcome page is to persuade readers to make use of the documents that NARA provides.

4. Sample response: The purpose of this Web site might be to inform people about the history and development of airplanes.

"The Treasure of Lemon Brown"
Walter Dean Myers

p. 67 Note-taking Guide
Sample response:
Event: The bad men go after Lemon Brown.
Event: Lemon Brown tells Greg about his treasure.
Event: Greg understands a new meaning for treasure.
Climax: Lemon Brown and Greg scare off the men.
Resolution: Greg goes home with a better understanding of his father.
Conflict: Greg cannot accept what his father has to say.

p. 68 Activate Prior Knowledge
Students may write about a time when their parents were upset with them but were really just concerned about their safety.

p. 68 Short Story
Students should underline "Greg" and "his father." Greg is remembering a time they talked about Greg's poor effort at school and why, as a result, he can't play basketball.

p. 68 Reading Check
Students should underline "Now Greg cannot bring himself to go inside to hear more of the same."

p. 69 Short Story
Sample response: Greg doesn't want to listen to what his father has to say.

p. 69 Vocabulary and Pronunciation
Students should circle "For a moment" and "as soon as."

p. 69 Short Story
Sample response: **Characters:** Greg and his father; **Time:** late evening or night. **Place:** an old, empty building

p. 70 Short Story
Students should draw a box around the word "Ain't."

p. 70 Short Story
Sample response: Greg and Lemon Brown see three men breaking into the building. They are carrying pieces of pipe. They say that they want Lemon Brown's treasure.

p. 70 Reading Check
Students should circle "You ain't one of them bad boys looking for my treasure, is you?"

p. 71 Read Fluently
Students should circle a comma.

p. 71 Build English Skills
Students should draw a box around *eerier*. *Eerier* means "even scarier, more frightening."

p. 71 Short Story
Students should circle "Between the two of them, they scare the three men off."

p. 72 Short Story
Sample response: They are a treasure to Brown because his son valued them. They link Brown to his son.

p. 72 Stop to Reflect
Sample response: Greg has learned something about fathers and sons from his time with Lemon Brown.

p. 72 Reading Check
Students should underline "he will be heading west in the morning."

p. 73 Apply the Skills
1. Some students may say that Greg should not tell his father. Greg's father might not understand why Greg was in an abandoned building. Other students may suggest that Greg should tell his father about the lesson he learned from Lemon Brown. Doing so might resolve the conflict between them.
2. **Graphic Organizer**
Sample response:
Column 1: Brown's treasures are his harmonica, his newspaper clippings, and his memories.
Column 2: These were Brown's legacy to his son.
Column 3: Greg realizes that his father's lectures are his legacy.
3. Sample response: Greg has a conflict with his father because Greg doesn't want to work hard or listen to his father.
4. Sample response: Details about the stormy weather and the inside of the tenement building could be real.

"The Bear Boy"
Joseph Bruchac

"Rikki-tikki-tavi"
Rudyard Kipling

p. 75 Graphic Organizer
Sample response:
"The Bear Boy"
Exposition: Kuo-Haya's father mourns the death of his wife. He does not teach his son to wrestle or to run.
Event: Kuo-Haya follows bear tracks.
Event: Kuo-Haya plays with bear cubs.
Event: The villagers and Kuo-Haya's father find Kuo-Haya with the bears and try to get him back.
Climax: Kuo-Haya's father treats the bears with respect. He gives them honey.
Event: Kuo-Haya's father promises to be friendly with bears.
Event: Kuo-Haya agrees to go back with his father.
Resolution: Kuo-Haya becomes the best wrestler and greatest runner in the village.

"Rikki-tikki-tavi"
Exposition: A flood destroys Rikki's home.
Event: Teddy's family adopts Rikki.
Event: Rikki rescues Teddy by killing a small snake.
Event: Teddy's father and Rikki kill Nag.
Climax: Rikki chases Nagaina into a hole and kills her.
Event: The coppersmith announces that Rikki has killed Nagaina.
Event 2: Rikki eats a large meal.
Resolution: Teddy's family and Rikki are safe.

p. 76 Reading/Writing Connection
Sample response:
1. At the zoo, people <u>appreciate</u> seeing unusual animals.
2. Scientists <u>observe</u> wild animals to learn how these animals find food.
3. Lions might teach people how to <u>survive</u> when they are in danger.

p. 76 Note-taking Guide
Sample response:
Column 2, row 1: timid
Column 2, row 2: sad
Column 3, row 1: He learns to wrestle.
Column 3, row 2: He learns how to treat his son.

Column 4, row 1: He is confident.
Column 4, row 2: He is proud of his son.

p. 77 Activate Prior Knowledge
Sample response: They probably will not get along. Bears and people are usually enemies.

p. 77 Short Story
Sample response: A bear might find the boy. The boy could get hurt.

p. 77 Literary Analysis
Students should underline "As they played, however, a shadow came over them" or "Kuo-Haya looked up and saw the mother bear standing above him."

p. 78 Literary Analysis
Sample response: The paragraph shows that a conflict will arise between the bears and the humans.

p. 78 Read Fluently
Students could underline "to encourage," "to grab," "to know," "to be," and "to realize."

p. 78 Build English Skills
Sample response: The man who was getting rid of his puppy had a change of heart and kept it instead.

p. 78 Reading Check
Students should circle "But as soon as the mother bear caught their scent, she growled and pushed her cubs and the boy back into the cave."

p. 79 Stop to Reflect
Sample response: The father wants to get Kuo-Haya back.

p. 79 Literary Analysis
Students should underline "Kuo-Haya's father prays for help. Then he gets an idea after a bee flies past his face. He goes to a beehive, makes a fire, and blows smoke into the hive. The smoke puts the bees to sleep. He then takes some honey from the hive." Sample response: A reader can now predict how the problem will be solved.

p. 80 Literary Analysis
Sample response: Kuo-Haya comes home. The father teaches him. He shows Kuo-Haya love.

p. 80 Reading Check
Students should circle "It reminds parents how important it is to show their love for their children."

p. 81 Apply the Skills

1. Sample response: The mother bear encourages Kuo-Haya and teaches him to be strong. Kuo-Haya feels as if he belongs with the bears. In Kuo-Haya's village, where he is neglected by his father, the boy feels that he is an outsider.

2. Sample response: He will distract the bears with honey.

3. **Graphic Organizer:**
Sample response:
Story Details: The father decides to get his son back.
My Prior Knowledge: Bears like honey.
Prediction: The father will use honey to get his son back.

4. Sample response: These two plot events make the story more exciting: the mother bear's anger and the father's hunt for weapons.

p. 83 Reading/Writing Connection
Sample response:

1. Firefighters demonstrate bravery when they put out fires.

2. Police officers exhibit courage when they protect people from harm.

3. Acrobats in the circus display courage when they jump from one bar to another.

p. 83 Note-taking Guide
Sample response:
Why does Rikki leave his home? Rikki leaves his home because it has been flooded.
Where does Rikki go to live? Rikki lives with Teddy's family in India.
What creatures does Rikki meet in his new home? Rikki meets a tailorbird named Darzee, Darzee's wife, a muskrat named Chuchundra, Karait the dusty brown snakeling, and Nag and Nagaina, the cobras.
How does Rikki protect his adopted family? Rikki fights the cobras.

p. 84 Apply the Skills

1. Sample response: Rikki and the cobras are the same because they want to protect their families. They are different because Rikki is brave and good. The cobras are greedy and evil.

2. Students may say that this story deserves to be popular because its plot is suspenseful and exciting. Also, its hero is likable and its villains are evil.

3. **Graphic Organizer**
Sample response:
Story Details: Rikki hears the cobras' plot.
My Prior Knowledge: Cobras kill people.
Prediction: Rikki will protect Teddy and his family against the cobras.

4. Sample response: These events create more conflict: Rikki bites Nagaina. He also kills Karait.

Reading Informational Materials: Magazine Articles

p. 86 Graphic Organizer
Sample response:
Clue: The title is "Mongoose on the Loose."
Clue: A subhead reads "Population Explodes."
Clue: Another subhead reads "Scientist Studies Problem."
Prediction: The article will be about mongoose overpopulation and what a scientist is doing to solve the problem.

p. 87 Reading Magazine Articles
Mongooses were imported to eat the rats that were feeding on the crops in Jamaica.

p. 87 Reading Informational Materials
Students should predict that the article will be about mongoose overpopulation.

p. 87 Reading Check
The huge mongoose population is now threatening other animals. Students should underline ". . . the mongoose population exploded, and within a few years, they were killing not just rats, but pigs, lambs, chickens, puppies, and kittens."

p. 88 Stop to Reflect
Students may be interested in the project. Volunteers can see mongooses while helping solve a problem.

p. 88 Read Fluently
Students may circle "five-year, $60,000 study," "sponsored by Earthwatch Incorporated, a non-profit group," "Volunteers," "set out mongoose traps, study the animals, and keep records," "perform surgery," "implant the electronic devices," and "track the animal's habits."

p. 88 Reading Skill
It tells readers that the article refers to a unique situation.

p. 88 Reading Check
Students should underline "'I want to know what happens when you take a small animal and put him in an area with no competition.'"

p. 89 Stop to Reflect
Sample response: Yes, it is a good idea. Implanting tracking devices in animals can help scientists learn more about animal behavior.

p. 89 Reading Informational Materials
Students should underline the caption "A mongoose is tagged."

p. 89 Vocabulary and Pronunciation
Students should underline "permanently," "previously," or "extremely."

p. 89 Reading Check
Students should underline "Among them: mongooses have a life expectancy of six to ten years, much longer than the previously accepted figure of three years."

p. 90 Apply the Skills
Thinking About the Magazine Article
1. Sample response: The title, subheads, and photos and captions help the reader predict what a magazine article is about.
2. Sample response: The information tells how and why mongooses were brought to the Caribbean. It also explains their value to farmers.

Reading Skill
3. The subhead tells the reader that a problem exists with the mongooses and that a scientist is studying this problem.

from Letters from Rifka
Karen Hesse

"Two Kinds" *from* The Joy Luck Club
Amy Tan

p. 91 Graphic Organizer
Sample response:
from **Letters from Rifka**
Prediction: Something bad will happen.
Details: There is talk of death, prison, and escape.
Revised or Confirmed Prediction: Rifka and her family will make it to Poland.
New Details: They work together, take precautions, and are determined.
Actual Outcome: Their fate is still undetermined by the end of the story.

"Two Kinds" *from* **The Joy Luck Club**
Prediction: Jing-mei will become a prodigy.
Details: Jing-mei is just as excited as her mother at the idea of being a prodigy. Jing-mei thinks that she will become perfect.
Revised or Confirmed Prediction: Jing-mei will not become a prodigy.
New Details: Jing-mei does not learn the capitals. She cannot pass her mother's tests. She begins to hate the tests.
Actual Outcome: Jing-mei does not become a prodigy. She and her mother argue about this fact.

p. 92 Reading/Writing Connection
Sample response: Most people could adjust to life without television. They would adapt their lives without it by reading books. Some children might feel that their parents deprive them of their favorite television shows.

p. 92 Note-taking Guide
Sample response:
Beginning: Rifka's brother leaves the army.
Event: The family decides to leave the country.
Event: The family packs to leave.
Event: The family hides in a cellar.
Event: Rifka distracts the guards so that her family can hide.
Event: The guards search the train.

p. 93 Activate Prior Knowledge
Sample response: People write letters to relatives and friends to share family news. They also write to keep in touch with relatives and friends who live far away.

p. 93 Reading Skill
Sample response: The story will be about a family escaping from Ukraine or a country near Ukraine.

p. 93 Vocabulary and Pronunciation
backpack, candlesticks

p. 93 Reading Check
Students should circle "My Dear Cousin Tovah."

p. 94 Literary Analysis
Sample response: She does not tell because no one must know that the escaping family is on the train.

p. 94 Build English Skills
Sample response: Those who have helped him will die, too.

p. 94 Reading Skill
Sample response: Nathan has committed a crime.

p. 94 Reading Check
Students should circle "I think the guards missed seeing me at first because they were so busy in their search of the train."

p. 95 Read Fluently
Students should circle "no matter how frightened I was."

p. 95 Literary Analysis
Sample response: They need a safe place to plan their escape.

p. 95 Culture Note
Sample response: One benefit would be that your pen pal would show you what it is like to live in another culture. Your pen pal could give you information that you might not be able to learn from a book.

p. 96 Apply the Skills
1. Students may say that Nathan felt relieved when he saw his family because he could warn them about the soldiers.
2. Some students may say that because she is young, Rifka is more afraid of what might happen. Others may say that Rifka's youth helps her get caught up in the excitement of the journey.
3. Students probably determined that the family was leaving Russia when they read that the Russian army shoots deserters. Students should have made the connection between Rifka's brothers and the army.
4. Students may identify Rifka as young, brave, small, poor, and loving.

Graphic Organizer
Sample response:
Rifka is young: She twelve years old in the story.
She is brave: She distracts the guards so her family can hide.
She is small: The guards do not notice her at first.
She is poor: She does not have many things.
She loves her family: She wants everyone to be safe, even the brother she says she dislikes.

p. 98 Reading/Writing Connection
Sample response:
1. One day, I would like to <u>achieve</u> success as a great Olympic diver.

2. To <u>pursue</u> a Nobel Prize is another day-dream I have.
3. Sometimes I dream that I can <u>attain</u> the status of a legendary actor.

p. 98 Note-taking Guide
Sample response:
Mother's Plans: [row 2] She wants her daughter to be remarkable and smart. [row 3] She wants her daughter to play the piano well.
Daughter's Response: [row 1] Jing-mei looks forward to her future fame. [row 2] Jing-mei begins to hate the tests her mother gives her. [row 3] Jing-mei does not put in the effort necessary for playing the piano well.

p. 99 Apply the Skills
1. Sample response: The daughter believes she can never meet her mother's expectations, and the mother is angry because her daughter refuses to try.
2. Students may suggest that the mother pushed her daughter too hard. The mother's efforts backfired. Her daughter believed that she would never be good enough to meet her mother's expectations and stopped trying.
3. **Graphic Organizer**
Sample response:
sad, angry, powerful, willful, bored, lazy
She is sad and angry when she cries in the bathroom. She becomes powerful and willful after she realizes that she does not have to do as her mother says. She is bored and lazy when practicing the piano.
4. Sample response: The daughter will perform poorly because she is not interested in playing, and her teacher is not a good one. The prediction was accurate.

"The Third Wish"
Joan Aiken

"Amigo Brothers"
Piri Thomas

p. 101 Graphic Organizer
Sample response:
"The Third Wish"
Details: Mr. Peters offers to turn Leita's sister into a human. Mr. Peters uses his second wish to turn Leita back into a swan.
Inference: Mr. Peters loves his wife and wants her to be happy.

"Amigo Brothers"

Details: Antonio waves to Felix from the dressing room. The boys stop in mid-punch as the bell rings.

Inference: Antonio still thinks of Felix as a friend. The two respect the match and play by the rules.

p. 102 Reading/Writing Connection

Sample response:

1. A person would be wise to <u>maximize</u> three wishes by asking for more wishes.
2. Some students might want teachers to <u>grant</u> them freedom from homework.
3. Some people might want money, but I want to <u>obtain</u> happiness.

p. 102 Note-taking Guide

Sample response:

1. Wish: Mr. Peters wishes for a wife. **Result:** His wife loves him, but she misses her swan sister.

2. Wish: Mr. Peters uses his second wish to turn his wife back into a swan. **Result:** The swans keep Mr. Peters company when he grows old.

3. Wish: Mr. Peters does not make a third wish. **Result:** The unexpected effects of another wish do not disappoint him.

p. 103 Activate Prior Knowledge

Students may wish for money, good friends, happiness, or other things of value.

p. 103 Reading Skill

Sample response: Mr. Peters is curious, brave, and kind. He is curious when he hears a strange noise. He is brave and kind enough to try to free the trapped swan.

p. 103 Culture Note

Students should name and describe an imaginary character.

p. 104 Read Fluently

Students should put a box around each of the three dashes.

p. 104 Build English Skills

Students should place a star next to "leaves."

p. 104 Reading Check

Students should underline "The only thing that troubled him was that he was a little lonely, and had no companion for his old age."

p. 105 Literary Analysis

Sample response: Leita wants to make Mr. Peters happy; however, she misses her swan sister.

p. 105 Vocabulary and Pronunciation

Students should circle "rhymes with *fears*."

p. 105 Reading Skill

Sample response: The marriage will not work out because both people cannot be happy.

p. 106 Reading Skill

Sample response: Leita wants to stay near the river. She wants to be close to her sister.

p. 106 Literary Analysis

Sample response: Mr. Peters loves his wife and wants her to be with him always, yet he knows that she longs to be a swan again. He struggles with loving her but letting her go.

p. 106 Reading Check

Students should number as follows: 1. "taking her for drives in the car"; 2. "finding beautiful music for her to listen to on the radio"; 3. "buying clothes for her"; 4. "suggesting a trip round the world." Some students may label the sentence stating that Mr. Peters builds his wife a special seat by the river.

p. 107 Stop to Reflect

Sample response: Mr. Peters spent all of his time with the swans, which is not something people usually do.

p. 107 Literary Analysis

Sample response: He uses his second wish to turn Leita back into a swan. He decides not to use his third wish. Instead, he lives near the swans for the rest of his life.

p. 107 Reading Skill

Sample response: The feather is probably one of Leita's feathers that Mr. Peters kept.

p. 108 Apply the Skills

1. He is already content with the material things he has.
2. Sample response: Mr. Peters uses his second wish for Leita instead of for himself.
3. Sample response: She spends a great deal of time with him.
4. **Graphic Organizer**

Sample response:

Smaller Conflict: Mr. Peters suffers from loneliness. Leita is unhappy as a human.

Resolution: Mr. Peters wishes for and receives a wife. He wishes that his wife be turned back into a swan.

Main Conflict: Mr. Peters has to decide whether to use a wish to turn Leita back into a swan (to make her happy) or to keep her to lessen his loneliness.

p. 110 Reading/Writing Connection

Sample response:

1. Fighting against a friend for the same prize involves being <u>determined</u> to win.
2. You must <u>isolate</u> yourself from troublesome people.
3. To <u>accomplish</u> your goal, you may have to make difficult decisions.

p. 110 Note-taking Guide

Sample response:

Physical traits/ Felix: dark, short, and husky
Fighting style/ Felix: short, muscular frame (better slugger)
Fighting gear/ Felix: sky-blue trunks, red socks, white shoes
Physical traits/ Antonio: fair, lean, and lanky
Fighting style/ Antonio: lean form, long reach (better boxer)
Fighting gear/ Antonio: white trunks, black socks, black shoes

p. 111 Apply the Skills

1. Sample response: It is a good idea. Training apart helps them focus on their training, rather than on fighting each other.
2. Some students may say that the solution was a good one because the boys remained friends. Other students may believe that the solution was not good because the boys did not really want to fight.
3. **Graphic Organizer**

Sample response:

Smaller Conflict: The boys need to focus on their fight; the boys want to remain friends.
Resolution: They decide to train apart; they agree to fight as hard as they can. Each accepts that the other will fight hard but still remain a friend.
Main Conflict: Both Antonio and Felix want to win, but only one can win.
4. Sample response: Each boy is bothered by the thought of hurting the other. The boys leave the fight together, arm in arm, without caring to learn who won.

Reading Informational Materials: Government Publications

p. 113 Graphic Organizer

Sample response:

Evidence: Walking is a popular form of exercise.
Evidence: Walking is popular with older people.
Evidence: Walking has been popular for a long time.
Generalization: Many older people enjoy walking, an exercise that has never lost popularity.

p. 114 Reading Government Publications

Students should circle "The President's Council on Physical Fitness and Sports."

p. 114 Reading Informational Materials

Students should underline "Walking for Exercise and Pleasure" and "Walking: An Exercise for All Ages."

p. 114 Read Fluently

Students should put an asterisk next to "(18 years of age and older)" or "(39.4%)."

p. 114 Reading Check

Students should draw an arrow next to 39.4%. Men who are 65 and older make up the highest percentage of regular walkers.

p. 115 Reading Skill

Sample response: People who walk are almost always healthier than people who do not walk. Walking can improve the body's ability to use oxygen during exertion, lower the resting heart rate, lower blood pressure, and increase the efficiency of the heart and lungs.

p. 115 Reading Informational Materials

Students may circle "It also helps burn excess calories."

p. 115 Reading Check

Students may underline "improve the body's ability to consume oxygen during exertion," "lower the resting heart rate," "reduce blood pressure," and "increase the efficiency of the heart and lungs." Students may also underline "burn excess calories." Some students may underline "Almost everyone can do it," "You can do it almost anywhere," "You can do it almost anytime," and "It doesn't cost anything."

p. 116 Reading Skill
Students should underline "You can do it almost anywhere."

p. 116 Reading Informational Materials
Sample response: Pay attention to your body when you walk.

p. 116 Reading Check
Students should underline "The variety of settings available is one of the things that makes walking such a practical and pleasurable activity."

p. 117 Apply the Skills
Thinking About the Government Publication
1. Sample response: When done briskly on a regular schedule, walking can improve the body's ability to consume oxygen during exertion.
2. You should slow down if you develop dizziness, pain, nausea, or any other symptoms. These symptoms tell you that your body is working too hard.

Reading Skill
3. You can make the generalization that most people walk because it is good for them.
4. Sample response: It is possible to develop dizziness, pain, nausea, or other symptoms when walking.

"Zoo"
Edward D. Hoch

"Ribbons"
Laurence Yep

p. 118 Graphic Organizer
Sample response:
"Zoo"
Why Does the Writer tell the ticket price and the number of people who see the zoo?
Answer (inference): to suggest that Professor Hugo makes a lot of money from the zoo
Why Does the Writer describe the behavior of the horse-spider people of Kaan?
Answer (inference): to compare it with the behavior of the humans at the zoo

"Ribbons"
Why Does the Writer keep what happened to the grandmother's feet a secret?
Answer (inference): to make the reader wonder what happened to her feet

Why Does the Writer have the grandmother show affection to Ian but not to Stacy?
Answer (inference): to develop a conflict for the story

p. 119 Reading/Writing Connection
Sample response:
1. The border around my elephant habitat minimizes outside contact.
2. One benefit of being in the zoo is that animals cannot attack one another.
3. Overall, the people who run my zoo like to emphasize animal safety.

p. 119 Note-taking Guide
Sample response:
The Earth People: They walk on two legs. They walk on the ground. They wear clothes.
The Horse-Spider People: They walk on many legs. They walk in any direction. They wear no clothes.
Same: They have families. They like to see new things. They think that other ways of living are strange.

p. 120 Activate Prior Knowledge
Sample response: Zoos have animals from far-off places. People visit zoos to see these animals.

p. 120 Reading Skill
Sample response: The children know that the special zoo is coming, and they want to go see it.

p. 120 Build English Skills
Students should circle *twenty-third* and *horse-spider*.

p. 120 Reading Check
Students should underline "move around quickly and make a high-pitched chattering noise" and/or "looked like horses but ran up the walls of their cages like spiders."

p. 121 Read Fluently
Students may circle *announces*, which means to say something publicly.

p. 121 Literary Analysis
Sample response: The creatures are telling what is unusual about Earth creatures. This description shows the theme that people are often afraid of something that seems different.

p. 121 Culture Note
Sample response: By learning about animals from other countries people also can learn

more about the countries and the people in them.

p. 122 Apply the Skills

1. Sample response: The crowd views the creatures as a nightmare because the creatures are totally unfamiliar.

2. Sample response: This quotation indicates that humans fail to accept or be open-minded when faced with living creatures that look different from themselves.

3. Sample response: The children behave themselves so that their parents will let them go to the Interplanetary Zoo.

4. **Graphic Organizer**

Sample response:

Theme: People view foreign creatures as strange or weird.

Setting: People in Chicago see the spaceship as a zoo, and the creatures on the spaceship see Chicago as a zoo.

Character: People on Earth are frightened of and curious about the horse-spider people. Horse-spider people are wary of and curious about Earth people.

p. 124 Reading/Writing Connection

Sample response:

1. A way to <u>maximize</u> your learning is to study other <u>cultures</u>.

2. <u>Ignore</u> your differences and pay attention to your <u>similarities</u>.

3. <u>Rely</u> on good manners to break down cultural <u>barriers</u>.

p. 124 Note-taking Guide

Sample response:

What does . . . Ian? She teaches him to speak Chinese.

What does . . . Stacy? She takes away Stacy's ribbons. She tells Stacy that she (Stacy) can dance.

p. 125 Apply the Skills

1. Students may suggest that the hardest changes for Stacy come when she has to change her behavior and give up her ballet lessons.

2. Sample response: Stacy's mother explains Grandmother's behavior to Stacy, and Stacy is finally able to explain her love of dancing to Grandmother.

3. Sample response: Why does the author include the detail about Grandmother's carrying her daughter on her back? Why does he include the detail about Grandmother's walking such a great distance?

4. **Graphic Organizer**

Sample response:

Theme: The theme might be understanding and overcoming differences.

Traits: Stacy tries hard and is loving and dedicated.

Motives: Stacy wants to dance and wants her grandmother to like her.

"What Makes a Rembrandt a Rembrandt?"
Richard Mühlberger

p. 129 Note-taking Guide
Sample response:
Circle 1: shows commotion in the scene
Circle 2: highlights person's rank
Circle 3: leads viewers to center of painting

p. 130 Activate Prior Knowledge
Students may say that they would make the scene more interesting by painting different expressions on people's faces, rather than all smiles.

p. 130 Nonfiction
Students should underline "In all of these group portraits, the men were evenly lined up so that each face got equal attention, just as they had been in traditional anatomy lesson paintings." Rembrandt's solution was to show the scene before a parade. He added people who were not in the military to add realism to the scene. He showed the excitement and activity before a military parade began.

p. 130 Reading Check
Students should underline "his militia company."

p. 131 Nonfiction
The officers are illuminated, or in the light. Everything else is in shadow.

p. 131 Nonfiction
Sample response: The captain is dressed in black. He wears a red sash. The captain is giving orders to his lieutenant.

p. 131 Vocabulary and Pronunciation
Students should circle: "His lieutenant stands next to him in a yellow uniform with a silk sash, cavalry boots, and a hat with a white ostrich feather," and "Rembrandt shows the captain giving orders to his lieutenant, who is listening to him with respect." Sample response: The artist shows the captain giving orders to another military officer, who respectfully listens to him.

p. 132 Read Fluently
Students should circle "and" and "and."
Students should place a box around

"drummer" and "dog," and "Rembrandt" and "he."

p. 132 Reading Check
Students should underline "there are shadows that show daylight" and "No one seems to be on watch."

p. 133 Stop to Reflect
Sample response: Students may say that the way Rembrandt highlights figures in the background and his attention to individuals shows his greatness.

p. 133 Reading Check
Students should circle "red."

p. 133 Build English Skills
Students may underline "Light illuminates," "dark shadows hide," "red," "posed informally," and "portraits of individuals." Sample response: The artist uses light to illuminate men's faces and other important details. Dark shadows are used to hide unimportant details. The only bright color the artist uses is red. The men in the portrait are posed informally. Each face is a portrait of an individual.

p. 134 Apply the Skills
1. Sample response: Students may name the painting *The Militia Parade*, or *Citizen Soldiers*.
2. Rembrandt wanted to make his painting more realistic. He wanted to show the excitement before a parade. He included people moving and doing things.
3. The two highest-ranking men are at the front of the portrait. One officer's face is illuminated against a dark background. The other's entire figure is painted in bright colors.
4. **Graphic Organizer**
Sample response:
Examples of Description: describing Banning Cocq; describing the other officer; describing the girls.
Examples of Exposition: explaining the use of color to create contrasts between light and dark; explaining how Rembrandt included activity and excitement to make the scene seem real.

"Life Without Gravity"
Robert Zimmerman

"Conversational Ballgames"
Nancy Masterson Sakamoto

p. 137 Graphic Organizer
Sample response:
"Life Without Gravity"
Column 3, row 1: weightlessness
Column 3, row 2: "In space, bodies change."
Column 3, row 3: spines

"Conversational Ballgames"
Column 3, row 1: "A western-style conversation between two people is like a game of tennis."
Column 3, row 2: "If I introduce a topic, a conversational ball, I expect you to hit it back."
Column 3, row 3: elaboration

p. 137 Reading/Writing Connection
Sample response: Gravity will require you to be careful when you are jumping on a trampoline. Gravity forces you to react if you were to fall off your bicycle. Can you predict what would happen without gravity?

p. 137 Note-taking Guide
Sample response:
Effects on Blood: Blood flows to head and not to legs.
Effects on Stomach: The stomach gets upset.
Effects on Eating: Astronauts must drink out of a special straw.

p. 138 Activate Prior Knowledge
Students may say that they would like to be an astronaut. They may think it would be exciting to go places where few people have been.

p. 138 Literary Analysis
The words "being weightless in space," "Zero gravity," and "Living in space" tell the topic of this essay.

p. 138 Build English Skills
Students should circle "shortest."

p. 138 Reading Check
Students should circle "Blood flows from the feet to the head," "legs to become thin," "the head to swell," "Bones and muscles weaken," "upset stomachs," and "disks between the bones in the spine spread."

p. 139 Reading Skill
Students should underline "In space, you cannot pour milk into a bowl of cornflakes."

p. 139 Read Fluently
Students should draw a box around "in space" and "in orbit."

p. 140 Apply the Skills
1. Sample response: People get dizzy and feel sick to their stomachs because they lose their sense of balance without gravity.
2. Sample response: An astronaut can choose to move up or down, or left or right, just by moving his or her head. He or she must also choose to store away tools or let them float way and possibly get lost.
3. The main idea is that weightlessness has negative effects, but these effects can be overcome.
4. **Graphic Organizer**
Sample response:
Column 2: It is fun to float around. A person can use every inch of space to work. A person can change direction just by moving his or her head.
Column 3: Weightlessness can make a person feel dizzy and sick to his or her stomach. It causes the head to swell and the muscles to weaken.
Column 4: Weightlessness can be fun, and its effects are quickly reversed on Earth. It is important to know about the effects of weightlessness if astronauts are going to explore outer space.

p. 142 Reading/Writing Connection
Sample response: Newcomers to American culture may not comprehend that *cool* means "cold" or "very good." They may try to communicate using formal language. Americans may respond to them with confusion.

p. 142 Note-taking Guide
Sample response:
Column 2, row 3: Players take their own turn to hit the ball; the game does not stop for them to take their turn.
Column 3, row 3: People speak one at a time.
Column 4, row 1: bowling ball
Column 4, row 2: A player bowls and his or her turn ends.

p. 143 Apply the Skills

1. The author did not understand that she should wait her turn to speak, and that she should not respond to people's comments.

2. Sample response: The newcomer should respect the rules of the other culture; the native speakers should be tolerant of the newcomer's style.

3. The main idea is that Western and Japanese-style conversations are very different.

4. **Graphic Organizer**

Sample response:

Describe Polite Conversation in Japan: It allows only one speaker at a time, according to his or her social standing. While the speaker talks, the others listen quietly. When it is time for a new speaker, he or she starts with a new topic.

"I Am a Native of North America" Chief Dan George

from In Search of Our Mothers' Gardens Alice Walker

p. 145 Graphic Organizer

Sample response:

"I Am a Native of North America"

Main Idea: People of Chief Dan George's culture and people of white culture must love one another.

Left Key Point: Love is necessary for human life.

Detail 1: George's culture taught him to love and respect people.

Detail 2: George's father taught him to love and respect animals and nature.

Right Key Point: George wonders whether people from white culture know how to love.

Detail 1: The white man loves the things he owns rather than each other.

Detail 2: White culture abuses Earth.

***from* In Search of Our Mothers' Gardens**

Main Idea: Throughout history, women have often been forced to express their creativity in modest ways, such as storytelling, gardening, and quilting, but they have passed down the creative spirit to the next generation of women.

Left Key Point: The stories people tell are often the ones they heard and absorbed from their parents.

Detail 1: Many of the stories Walker has written are her mother's stories.

Detail 2: Through the years of listening to her mother's stories, Walker absorbed her mother's manner of storytelling.

Right Key Point: Gardening was an important means of self-expression for Walker's mother.

Detail 1: Whatever Walker's mother planted grew as if by magic.

Detail 2: In searching for her mother's garden, Walker found her own.

p. 146 Reading/Writing Connection

Sample response:

1. My cultural background has helped enrich my ability to respect others' opinions.

2. Many cultures stress that it is important to cooperate with one another.

3. People should evaluate how their cultural backgrounds influence their lives.

p. 146 Note-taking Guide

Sample response:

Native American Culture: values community; has learned much from white American culture

White American Culture: overtaking Native American culture; has not learned from Native American culture

[overlapping circle] Both groups must forgive each other.

p. 147 Activate Prior Knowledge

Students may suggest goals such as ending hunger, cleaning up the environment, or ending crime.

p. 147 Vocabulary and Pronunciation

Students should circle any two of the following: "loved," "respected," "considered," "fished," "scolded," and "respected."

p. 147 Literary Analysis

The words are in the past tense.

p. 148 Reading Skill

Students should circle "they stripped the land and poisoned the water and air."

p. 148 Stop to Reflect

Students may say that the only thing separating humans from animals is humans' ability to love. Some students may agree with this statement and say that only humans have the mental ability to feel this emotion. Others may disagree and say that they believe animals can love as much as humans can. They may have pets that they believe love their human families.

p. 148 Build English Skills

Students should circle "everyone's."

p. 149 Literary Analysis

His culture believes that all things belong to nature and should be shared.

p. 149 Read Fluently

Students should circle each period, comma, dash, and ellipsis.

p. 150 Apply the Skills

1. Sample response: By "brotherhood," Chief Dan George means love, patience, trust, acceptance, peace, and forgiveness among all people.
2. Sample response: He means that his "white brothers" have been more successful in spreading their values than his culture has been.
3. Sample response: The author believes it is important for all Americans to love, respect, care for, and forgive one another and to live in peace.
4. **Graphic Organizer**
Sample response:
Chief George's Reflections: How his culture is fading
My Responses: Students' responses may include empathy or confusion.
After Rereading: Students may agree that the world would certainly benefit from people of different cultures showing more love, respect, and forgiveness to each other.

p. 152 Reading/Writing Connection

Sample response: I do not think that I can fully appreciate everything that my mother has done for me. She is the first person to contribute help when I need it. She has demonstrated love to me.

p. 152 Note-taking Guide

Sample response:
Anonymous Women: names unknown; lived hard lives; created beauty from everyday things: quilts, songs, and so on.

Alice Walker: very famous; lives much easier life; uses words and ideas to write

p. 153 Apply the Skills

1. Sample response: Walker's mother shares a creative spirit with all women and she has passed on the spirit of creativity to the next generation, just as other women before her have done.
2. Sample response: It is a tribute to all mothers, not just her own.
3. Sample response: The main idea is that throughout history, women have often been forced to express their creativity in modest ways. They garden, quilt, or tell stories. By doing so, they have passed down the creative spirit to the next generation of women.
4. **Graphic Organizer**
Sample response:
Walker's Reflections: The quilt by the "anonymous" black woman in Alabama is a work of art; Mother created beautiful gardens that were greatly admired.
My Responses: Students responses may include memories of quilts, stories, or gardens created by women in their families, or memories of other ways in which the women in their families have expressed creativity.
After Rereading: Students should identify ways their thinking has changed. For example, they may not have thought that quilts or gardens were creative outlets. After reading the essay, they may think otherwise.

Reading Informational Materials: Problem-and-Solution Essays

p. 156 Reading Problem-and-Solution Essays

Students should underline "As many as 9 million Americans have hearing loss caused by noise."

p. 156 Reading Skill

Students should circle "prevent hearing loss" and should number "using ear protectors," "buy quieter machines," "avoid using lawnmowers or power tools at quiet times of the day," and "turning down the volume on headphones for radios and CD players."

p. 156 Read Fluently

Students may write "motorbike."

p. 156 Reading Check
Students should draw a box around "120 decibels."

p. 157 Reading Skill
Students may choose "What Can Communities Do?" Students may number "locate airports away from dense populations," "prohibit late-night flights," "have laws against noise that exceeds a certain decibel level," and "give fines to people who use noisy equipment."

p. 157 Reading Informational Materials
The last paragraph tells about things that the government can do that affect everyone. It says the federal government could bring back laws that set limits on noise. It says the best way to fix the problem of noise pollution is to have the government pay for research to make machines quieter.

p. 158 Apply the Skills
Thinking About the Problem-and-Solution Essay
1. Cars, trains, trucks, and planes are the largest source of noise pollution. About 15 million Americans live near an airport or under a flight path.
2. Noise that does not cause pain can still damage your hearing. Household appliances such as a kitchen blender can slowly damage the hair cells in your cochlea.

Reading Skill
3. The author uses facts to support each idea logically.
4. The effect is that the essay is logical and believable.

"The Eternal Frontier"
Louis L'Amour

"All Together Now"
Barbara Jordan

p. 159 Graphic Organizer
Sample response:
"The Eternal Frontier"
Appeals to Emotion: "And today is the past."
Appeals to Reason: "Computers, new medicines, and new ways of keeping healthy are results of space exploration."

"All Together Now"
Appeals to Authority: "President Lyndon B. Johnson pushed through the Civil Rights Act of 1964, which remains the fundamental piece of civil rights legislation in this century."
Appeals to Emotion: "I care about you because you are a fellow human being and I find it okay in my mind, in my heart, to simply say to you, I love you."
Appeals to Reason: "Each of us can decide to have one friend of a different race or background in our mix of friends."

p. 160 Reading/Writing Connection
Sample response:
1. People will have to invest too much time and money for space exploration.
2. The decision to undertake more space exploration could benefit the world.
3. Scientists will obtain new knowledge as a result of space exploration.

p. 160 Note-taking Guide
Sample response:
Circle 3: "The human mind has no limits . . . ."
Circle 4: ". . . if humans had not looked to new frontiers, we would still be hunters and food gatherers."
Circle 5: "It is our destiny to move out . . . ."

p. 161 Activate Prior Knowledge
Sample response: In the future people may live on other planets, travel in outer space on space shuttles, or spend time at space stations as a result of space exploration.

p. 161 Reading Skill
Students should circle "All space exploration in the past has been preparation for the future," and underline "People have already imagined and developed many things, from cars and paved roads to electricity and television."

p. 161 Reading Check
Students should circle "Outer space."

p. 162 Read Fluently
Students should underline "to move," "to accept," "to dare," "to achieve," and "to live." Students should underline "to move out," "to accept the challenge," "to dare the unknown," and "to live in the past."

p. 162 Build English Skills
Students should underline any two of the following: "Industries," "Computers," "medicines," "ways," "results," "developments," and "lives."

p. 163 Apply the Skills

1. Sample response: These leaders may vote for legislation and funding that support space travel.

2. Sample response: The essay conveys the message that exploring outer space is our human destiny. It paints a noble picture of humankind. This is a positive message.

3. **Graphic Organizer**
Row 1: "all"
Row 2: "must"

4. Sample response: Students may write "Industries are growing because of our exploration of outer space."

p. 165 Reading/Writing Connection

Sample response: Many laws help integrate our society. However, it is impossible to legislate people's feelings. Each person must promote tolerance in the community. Then, people will begin to understand one another.

p. 165 Note-taking Guide

How can we achieve it? through laws and personal actions

Why is it important? It brings peace to the world and helps us appreciate differences among people.

p. 166 Apply the Skills

1. Sample response: Jordan means that a baby has not yet been influenced by society.

2. Sample response: Jordan's ideas could work if all people were as optimistic as Jordan.

3. **Graphic Organizer**
Sample response:
Clue 2: "need"
Clue 3: "best way"

4. Sample response: Appeal to reason: "Each of us can decide to have one friend of a different race or background in our mix of friends."

"The Real Story of a Cowboy's Life"
Geoffrey C. Ward

"Rattlesnake Hunt"
Marjorie Kinnan Rawlings

p. 168 Graphic Organizer

Sample response:
"The Real Story of a Cowboy's Life"
atlas or map: route of a typical cattle drive
dictionary: difficult words, such as *escorts*
encyclopedia: information about cattle drives

reliable Web site: information about the author, Geoffrey C. Ward

"Rattlesnake Hunt"
almanac: the burning of the countryside at that time of year in order to create cattle forage
atlas or map: the location of Big Prairie, the rattlesnake hunting ground
biographical dictionary: "Ross Allen, a young Florida herpetologist, invited me to join him on a hunt in the upper Everglades—for rattlesnakes."
dictionary: difficult words, such as *herpetologist*
encyclopedia: information about rattlesnakes
reliable Web site: information about the author, Marjorie Kinnan Rawlings

p. 169 Note-taking Guide

Sample response:
Inconveniences: dust; homesteaders
Dangers From Animals or Nature: stampede at night; prairie dog holes; deep cuts in the ground
Benefits: beautiful views

p. 170 Activate Prior Knowledge

Students may list herds of cattle, riding horses, dusty ground, cowboy hats and boots, and so on.

p. 170 Reading Skill

Students should check "Encyclopedia" and "Reliable Web site."

p. 170 Literary Analysis

Students should underline "chair," "workbench," and "pillow at night."

p. 171 Read Fluently

Students should circle "–the Nueces, the Guadalupe, the Brazos, the Wichita, and the Red" and "—payable in money or beef." The words following the first dash explain which rivers the herd crossed. The words following the second dash explain how the cowboys paid tolls.

p. 171 Reading Check

Students should circle "the homesteaders settled near water and then charged the cowboys for the water," and "When the cattle got into their crops, they came with guns and demanded payment for the damage."

p. 172 Apply the Skills

1. Teddy Blue participated in several cattle drives.

2. Sample response: Successful cowboys worked as a team. They loved the open trail.

3. Sample response: If opinions were not included, the author would not give as colorful a picture of cowboy life.

4. **Graphic Organizer**

Sample response:

Informal Language: ". . . it sure was a pretty sight to see them strung out for almost a mile, the sun shining on their horns."

p. 174 Reading/Writing Connection

Sample response: One way to respond to something that frightens you is by turning away from it. It is difficult to acquire a deeper respect for what you fear. Facing something scary can benefit a person by making him or her get over the fear.

p. 174 Note-taking Guide

Sample response:

Box 3: She describes the snakes' behavior in an unemotional way.

Box 4: She heads off by herself to hunt a snake.

p. 175 Apply the Skills

1. Rawlings has won because she has conquered a fear.

2. Rawlings views herself as more courageous, and she views nature as less dangerous.

3. The facts show what Rawlings learned about snakes.

4. **Graphic Organizer**

Sample response:

Technical Vocabulary: coupe; arid

Formal Language: "I felt an upsurgence of spirit." "As I had discovered with the insects and the varmints, it is difficult to be afraid of anything about which enough is known, and Ross' facts were fresh from the laboratory."

Informal Language: "I've got one"; "Well, pick it up."

Reading Informational Materials: Manuals

p. 177 Graphic Organizer

Which details can be verified as facts? The copperhead has diamond shaped markings; Pit vipers puncture their victims with fangs; Coral snakes are red, yellow, and blue.

Which details are opinions? It is the most striking of the pit vipers; Pit vipers are the most frightening snakes; Coral snakes are beautiful.

p. 178 Reading Manuals

This snake is venomous. The snake has pits between its eyes and its nostrils, fangs, a triangular head, and eyes with narrow pupils.

p. 178 Read Fluently

Students should underline "triangular," "narrow," "vertical," "round," "visible," "nonvenomous," and "round."

p. 178 Reading Manuals

Sample response: Most manuals include pictures because manuals are meant to give information.

p. 178 Reading Check

Students should underline "the water moccasin."

p. 179 Reading Informational Materials

Sample response: What to do in a fire. How to treat a cut or a burn.

p. 179 Reading Manuals

Students should circle any three of the following: "cut into a snake bite"; "apply cold compresses"; "apply a tourniquet"; "raise the site of the bite above the level of the victim's heart"; "give the victim aspirin, stimulants, or pain medication"; "allow the person to exercise"

p. 179 Reading Check

Students should circle "venomous snakes can bite reflexively even after they die."

p. 180 Reading Skill

Sample response: The statement is an opinion because it says that "the bitten area may swell." It is not certain that the bitten area *will* swell. Even so, it would be a good idea to complete step five when assisting a bite victim.

p. 180 Reading Check

Students should underline two of the following: "lay the victim flat," "raise his or her feet 8 to 12 inches," or "cover the victim with a coat or blanket." Students should circle one of the following: "elevate the bitten area above the person's heart," or "place the victim in this position if you suspect any head, neck, back, or leg injury or if the position makes the victim uncomfortable."

p. 181 Apply the Skills
Thinking About the Manual

1. Anxiety can aggravate his or her reaction to the bite. This can make the bite more painful and more difficult to treat. It can also make recovery harder.

2. In North America, all venomous snakes—except the coral snake—are pit vipers. Pit vipers have triangular heads, fangs, narrow vertical pupils and pits between their nostrils and eyes. Nonvenomous snakes do not have these characteristics.

Reading Skill

3. You could use encyclopedias, other manuals, reliable Internet sources, or reference books from the library to check facts about venomous snakes.

4. Manuals are reference materials. Reference materials must have facts to provide reliable information.

"Maestro"

"The Desert Is My Mother"

"Bailando"
Pat Mora

p. 184 Note-taking Guides
Sample response:
"The Desert Is My Mother"
Speaker: A woman who loves the desert.
Memories or Commands: She commands the desert to feed, tease, frighten, hold, heal, caress, sing, and teach her, and to make her beautiful.

"Bailando"
Speaker: A grown adult remembering her aunt.
Memories or Commands: She remembers her aunt dancing as a young woman, dancing with her, dancing with her children, and dancing on her ninetieth birthday.

p. 185 Activate Prior Knowledge
Some students may say that baking cookies reminds them of a time when a grandmother taught them how to make cookies. Other students may say that a day at the lake reminds them of a time when their father taught them how to fish.

p. 185 Poetry
Students should write "singing" and "songs."

p. 185 Poetry
Students should circle "smile" and "slid."

p. 185 Reading Check
Students should underline "when he bows."

p. 186 Read Fluently
Students should underline "I say" and "She."

p. 186 Vocabulary and Pronunciation
Students should underline "frighten" and "lightning."

p. 186 Poetry
"She" is the desert.

p. 186 Poetry
Students should list "silence" and "driest."

p. 187 Poetry
Students could underline "Le digo," or "Me."

p. 187 Poetry
Students may notice "susurra" in the fourth stanza. It is an example of onomatopoeia because it sounds like "whisper," which is what it means in English.

p. 187 Stop to Reflect
Sample response: Spanish is often spoken in the American Southwest, where deserts are found. This might be another way to connect the speaker to the desert.

p. 188 Poetry
Sample response: This poem is free verse because the lines do not rhyme. There are no stanzas. The lines have different numbers of syllables.

p. 188 Poetry
Students should circle "spinning round and round."

p. 188 Build English Skills
Students should circle "Bailando." They should also circle three words such as "dancing," "spinning," or "swaying."

p. 188 Reading Check
Students should underline "my dear aunt."

p. 189 Apply the Skills
1. Sample response: The musician feels grateful to his parents. He is comforted when he thinks about them. They inspired him to become a musician.
2. The poem is about the speaker's aunt.
3. In "Maestro," "again and again," "bit by bit," and "note to note" are repeated. In "The Desert Is My Mother," "I say" and "Le digo" are repeated. In "Bailando," "spinning round and round" is repeated.
4. **Graphic Organizer**
Sample response:
. . . a woman: serves, shouts, whispers, gives, strokes, offers, chants
. . . a hot and dry region: spiked cactus, sunny day, thunder and lightening, pink blossoms, windy, sun's glare, driest sand
both: "She gives me chamomile and other spices" and "warm breath."

Poetry Collection 1

Poetry Collection 2

p. 191 Graphic Organizer
Sample response:
Poetry Collection 1
"Haiku"
Detail 1: The pond is watched by a weasel.
Detail 2: The moon sets.
Detail 3: Shadows drift.
How are the details related? They all take place in a woodsy area.
Conclusion: The poet is concerned with nature.

Poetry Collection 2:
"Winter"
Detail 1: Frogs burrow in the mud.
Detail 2: "Snails bury themselves."
Detail 3: The speaker airs quilts.
How are the details related? All of the details describe how animals and people prepare for winter.
Conclusion: Animals and people want to stay warm, cozy, fed, and healthy during the winter.

p. 192 Reading/Writing Connection
Sample response: People write poems because poetry helps communicate feelings, ideas, and action in few words. The images in poetry can generate feelings of love, curiosity, anger, or longing. Poetry reinforces a love of words and wordplay.

p. 192 Note-taking Guide
"The Rider"
Topic of Poem: The topic is a person riding a bicycle.
Actions in Poem: Action in the poem includes pedaling hard, leaving loneliness, panting, and floating free.

"Seal"
Topic of Poem: The topic is a seal swimming through the water.
Actions in Poem: Action in the poem includes dives, darts, a swerve, a twist, a flip, a flick, plunges, and plops.

"Haiku"
Topic of Poem: The topics are ducklings in pond, the woods, and shadows in the forest.

Actions in Poem: Action in the poem include pond is watched, not one leaf moves, moon sets, and shadows drift and disappear.

p. 193 Activate Prior Knowledge
Students may say that they have been inspired by the image of an actor performing in a Shakespearean play. The actor's talent and dedication to his art would be a good subject for a poem.

p. 193 Reading Skill
Students may underline "float free," "a cloud of sudden azaleas," and "luminous pink petals."

p. 193 Build English Skills
Students should circle "pedaling" and "panting." Students should underline "pedaling hard down King William Street" and "panting behind you on some street corner."

p. 194 Literary Analysis
Students should say that a concrete poem focuses on a visual image. The poet places the letters and lines in a way that looks like that image. Some students may say the poet chose this form because the poem's lines look like a seal. Others may say that the lines resemble the seal's movement as it swims and dives.

p. 194 Reading Skill
Sample response: The speaker admires the seal for its graceful movements in the water.

p. 194 Reading Check
Students should draw a box around "A whoop, a bark."

p. 195 Vocabulary and Pronunciation
Students should circle "green" and either "weasel" or "leaf."

p. 195 Reading Skill
Students should say the speaker is worried about the ducklings. If they swim in the pond, the weasel will catch and eat them.

p. 195 Stop to Reflect
Students may say that it seems as if the woods themselves are afraid. The wind does not blow, and the leaves do not dare to move. Some students may say a predator is hunting in the woods. Other students may say that the woods are afraid of people who might do harm.

p. 195 Read Fluently

Students should circle "shadows" and "drift." Some students may also circle "disappear."

p. 196 Apply the Skills

1. Sample response: Rollerskating and bicycle riding are discussed in "The Rider." The two sports have wheels, movement, and speed in common.
2. Sample response: These words create a playful mood.
3. Sample response: Why does the speaker in "The Rider" include such colorful details about speed and movement?
4. **Graphic Organizer**
"The Rider" checkmarks under Musical language, Single image or idea, and Thoughts of one speaker
"Seal" checkmarks under Lines shaped like subject
"Haiku" checkmarks under Thoughts of one speaker; Three-lines; 17 syllables

p. 198 Reading/Writing Connection

Sample response: People might write a poem to capture their feelings about the desert. They could concentrate on details about animals, plants, and the climate of the desert. The poem would emphasize the variety and beauty of living things in the desert.

p. 198 Note-taking Guide

Sample response:
"Winter"
Supporting Details: "Chipmunks gather nuts." The speaker collects books.

"Forsythia"
Main Idea: Forsythia is a messenger of spring.
Supporting Details: "FORSYTHIA OUT" and "SPRING'S YELLOW TELEGRAM"

"Haiku"
Main Idea: Flowers are a sign of spring on a mountain.
Supporting Details: "sweet plum blossoms," "fragrant blossoms," and "Has spring come indeed?"

p. 199 Apply the Skills

1. Sample response: The words suggest that forsythia plants burst out in early spring. They let everyone know that spring is on its way.
2. Sample response: He respects nature. Nature inspires and amazes him.

3. Sample response: How are the words about forsythia related?
4. **Graphic Organizer**
"Winter" checkmarks under Musical language, Single image or idea, and Thoughts of one speaker
"Forsythia" checkmarks under Lines shaped like subject
"Haiku" checkmarks under Thoughts of one speaker, and Three lines; 17 syllables

Poetry Collection 1

Poetry Collection 2

p. 201 Graphic Organizer

Sample response:
Poetry Collection 1
Simile (from "The Courage That My Mother Had"): She had "courage like a rock."
Personification (from "Loo-Wit"): "She sprinkles ashes on the snow."
Metaphor (from "Life"): "Life is but a toy."
Symbol (from "Life"): The watch is a symbol that stands for life.

Poetry Collection 2
"The Village Blacksmith"
Simile: "the muscles of his brawny arms / Are strong as iron bands."
Personification: "the bellows roar"
Metaphor: Life is a "flaming forge" at which peoples' "fortunes must be wrought"
Symbol: The "tear" represents sorrow or grief.

p. 202 Reading/Writing Connection

Sample response: Though they occur rarely, volcanic eruptions are very dangerous and harmful. Smoke and ash indicate that a volcano is getting ready to erupt. It is not difficult for a volcano to impress most people.

p. 202 Note-taking Guide

Sample response:
Topic of the Poem:
"Life" The topic is life.
"The Courage That My Mother Had" The speaker's mother's courage is the topic.

Words Used to Describe Topic:
"Life" The poem uses the words "toy," "ticking," and "run down."
"The Courage That My Mother Had" The poem uses the words "granite," and "rock."
"Loo-Wit" The poem uses the words "old," "trembling," and "thin."

p. 203 Activate Prior Knowledge
Students may describe life as an exciting adventure. Life could lead them anywhere. They may describe courage as an attitude that can help them do things that would be impossible without it. They may describe a volcano as a sign of the power of nature.

p. 203 Reading Skill
Students may underline "Life is but a toy" and "to amuse a fascinated infant."

p. 203 Culture Note
A student from France may mention Bordeaux. It is known for its wine.

p. 203 Reading Check
Students should circle "lets the watch run down."

p. 204 Reading Skill
Sample response: The most important details are the old woman spitting "black tobacco" and sprinkling "ashes / on the snow."

p. 204 Read Fluently
Students should underline three prepositional phrases such as "from her bumpy bed," "to earth," and "on her neck."

p. 204 Vocabulary and Pronunciation
The poet uses the words "growls" and "snarls" to describe the sounds of the machinery.

p. 205 Literary Analysis
The poet uses personification to give human qualities to a volcano.

p. 205 Stop to Reflect
Sample response: Loo-wit's singing is the eruption of the volcano.

p. 205 Build English Skills
Students should circle "sleeping" or "clearing," and "shaking."

p. 205 Reading Check
Students should circle "but she heard the boot scrape, / the creaking floor, / felt the pull of the blanket / from her thin shoulder."

p. 206 Apply the Skills
1. Sample response: Both life and the watch stop after a while.
2. The scrape of a boot causes the eruption.
3. **Graphic Organizer**
Sample response:
Detail 2: The ticking of the watch amuses a child.

Detail 3: The old man, once an infant, is tired and lets the watch wind down.
4. Sample response: The rock is a symbol for strength.

p. 208 Reading/Writing Connection
Sample response: My older sister displays many qualities to admire, including a concern for others. It is easy to appreciate how she really listens when I talk to her about something important to me. This person makes others aspire to better themselves.

p. 208 Note-taking Guide
Sample response:
Topic of the Poem:
"The Village Blacksmith" The topic is life.
"Fog" The topic is fog.

Words Used to Describe Topic:
"The Village Blacksmith" "Thus at the flaming forge of life / Our fortunes must be wrought; / Thus on its sounding anvil shaped / Each burning deed and thought."
"Fog" "The fog comes / on little cat feet"; "It sits . . . on silent haunches."

p. 209 Apply the Skills
1. Sample response: Fog makes the atmosphere seem mysterious. This quality makes it a good subject for a poem.
2. Sample response: The mother demonstrates the qualities of strength and determination.
3. **Graphic Organizer**
Sample response:
Detail 1: The staircase often had splinters, torn up boards, and bare places
Detail 3: The mother tells her son that even though life is hard, she keeps climbing, and so should he.
4. Sample response: The lines include a simile. The blacksmith's blows create a beat like a sexton ringing the village bell.

Reading Informational Materials: Advertisements

p. 214 Apply the Skills
Thinking About the Advertisements
1. Sample response: Words such as "amazing," "miracle," and "astonishing" in the advertisements appeal to the reader's emotions.
2. Sample response: The prices are probably not mentioned so the reader will focus on how "great" the sole is instead of how much it might cost.

Reading Skill

3. Sample response: The claim, "Never before has scientific research come up with such a remarkable combination," cannot be proved.

4. Sample response: The goal of the Neolite ad is to convince readers to buy Neolite soles for their shoes.

Poetry Collection 1
Poetry Collection 2

p. 215 Graphic Organizer

Sample response:

Poetry Collection 1:

Onomatopoeia (from "Weather"): "Dot a dot dot dot a dot dot / Spotting the windowpane."

Alliteration (from "Sarah Cynthia Sylvia Stout Would Not Take the Garbage Out"): "Sarah Cynthia Sylvia Stout" is alliteration.

Repetition (from "Sarah Cynthia Sylvia Stout Would Not Take the Garbage Out"): She "*would not take the garbage out*" repeats throughout the poem.

Poetry Collection 2:

Onomatopoeia (from "Onomatopoeia"): "The rusty spigot *sputters*"

Alliteration (from "Full Fathom Five"): "*Full fathom five thy father lies*"

Repetition (from "Train Tune"): "*Back through* clouds / *Back through* clearing / *Back through* distance / *Back through* silence.*"

p. 216 Reading/Writing Connection

Sample response:

1. People react with shock and surprise when people see how I dress.

2. I dedicate myself to practicing very hard to stand out from the crowd.

3. My attitude is that everyone should strive to be unique.

p. 216 Note-taking Guide

Sample response:

Topic of the Poem:

"Sarah Cynthia Sylvia Stout Would Not Take the Garbage Out" a girl who refuses to take out the garbage

"One" individuality

Words Used to Describe the Topic:

"Sarah Cynthia Sylvia Stout Would Not Take the Garbage Out" "It filled the can, it

covered the floor," "It raised the roof, it broke the wall"

"One" "Only one," "nobody can get a second one"

p. 217 Activate Knowledge

Students may recall words such as "carbuncle" or "squish," as in "Did you *squish* your *carbuncle* today?"

p. 217 Reading Skill

Students should circle the words "She'd," "out," "And," and "cheese." Students should also circle the commas after "pans," "hams," "shout," "grounds," "peelings," "bananas," and "peas"; periods after "out" and "cheese"; and the colon after "ceilings."

p. 217 Read Fluently

Students should circle: "With," "bacon rinds," "chicken bones," "ice cream cones," "prune pits," "peach pits," "orange peel," "oatmeal," "pizza crusts," "greens," "beans," "tangerines," "crusts," and "roasts."

p. 218 Literary Analysis

Students should circle the letters "s" and "c" at the beginning of "Sarah" "Cynthia" "Stout" and "said."

p. 218 Reading Skill

Sample response: The garbage piled up very high. Sarah's neighbors moved away and no one would come to play with her. Sarah finally agreed to take out the garbage.

p. 219 Build English Skills

Students should list "outside" and "bumbershoot."

p. 219 Read Fluently

Students may underline "juddle," "luddle," and "puddmuddle."

p. 219 Literary Analysis

Students should circle the words "slosh," "galosh," "puddle" and "jump." Sample response: The poet might mean that people are sloshing through water in rubber boots.

p. 220 Literary Analysis

Students should circle the two uses of "nobody," the three uses of "my," and the two uses of "or."

p. 220 Build English Skills

Students should underline "anybody."

p. 220 Vocabulary and Pronunciation
Sample response: "Act" and "copy" have the same meaning as mimic.

p. 220 Reading Check
Students should underline "Only one of me."

p. 221 Apply the Skills
1. Sample response: The poem is funny and not preachy. The poem was intended to entertain, not to teach a lesson.
2. Sample response: The poet feels bad about all three words. "Mimic" and "act" are especially bad actions that involve others making fun of the speaker.
3. **Graphic Organizer**
Sample response:
"Sarah Cynthia Sylvia Stout . . . "
Example from Poem: "It cracked the window and blocked the door / With bacon rinds and chicken bones."
Paraphrase: The garbage cracked the window. It also blocked the door.

"Weather"
Example from Poem: "Dot a dot dot dot a dot dot / Spotting the windowpane."
Paraphrase: Dots of rain are all over the windowpane.
4. Sample response: "Splatter" and "slosh" are two words that imitate the sound of water.

p. 223 Reading/Writing Connection
Sample response:
1. The sound of flowing water can affect how a person feels.
2. If it persists, the sound of a jackhammer can be very irritating.
3. The sound of birds singing generates a feeling of happiness in many people.

p. 223 Note-taking Guide
Sample response:
"Onomatopoeia"
Visual Details: "rusty spigot," "smattering of drops"
Aural (sound) Descriptions: "splutter," "splatters," "scatters," "plash!"

"Train Tune"
Visual Details: "clouds," "groves," "lightning"
Aural (sound) Descriptions: "silence"

p. 224 Apply the Skills
1. Sample response: The father's bones have turned into coral. His eyes have turned into pearls. Coral and pearls are precious items,

so the changes might be called special or "rich." The changes might be called unusual or "strange" because the human form of the father appears to have become part of the sea.
2. Sample response: The poet may be remembering a love that has ended or a loved one who has died.
3. **Graphic Organizer**
Sample response:
"Full Fathom Five"
Example from Poem: "Nothing of him that doth fade / But doth suffer a sea change / Into something rich and strange"
Paraphrase: His whole body is transformed as it decays.

"Onomatopoeia"
Example from Poem: "The rusty spigot / sputters, / utters / a splutter, / spatters a smattering of drops, / gashes wider"
Paraphrase: The old faucet makes a hissing noise. It spits some drops of water, and the water spreads.

"Train Tune"
Example from Poem: The poem has no punctuation and is meant to be read without pausing.
Paraphrase: The train travels fast across time and place.
4. Students may suggest words such as "slosh," "glug," and "dribble."

Poetry Collection 1

Poetry Collection 2

p. 226 Graphic Organizer
Sample response:
Poetry Collection 1:
"Annabel Lee"
Original: "The angels, not half so happy in Heaven, / Went envying her and me."
Unfamiliar Words: "envying"
Dictionary Definitions: "Envying" means wanting to have something that someone else has.
Paraphrase: The angels were not as happy as the speaker and Annabel Lee. They wanted what the lovers had.

Poetry Collection 2:
"Father William"
Original: "In my youth,' said the sage, as he shook his gray locks, / 'I kept all my limbs very supple'"

Unfamiliar Words: *sage, locks, supple*
Dictionary Definitions of Unfamiliar Words: *sage* = wise man, *locks* = hair, *limbs* = arms and legs, *supple* = flexible
Paraphrase: "When I was young," the wise man said as he shook his gray hair, "I kept my body very flexible."

p. 227 Reading/Writing Connection
Sample response: The president has dedicated his/her life to helping Americans. He/She represents the people of the United States. His/Her actions affect the entire world.

p. 227 Note-taking Guide
Sample response:
"Martin Luther King"
Topic of Poem: Martin Luther King
Feelings the Speaker Has for the Topic: admiration; hope

"I'm Nobody"
Topic of Poem: Being a normal person instead of famous.
Feelings the Speaker Has for the Topic: dislike; finds fame boring

p. 228 Activate Prior Knowledge
A student may recall the words to "Pride (In the Name of Love)" by U2: "One man come in the name of love / One man come and go / One man come, he to justify / One man to overthrow."

p. 228 Literary Analysis
Students should circle the following syllables: "man-," "year," and "-go" in the first line; and "king-," "by," and "sea" in the second line.

p. 228 Vocabulary and Pronunciation
Students should circle "sepulcher," in which "ch" is pronounced "k." They should also circle "child" or "chilling," in which "ch" is pronounced "ch."

p. 229 Read Fluently
Students should circle "the wind."

p. 229 Reading Skill
Students may find words and phrases such as "Heaven above," "demons," "dissever," and "my soul from the soul" confusing. Students may paraphrase with these words: "Nothing can separate my soul from Annabel Lee's soul."

p. 229 Reading Check
Students should underline "I see the bright eyes / Of the beautiful Annabel Lee."

p. 230 Culture Note
Students from South Africa may compare Nelson Mandela to King. Both men fought for the rights of their people.

p. 230 Literary Analysis
Students should circle the following syllables: "came," "-on," and "age" in the first line; "-set," "grief," and "rage" in the second line.

p. 230 Build English Skills
Students should circle "dreary," "public," "livelong," and "admiring."

p. 231 Apply the Skills
1. Sample response: The poet means that King's passion was very strong and powerful.
2. Sample response: "I'm Nobody" talks about how celebrities are always in public. They never have private time. They have to keep their admirers happy. This lifestyle can become boring and annoying.
3. Sample response: Annabel Lee's relatives took her body from the speaker. They buried it in a tomb by the sea.
4. **Graphic Organizer**
Sample response:
"Annabel Lee" ago, know; sea, Lee, me; we, sea, Lee; beams, dreams; rise, eyes; nighttide, side, bride.

p. 233 Reading/Writing Connection
Sample response:
1. A person's outlook on life can affect how well you remember him or her.
2. Someone with a positive attitude can enrich the lives of others.
3. He or she can teach others to appreciate simple pleasures.

p. 233 Note-taking Guide
Sample response:
Characters in Poem:
"Father William" Father William, his son
"Stopping by Woods . . . " a traveler

Actions in Poem:
"Jim" The sun shines on Jim. Jim brings his mother cocoa, broth, bread, and medicine. Jim tiptoes and tidies her room. He misses his baseball game.
"Father William" Father William and his son discuss the father's behavior. Father William stands on his head, turns a somersault, eats goose bones, and balances an eel on the end of his nose.

"**Stopping by Woods . . .** " A traveler stops to watch the woods fill up with snow. The person wonders at the beauty and quiet of the snow and then continues the journey.

p. 234 Apply the Skills
1. Sample response: Jim's decision to give up his baseball game to take care of his mother shows that he is not selfish.
2. Students may say that they are surprised by Father William's actions. He seems too old and too large to stand on his head, or do somersaults.
3. Sample response: The only other sound in the wood is the wind blowing gently and the snow falling softly.
4. **Graphic Organizer**
Rhyming Words:
"Father William" said, head; white, right; son, none; brain, again; before, door; fat, that; locks, box; supple, couple; weak, beak; suet, do it; law, jaw; wife, life; suppose, nose; ever, clever; enough, stuff; airs, downstairs
"Stopping by Woods . . . " know, though, snow; here, queer, year; lake, shake, mistake, flake; sweep, deep, keep, sleep

Reading Informational Materials: Magazine Articles

p. 236 Graphic Organizer
Sample response:
Sentence or Passage: It could be the hammering lyrics of a rap artist.
Replacement Words: hammering = pounding; lyrics = words
Paraphrase: It could be the pounding words of the rap artist.

p. 237 Reading Magazine Articles
Sample response: The people dancing are interesting to look at.

p. 237 Reading Skill
Students should circle "*Odyssey Magazine*, March 2002."

p. 237 Reading Check
Students should underline "Rap as a popular music style started in the late 1970s."

p. 237 Reading Magazine Articles
Sample response: The title catches a reader's attention. The title uses alliteration to help the reader understand that rap music is like poetry.

p. 238 Stop to Reflect
Sample response: Reading a poem and reading Dr. Seuss are like rap music. They use strong rhythmic phrasing.

p. 238 Reading Magazine Articles
Sample response: The main idea is "Sampling serves up yet more rhythms in rap."

p. 238 Reading Check
Students should circle "'MC' is the same as 'emcee' and stands for 'master of ceremonies'"

p. 239 Read Fluently
Students should put a 1 next to "ONE" and a 2 next to "Three."

p. 239 Reading Skill
Sample response: Listeners need interesting rhythm patterns to enjoy music. Rap music uses a mix of rhythms. It also has unpredictable lyrics and syncopation. Rap music is fun because it pleases and amazes listeners.

p. 239 Reading Informational Materials
Sample response: The last paragraph ties together the ideas in the article. It also lets the reader know that this paragraph is the end of the article.

p. 239 Reading Check
Students should circle "Too fast, and the brain can't perceive individual sounds. The music becomes one big blur."

p. 240 Apply the Skills
Thinking About the Magazine Article
1. Sample response: Tempo sets the mood for music. Tempo must not be too fast or too slow, or the song will not sound right.
2. Sample response: The brain remembers groups or patterns of rhythms in music. Music must use patterns or the brain will not process the sounds.

Reading Skill
3. Sample response: Rap is about people. Some rap songs get noticed.
4. Sample response: Sampling is taking a small part of one song and using it over and over to add background to a new song.

from Dragonwings
Laurence Yep

p. 243 Note-taking Guide
Sample response:
Novel: The narrator gets out of bed to answer the door.
Drama: Moon Shadow writes to his mother. Windrider and others pull Dragonwings to the top of the hill. Windrider flies and then falls to the ground. Windrider tells Moon Shadow that he will not fly again.
Both: Moon Shadow learns that Uncle and others have come to help Father get the flying machine up the hill.

p. 244 Activate Prior Knowledge
Some students may describe a place on a mountain. It would be a flat area, and not high enough for snow to be present. Other students may describe an airport runway, long and flat and surrounded by grass.

p. 244 Fiction
Sample response: The actor playing Moon Shadow would have to show his surprise and happiness with facial expressions. He would smile and his eyes would grow wide with surprise. The actors playing the other characters would have to use body language to show that they are tired from coming up the hill. They would try to catch their breath, and their shoulders might be slumped.

p. 244 Stop to Reflect
Sample response: Uncle's actions show that he cares about his brother.

p. 245 Build English Skills
Sample response: Uncle said, "I'll be there to haul your machine up the hill, and I'll be there to haul it back down when it does not fly."

p. 245 Reading Check
Students should circle "he had come to help because he wanted to make up for the bad things his son had done to us."

p. 246 Drama
Students should circle "Miss Whitlaw."
Sample response: White Deer is the third laundry owner.

p. 246 Read Fluently
Students should underline "Windrider," "Uncle Bright Star," and "Moon Shadow."

Students should write: Uncle: Uncle Bright Star; Narrator: Moon Shadow; Father: Windrider.

p. 246 Drama
Sample response: Uncle cares about his brother. He is helping even though he does not believe in flying machines. He notices how thin and ragged his brother has become.

p. 247 Drama
Students should underline "In pantomime, Windrider illustrates to the others how to put the heavy ropes over their shoulder to pull the airplane up the hill," "Windrider positions himself as if on board a plane, while Miss Whitlaw pantomimes turning the right propeller, and Moon Shadow pantomimes turning the left propeller. Through sound effects, we hear the roar of the plane's engine, and Windrider begins a ballet to simulate flying." Sample response: These lines would make good stage directions because no one is talking. The lines are just describing how people are moving and what the sound effects should be, which is what stage directions do.

p. 247 Reading Check
Students should underline "He's really flying" and "A human up in the sky. Off the ground."

p. 248 Vocabulary and Pronunciation
Students should underline "directly."
Students should circle "speaks."

p. 248 Drama
Students should underline "speaks directly to the audience." Students may say that they know it is a monologue because Moon Shadow is not talking with any other characters.

p. 248 Read Fluently
Students should list "as an adult," "the adult Moon Shadow," "the scene shifts back to Moon Shadow's childhood," and "Then the scene shifts again."

p. 248 Reading Check
Students should underline "He wants to become a merchant so that he will be able to bring his wife, Moon Shadow's mother, here from China."

p. 249 Stop to Reflect
Sample response: He will not fly Dragonwings again. Windrider feels that his son is more important to him than flying.

p. 249 Build English Skills
Sample response: The gymnast had to strike a pose when she was done with her routine.

p. 250 Apply the Skills
1. Sample response: The audience knows that the actors move Dragonwings up the hill because the actors pantomime putting the ropes over their shoulders and pulling.
2. Sample response: Moon Shadow is saying that he and his father never forgot about building another airplane. Even though they did not, they still dreamed of doing so.
3. Sample response: The drama enhances the emotion of the situation because actors add tone, facial expressions, and body language to the scene, and these all enhance the emotion of a situation. Drama also enhances emotion because the audience can see the scene unfold before them, not just read about it.
4. Graphic Organizer
Sample response:
To Show Action: "He's really flying."
To Reveal Thoughts and Feelings: "I thought he'd fly forever and ever."
To Describe Setting: "And I'll haul that thing back down when it does not fly."

A Christmas Carol: Scrooge and Marley, Act I
Israel Horovitz
from A Christmas Carol
by Charles Dickens

p. 252 Graphic Organizer
Sample response:
What Is Suggested About the Work?
Picture: It will be set in the past.
Organization, Structure, Literary Form: It will be a play with many characters, acts, and scenes, and a story told through dialogue.
Beginnings of Passages: There will be ghosts and supernatural events.

p. 253 Reading/Writing Connection
Sample response:
1. A scrooge is someone who cares only about himself or herself.
2. Being a scrooge does not involve being generous to others.
3. A scrooge does not appreciate family and friends.

p. 253 Note-taking Guide
Sample response:
Evidence 1: He refuses to spend Christmas Eve with his nephew's family; he will not give money to help the poor.
Evidence 2: As a boy, he loved his sister; as a young man, he was happy with his friends and his boss.
Evidence 3: He wishes he had treated Cratchit more kindly; he wishes he had not chosen greed over the woman he loved.

p. 254 Activate Prior Knowledge
Some students may say that ghosts appear in stories to frighten readers. Other students may say that the role of a ghost is to give a warning to the living. Some may also say that ghosts act as observers in stories. Students may say that they remember the story of the Headless Horseman or a cartoon ghost.

p. 254 Reading Skill
Students may circle "Ebenezer Scrooge," "Scrooge's lost love," "A Corpse," "The Ghost of Christmas Past," "The Ghost of Christmas Present," or "The Ghost of Christmas Future."

p. 254 Vocabulary and Pronunciation
Students should circle "B." Students may say that a joke is something people tell in order to make other people laugh cheerfully.

p. 255 Reading Skill
Students may say that they looked at how long the play is and how many characters are in it. Some students may say that their purpose is to be entertained. Other students may say that their purpose is to be inspired because the play takes place on a day that is an important spiritual holiday for some people.

p. 255 Read Fluently
Students should underline "Ghostly music in the auditorium. A single spot light on Jacob Marley, D. C. He is ancient; awful, dead-eyed. He speaks straight out to auditorium," "Cackle-voiced," "He laughs" and "Pause; remembers."

p. 255 Reading Check
Students should underline "Scrooge was too stingy to remove Marley's name from the sign on their office."

p. 256 Literary Analysis

Some students may say the lines show that Scrooge is selfish and mean.

p. 256 Build English Skills

Students should choose "to celebrate or observe." Sample response: It is the second definition because the text is talking about Christmas, and people cannot physically hold a holiday.

p. 256 Reading Check

Students should circle "A Merry Christmas to you, Uncle! God save you!" and "What reason have you to be morose? You're rich enough."

p. 257 Reading Skill

Sample response: Scrooge will probably learn a lesson about the true meaning of Christmas and how good it is to be kind and giving.

p. 257 Culture Note

Sample response: As in America, the work day ends at 5 P.M.

p. 257 Literary Analysis

Sample response: Some students may say the lines show that Scrooge is a bully. Students may also say that Scrooge is needlessly stingy.

p. 257 Stop to Reflect

Sample response: Cratchit is a good and giving man. He worries about other people's hardships more than he worries about his own.

p. 258 Literary Analysis

Sample response: The audience can tell that Scrooge is in a bad mood and that he does not feel the holiday spirit.

p. 258 Reading Skill

Students may underline "the door knocker changes into Marley's face," "the face disappears," "The pictures on the walls show Marley's face," "all the bells in the house begin to ring," and "hears a loud chain dragging across his basement floor and up the stairs. He hears doors fly open."

p. 258 Culture Note

Some students may say that basements are common and that they are used for storing food. Others may say that basements are not common.

p. 259 Build English Skills

Students should write: Present tense: I am; Past tense: You were.

p. 259 Literary Analysis

Sample response: Scrooge's words suggest he is neither impressed nor frightened by the strange visions and sounds at the beginning of the scene.

p. 259 Stop to Reflect

Sample response: Marley is the first ghost to appear to Scrooge because he knew Scrooge when he was alive.

p. 259 Reading Check

Students should circle "Marley screams a ghostly scream and removes his head from his shoulders."

p. 260 Reading Skill

Sample response: Scrooge comes home and Marley's ghost appears to him. Scrooge is frightened but does not truly believe in Marley's ghost. Marley screams and Scrooge believes. Marley tells Scrooge that he will be visited by Three Spirits. Marley leaves and Scrooge begins to think that he might have imagined the whole thing. Students' questions may include: Will any ghosts visit Scrooge? Why will they visit? What will they do with Scrooge? Will it change him?

p. 260 Literary Analysis

Sample response: Marley talks directly to the audience because he has to inform them about the change they will see in Scrooge.

p. 260 Build English Skills

Students should circle the exclamation points following "heed," "Rise," "me," and "fly."

p. 261 Stop to Reflect

Some students may say they would be scared to meet a ghost. Other students may say that they would like to meet a ghost who could show them their past.

p. 261 Build English Skills

Students should underline "open," "soft," "downy," and "country." Students should circle "open."

p. 261 Literary Analysis

Sample response: Remembering his own lonely experience as a boy allows Scrooge to relate to the singing boy.

p. 261 Reading Check
Students should circle "Bear just a touch of my hand here" and "touches the spirit's heart."

p. 262 Culture Note
Students may list white, purple, or gold as a color of mourning from their country.

p. 262 Build English Skills
Students could circle "crying."

p. 262 Vocabulary and Pronunciation
Sample response: Family members aspire to make each other proud.

p. 263 Read Fluently
Sample response: The woman shows that this conversation is very difficult for her because she loves Scrooge very much. The woman is both angry and sad.

p. 263 Reading Skill
Students may say they look forward to seeing where the Ghosts take Scrooge next and that their purpose is to be entertained. They may also want to see whether Scrooge's behavior will change. Students may say that their purpose for reading Act II is to be entertained and inspired. Sample response: Will Scrooge learn to be kind and giving to others? Will Scrooge be kinder toward his nephew and Bob Cratchit?

p. 263 Reading Check
Students should underline "Don't release me, madam . . ."

p. 264 Apply the Skills
1. Sample response: No, Scrooge is a lonely and bitter man because he has replaced kindness and a giving spirit with greed.
2. Sample response: Scrooge currently treats people harshly. In the future, he might try to build friendly relationships with the people around him.
3. Some students may say that they are reading this play in order to be entertained. Others may be reading to be inspired. Some students may expect both.
4. **Graphic Organizer**
Sample response:
What Does It Say? "If I could work my will, every idiot who goes around with 'Merry Christmas' on his lips, should be boiled with his own pudding, and buried with a stake of holly in his heart."

What Does It Mean? Scrooge wants all people who celebrate Christmas to be punished.
Why Is It Important? It shows how mean and heartless Scrooge is at the beginning of the play.

A Christmas Carol:
Scrooge and Marley, Act II
Israel Horovitz
from **A Christmas Carol**
by Charles Dickens

p. 266 Graphic Organizer
Sample response:
Types of Reading Material: Dialogue
Purpose for Reading: To be entertained
Reading Rate: Read quickly to imitate conversation.

p. 267 Note-taking Guide
Sample response:
Details That Support These Statements:
Row 1: Scrooge says, "Spirit, tell me if Tiny Tim will live."
Row 2: "A nervous giggle here," "Oh, Ghost of the Future, I fear you more than any Specter I have seen!"
Row 3: "I am as happy as a schoolboy," "An act of kindness is like the first green grape of summer: it leads to another and another and another."

p. 268 Apply the Skills
1. Sample response: Scrooge feels drawn to the caring young boy.
2. Sample response: Scrooge's actions suggest that he has taken the lessons to heart. His Christmas generosity shows that he thinks of others and that he now enjoys giving.
3. Students may say that they read long speeches with difficult vocabulary slowly and carefully to improve their understanding of the text.
4. **Graphic Organizer**
Sample response:
Characters on Stage: Scrooge, Marley
Movement of Characters: Marley moves close to the sleeping Scrooge.
Description of Lighting: a spotlight on Scrooge and one on Marley, lightning flashes, candle, colors change
Description of Sound: singing, thunder, ghostly music; Marley laughs and speaks.
Other Special Effects: A flame shoots from Marley's hand.

Reading Informational Materials: Literary Criticism

p. 270 Graphic Organizer
Sample response:
TNT
Critic's summary: none
Positive comments: "But TNT's *Carol* would be worth watching if only for the lead performance of Patrick Stewart."
Negative comments: "gratuitous special effects"
Critic's overall opinion: "Old story well told."

Meadow Brook Theater
Critic's summary: none
Positive comments: "Wicks has infused the show with new energy," "a more palatable holiday treat for adults and children"
Negative comments: "paying only passing attention to his English accent"
Critic's overall opinion: "A well-produced, grand-scale event that is as much pageant as play."

p. 271 Reading Check
Students should underline "But TNT's *Carol* would be worth watching if only for the lead performance of Patrick Stewart."

p. 271 Reading Literary Criticism
Students should underline: "TNT" and "Sun., Dec. 5, 8 P.M., ET." Sample response: The audience for this review is people who have televisions and who might want to watch *A Christmas Carol*.

p. 271 Reading Skill
Students should circle "Bottom line: Old story well told." Sample response: The critic would recommend that people watch this show. The critic thinks that this show is different from other versions of *A Christmas Carol* and therefore should be watched.

p. 272 Reading Skill
Sample response: The writer is positive about the change made by the director and will probably write a good review. Students may underline "make the old holiday fruitcake seem fresh."

p. 272 Reading Literary Criticism
Students may underline "The audience is still serenaded by a band of merry carolers in the lobby before the show," "the set and costumes are unchanged from these many Christmases past," and "set design for the show is, as always, enormous and gorgeous." Sample response: Kelleher discusses the actors more than the scenery and the atmosphere of the production because people will probably watch the show on television to see the famous actors. For the local production, audiences want to know about the actors, but the set and atmosphere are also important.

p. 272 Stop to Reflect
Sample response: The sets for this play had to show many different locations and some of these had to show both past and future events. It might have been difficult for the stage crew to change the scenes without interrupting the actors' performances. It would also have been difficult for the technical crew to make sure that the ghosts' appearances, disappearances, and scary voices sound real and happen at the correct times.

p. 273 Reading Check
Students should circle "pageant" and "beautifully wrapped gift under a well-decorated tree."

p. 273 Reading Informational Materials
Some students may say that hearing about the wonderful lights and staging of the play makes them want to see the production in the theater. Other students may say that the description of Patrick Stewart's performance makes them want to watch the TNT version.

p. 273 Culture Note
Students may say they enjoy celebrating Cinco de Mayo or the Chinese New Year with their families.

p. 273 Reading Skill
Students should underline "A well-produced, grand-scale event that is as much pageant as a play." Sample response: The production is large and impressive, which shows that it was done with care.

p. 274 Apply the Skills
Thinking About the Literary Criticism
1. Sample response: *People Weekly*: "So you muttered 'humbug' when you spied yet another version of *A Christmas Carol* on the TV schedule." *Oakland Press*: "Director Debra Wicks has tinkered with Meadow Brook's recipe for *A Christmas Carol* just enough to make the old holiday fruitcake seem fresh."

2. Sample response: Kelleher believes that people should watch the production if only to see Patrick Stewart's portrayal of Scrooge.

Reading Skill

3. Sample response: The phrase "like a beautifully wrapped gift under a well-decorated tree, it suits the season to a tee," summarizes Sousanis's opinion.

4. Sample response: Kelleher thinks that the story has been done too many times.

The Monsters Are Due on Maple Street
Rod Serling

p. 275 Graphic Organizer

Sample response:

Character: Charlie
Action 1: says Les needs to be watched
Motive 1: thinks Les may be dangerous
Action 2: takes gun from Steve
Motive 2: wants to protect neighborhood
Action 3: shoots Pete
Motive 3: is afraid that Pete is an alien

p. 276 Reading/Writing Connection

Sample response:

1. It is easy to arouse suspicions by being different.
2. Too often, we contribute to rumors by repeating them without thinking.
3. Sadly, if you try to dispute a rumor, you will often become the object of another rumor.

p. 276 Note-taking Guide

Sample response:

Box 1: The neighbors turn on Charlie.
Box 2: People get scared.
Box 3: The figures in the space craft wait for the people to destroy themselves.
Box 4: Figure 1 explains to Figure 2 how to take over the world.

p. 277 Activate Prior Knowledge

Some students may have noticed that people in groups can get out of control quickly. Other students may have noticed that people sometimes do not express their opinions freely in large groups.

p. 277 Literary Analysis

Sample response: Goodman's motive in telling Steve not to step on the porch is that Goodman does not want anything to happen to his house and family.

p. 277 Reading Check

Students should circle "the Goodman house."

p. 278 Vocabulary and Pronunciation

Students should circle "Noun."

p. 278 Literary Analysis

Sample response: Steve becomes anxious and sarcastic. This tells readers that Steve sees that things are getting out of control and that he thinks Charlie is not making sense.

p. 278 Reading Check

Students should underline "self-appointed hanging judge."

p. 279 Build English Skills

Students should circle "it's," "It's," "It's," "didn't," "didn't," "We're," "that's," "that's," "didn't," and "didn't."

p. 279 Literary Analysis

Sample response: Charlie reacts this way because Pete's death is a very serious consequence of Charlie's behavior. Charlie realizes he has just committed murder in front of many people.

p. 279 Reading Skill

Sample response: Charlie claims to have thought the person was a monster. He claims he was just protecting his home and that anyone else would have done it. He claims he did not know it was Pete.

p. 279 Reading Check

Students should circle "You killed him, Charlie. You shot him dead!"

p. 280 Reading Skill

Students should underline: "cut their electric power and communication devices, throw them into darkness, and then sit back and wait for them to panic, grow suspicious, and then destroy themselves." Sample response: Yes, this is a good summary of what happened on Maple Street because there really was not anything wrong on Maple Street, but the people turned on one another anyways.

p. 280 Read Fluently

Students should circle the three ellipses following: "It's," "it's," and "It's." Sample response: The ellipses are used to show that Charlie is panicking. He is trying to figure out who he can blame so that people stop blaming him.

p. 280 Stop to Reflect

Sample response: The author repeats these lines because he wants to show how scared Charlie is. Also, he might want to show that the choosing of others to blame is random and not motivated by real information.

p. 281 Reading Skill

Sample response: Figure One plans to let humans destroy themselves. Then, the aliens can take control of the planet.

p. 281 Reading Check

Students should circle "a very successful procedure for conquering humans."

p. 282 Apply the Skills

1. Sample response: Prejudices and attitudes lead people to destroy themselves; these are the tools of conquest.
2. Sample response: The monsters are the residents themselves.
3. **Graphic Organizer**
Sample response:

Important Details from the Beginning:
There is a flash across the sky; the electricity goes out; a boy suggests that aliens may be responsible.

Important Details from the Middle: Les Goodman is suspected of being an alien; it is revealed that Steve has a radio in his basement, and the crowd's suspicions turn to him; Charlie shoots a shadowy figure who turns out to be Pete Van Horn.

Important Details from the End: The crowd accuses Charlie; neighbors begin throwing rocks and smashing windows; Charlie accuses Tommy; the neighbors argue and fight, accusing one another; two aliens review the "procedure" used to get humans to destroy one another.

4. Sample response: Charlie keeps saying, "It's the kid." to throw suspicion off himself. They remember that it was Tommy who knew about the aliens in the first place.

Reading Informational Materials: Application

p. 285 Reading Informational Materials

Sample response: The playhouse wants to show the type and quality of its productions.

p. 285 Read Fluently

Students should underline "it," "its," "its," and "its." Sample response: The "It" stands for the Flat Rock Playhouse.

p. 285 Reading Applications

Sample response: The last sentence of the first paragraph suggests that the playhouse is looking for people who want to be apprentices and interns because a major purpose of the playhouse is to train people to perform there.

p. 286 Reading Applications

Sample response: This application requires an address and Social Security number.

p. 286 Stop to Reflect

Sample response: Most people who fill out this application are probably in high school or college because there is a space for "Parent/ Guardian Name."

p. 286 Reading Skill

Sample response: They are part of the same group because at the top of the application it says that people should contact the Flat Rock Playhouse for information about the Vagabond School.

p. 286 Reading Check

Students should circle "However, if one's schedule or geographic distance from the Playhouse makes a personal audition impossible, one may send a videotaped audition consisting of two monologues and if applicable examples of singing and dance work."

p. 288 Apply the Skills
Thinking About the Application

1. Sample response: Applicants do not need much space to write a name. More space is included for the applicants' previous instruction so that applicants can list complete information and because this information is important to the school.
2. Sample response: The Vagabond School of the Drama provides advantages for someone looking for a career in acting because it provides opportunities for networking with professionals and education for marketing oneself in the theater business.

Reading Skill

3. The school requires a headshot or snapshot.
4. The section titled "Instruction" is designed to determine the applicant's experience.

"Grasshopper Logic"

"The Other Frog Prince"

**"duckbilled platypus
vs. beefsnakstik®"**
Jon Scieszka and Lane Smith

p. 291 Note-taking Guide
Sample response:
"Grasshopper Logic"
Characters: Grasshopper, Mom Grasshopper
Problem: Grasshopper has waited too long
to do a big homework assignment.
Moral: "There are plenty of things to say
to calm a hopping mad Grasshopper mom.
'I don't know' is not one."

"The Other Frog Prince"
Characters: a frog, a princess
Problem: A frog says he is really a prince.
Moral: You should not believe everything
you hear.

"duckbilled platypus vs. beefsnakstik®"
Characters: Duckbilled Platypus,
BeefSnakStik®
Problem: Each character thinks it is better
than the other.
Moral: Just because you have a lot of stuff,
do not think you are so special.

p. 292 Activate Prior Knowledge
Sample response: A child lies. A child disobeys.
A child does not do his or her schoolwork.

p. 292 Oral Tradition
Sample response: My mom freaked out when
I forgot to call her.

p. 292 Oral Tradition
The assignment is exaggerated. It asks for
twelve musicals with designed and built sets.
One student cannot be expected to do all of
that work.

p. 292 Reading Check
Students should underline "Just one small
thing for History."

p. 293 Oral Tradition
Students should circle "frog."

p. 293 Oral Tradition
Sample response: In this story, the opposite
happens. The princess kisses the frog, but

the frog does not turn into the prince. The
frog lies to the princess to get a kiss.

p. 293 Vocabulary and Pronunciation
Spell is being used as a noun meaning
"a magical state."

p. 293 Reading Check
Students should underline "and the spell
can only be broken by the kiss of a
beautiful princess."

p. 294 Read Fluently
Sample response: I think the author uses
the ® because it adds humor to the story.

p. 294 Oral Tradition
Students should circle "Duckbilled Platypus."
Students should underline "BeefSnakStik®."

p. 294 Stop to Reflect
Sample response: The words in bold type
imply that the speaker is shouting or
speaking louder.

p. 295 Apply the Skills
1. Some students may prefer "Grasshopper
Logic" because they can relate to Grasshopper
procrastinating about his homework. Other
students may prefer "The Other Frog Prince"
because they are familiar with the original
fairy tale and like the funny ending. Others
may prefer the last story because it is very
silly and different from the original version.
2. Grasshopper wants his mother to allow
him to go out to play.
3. Sample response: Do not trust everything
you hear.
4. **Graphic Organizer**
Sample response:
"Grasshopper Logic"
Personification: talking grasshoppers;
a grasshopper that goes to school, carries
a backpack, plays with friends, and
has homework

"The Other Frog Prince"
Hyperbole: the princess kisses a frog
so quickly
Personification: a frog talks
"duckbilled platypus vs. beefsnakstik®"
Hyperbole: BeefSnakStik argues with a
duckbilled platypus

"Icarus and Daedalus"
Josephine Preston Peabody

"Demeter and Persephone"
Anne Terry White

p. 297 Graphic Organizer
Sample response:
"Icarus and Daedalus"
Cause: King Minos puts Daedalus and Icarus in prison on Crete.
Cause: Daedalus escapes his cell but cannot escape the island.
Cause: Daedalus sees seagulls flying.
Event: Daedalus builds wings to fly away.
Effect: Daedalus and Icarus fly away from Crete.
Effect: Icarus flies too close to the sun and crashes into the sea.
Effect: Daedalus names an island after his son and never flies again.

"Demeter and Persephone"
Sample response:
Cause: Aphrodite tells Eros to shoot an arrow at Pluto.
Cause: Eros shoots an arrow into Pluto's heart.
Cause: Pluto falls in love with Persephone.
Event: Pluto kidnaps Persephone.
Effect: Demeter makes Earth infertile.
Effect: Zeus sends Hermes to ask Pluto to release Persephone.
Effect: Pluto releases Persephone, but she must return during the winter months.

p. 298 Reading/Writing Connection
Sample response:
1. My dentist convinced me to <u>eliminate</u> candy before bedtime.
2. It was difficult to <u>modify</u> my free time so I could study and improve my grades.
3. It was easier to <u>adapt</u> to the new rules than it was to clean my room daily.

p. 298 Note-taking Guide
Sample response:
Second box: Daedalus uses bird feathers, thread, and wax to make wings for himself and his son.
Third box: Daedalus warns Icarus not to fly too close to the sun.
Fourth box: Daedalus and Icarus fly away, but Icarus flies too close to the sun. His wings melt, and he falls into the sea.

p. 299 Activate Prior Knowledge
A student may describe a time when he or she tried to play a very difficult piece of music on an instrument or tried to read a book that was too difficult.

p. 299 Vocabulary and Pronunciation
Students may circle "Crete," "cunningly," "could," and "clue."

p. 299 Reading Skill
Daedalus watches the seagulls flying. He realizes that they are free because of their ability to fly. This realization causes Daedalus to make wings so that he and his son can fly away from the island.

p. 299 Reading Check
Students should circle "Labyrinth."

p. 300 Build English Skills
Students should write "a pair of" on each blank line.

p. 300 Reading Skill
Sample response: Icarus wants to feel joy and freedom when he flies.

p. 300 Read Fluently
Students should circle the -em dashes after "vainly" and "falling."

p. 300 Reading Check
Students should circle "the fogs about the earth would weigh you down."

p. 301 Literary Analysis
Sample response: He tries to teach Icarus how to use the wings safely.

p. 301 Stop to Reflect
Students may say that they would have listened to the advice of their father.

p. 301 Reading Check
Students should underline "in memory of the child."

p. 301 Culture Note
Some students may know the myth of Pegasus, the flying horse. Students may provide other examples.

p. 302 Apply the Skills
1. Sample response: He makes wings from bird feathers, thread, and wax.
2. Sample response: Icarus shows that he is irresponsible. Icarus would rather have fun than be careful in a dangerous situation.

3. Daedalus names an island after his son. In his grief, he offers his wings to the temple of Apollo and never flies again.

4. Graphic Organizer
Sample response:
Icarus: Lesson: You should take warnings of danger seriously.
Daedalus: How Taught: through Icarus' death

p. 304 Reading/Writing Connection
Sample response: I appreciate my favorite season because I love to watch the leaves change color. It serves to unify the summer and the winter. It is hard to specify how beautiful the trees look.

p. 304 Note-taking Guide
Sample response:
Pluto: Falls in love with Persephone; kidnaps her
Demeter: Makes it so that the earth will not produce food
Persephone: Misses the flowers of the earth; eats a pomegranate from the underworld
Zeus: Sends Hermes to ask Pluto to release Persephone

p. 305 Apply the Skills
1. Sample response: Some students may say that Demeter's actions are right because she has lost someone she loves. Others may say that her actions are wrong because her actions will hurt innocent people.
2. Sample response: When Persephone returns to the underworld, Demeter grieves and vegetation dies. When Persephone returns to her mother, Demeter's joy brings life back to the fields.
3. Zeus intervenes, forcing Pluto to release Persephone.
4. Graphic Organizer
Sample response:
Demeter: How Taught: through Demeter's search for and grief for her lost daughter, which caused her to change the earth
Persephone: Lesson: Appearances may be deceiving. **How Taught:** through Pluto's love for Persephone and grief at her departure
Pluto: How Taught: through the death of vegetation brought on by Demeter and through Persephone's departure

Reading Informational Materials: Textbooks

p. 308 Reading Textbooks
Students should underline "The Seasons on Earth," "How Sunlight Hits Earth," and "Earth's Tilted Axis." Students should recognize that the headings tell them that they will learn how sunlight and the Earth's axis affect the seasons on Earth.

p. 308 Reading Skill
The Earth's tilted axis causes it to have seasons.

p. 308 Read Fluently
A list of the seasons follows the colon in the first sentence.

p. 308 Reading Informational Materials
Sample response: The headings tell me what I am reading about and help me understand the main idea of each section. The figure and its caption illustrate the ideas in the text.

p. 310 Apply the Skills
Thinking About the Textbook
1. As it is the beginning of summer at that time, one would expect warm weather in the Northern Hemisphere.
2. Because they receive the most direct sunlight all year, people living near the equator experience warmer temperatures.

Reading Skill
3. The tilt of Earth's axis causes the yearly cycle.
4. The season is summer.

"Tenochtitlan: Inside the Aztec Capital" Jacqueline Dineen

"Popocatepetl and Ixtlaccihuatl" Juliet Piggott Wood

p. 311 Graphic Organizer
Sample response:
"Tenochtitlan: Inside the Aztec Capital"
Cause/Effect: *Because* Tenochtitlan was built in a swamp, the city needed land to grow food.
Effect/Cause: The people built chinampas, or small islands, where they could grow food.
Cause/Effect: *Because* the chinampas were built on the swamp, the huts on them had to be light so that they would not sink.

"Popocatepetl and Ixtlaccihuatl"
Cause/Effect: *Because* some warriors were jealous of Popo's strength and success, they told the emperor that Popo had had been killed in battle.
Effect/Cause: The emperor told Ixtla that Popo had died, and Ixtla died of a broken heart.
Cause/Effect: *As a result of* Ixtla's death, Popo refused to become emperor and had two pyramids built, one for Ixtla and one for himself to watch over her.

p. 312 Reading/Writing Connection
Sample response: City planners should adapt old city centers for the needs of current residents. City roads need to maximize ways to travel through downtown. One can modify a city plan by reworking public transportation.

p. 312 Note-taking Guide
Sample response:
The Floating Gardens: made of piles of earth in the shallow parts of the lakes; called chinampas; supplied with fresh water by ditches and canals
The Homes: nobles' houses: large homes like palaces, one story high around a courtyard, built from adobe and whitewashed; poor people's houses: built on chinampas but not sturdy, grouped with other houses in compounds, had outdoor patio and gardens
The Furniture and Decoration: plain, dirt floor, mats of reeds for sleeping, clay cooking pots and utensils, household shrines with statues of the gods, no windows, no chimneys, no doors, open doorways

p. 313 Activate Prior Knowledge
Students may comment that ancient people lived more simply than people do today. They did not have electricity or toilets or cars. They had to grow their own food.

p. 313 Literary Analysis
Sample response: The Spaniards' first account of Tenochtitlan refers to it as "an enchanted vision." It talks about the city "rising from the water." The Spaniards were impressed with the city, and their account of it likely inspired many stories.

p. 313 Build English Skills
Students should underline "Cortés's soldiers."

p. 313 Reading Check
Students should circle "Stone waterways brought fresh water to the city from the mainland."

p. 314 Reading Skill
Students should mark "The land around the lakes was dry because there was very little rain."

p. 314 Reading Check
Students should circle "Some of the homes were built of adobe, or bricks of mud that had been dried in the sun."

p. 314 Read Fluently
Students should cross out "of flowers and vegetables," "in the courtyards," and "of rich Aztec homes." Students should circle "Gardens."

p. 315 Literary Analysis
Students should circle "What we do know has been pieced together from scattered historical records such as documents that record the sale of building sites on the chinampa gardens."

p. 315 Vocabulary and Pronunciation
Students should underline "A family lived together in one of these compounds." Sample response: The patio was probably a nice place for family members to gather outside. It gave them fresh air and more room to do things.

p. 315 Stop to Reflect
The houses of the rich people were like palaces, had courtyards, and were made from adobe. The houses of the poor people were smaller and built on chinampas. They were built in groups in walled compounds with gardens and patios.

p. 315 Reading Skill
The houses did not have windows or chimneys to vent smoke from cooking fires.

p. 316 Apply the Skills
1. **Graphic Organizer**
Sample response:
Questions: Why is there so little evidence about poor people's houses in Tenochtitlan?
Details: What we know has been pieced together from scattered documents.
Understanding the Article: No remains of poor people's houses survived to be studied.

2. Sample response: The Aztecs built chinampas, which allowed the people of Tenochtitlan to produce more of their own food. Each chinampa produced enough food to feed one family. The Aztecs also dug ditches and built canals to bring fresh water to the city.

3. Sample response: The Aztecs had water for irrigation.

4. Sample response: Two statements: Between one third and one half of people in Tenochtitlan were farmers; farmers' only tools were hoes and sticks. Facts: the Aztecs built three causeways over the swamp; Tenochtitlan was built in a huge valley; water flowed along stone aqueducts from the mainland to Tenochtitlan.

p. 318 Reading/Writing Connection
Sample response: My favorite family stories illustrate what life was like for my ancestors. I hope my children appreciate how difficult life was for our ancestors. These stories reinforce how much our family has struggled.

p. 318 Note-taking Guide
Sample response:

What Popo Does: He buries Ixtla under a heap of stones on one pyramid. He refuses to become emperor and climbs to the top of his own pyramid. He lights a torch and stays there to watch over Ixtla's body.

What Happens: Over the years, the pyramids become high, white-capped mountains.

p. 319 Apply the Skills
1. Graphic Organizer
Sample response:

Questions: Why does the Emperor care whether, after he dies, Ixtla rules alone or with a husband? Why does the Emperor offer his daughter to whoever defeats his enemies?

Details: The Emperor does not think anyone but his daughter will rule as he wants the city to be ruled. Enemies surround the city, and the Emperor is too weak to lead the fight against them.

Understanding the Legend: The Emperor is so proud that he wants to control what happens, even after his death. The Emperor does not think that his daughter can defend the city without help.

2. Sample response: The Aztecs admired people who displayed wisdom, honesty, bravery, and loyalty.

3. Popo's torch, still burning in memory of Ixtla, causes the volcano to smoke.

4. Sample response: Facts: Ixtlaccihuatl and Popocatepetl are volcanic mountains; Popocatepetl means "smoking mountain." The reader knows that they are facts because they can be proven true.

"Sun and Moon in a Box"
Richard Erdoes and Alfonso Ortiz

"How the Snake Got Poison"
Zora Neale Hurston

p. 321 Graphic Organizer
Sample response:

"Sun and Moon in a Box"
Story Title: "Sun and Moon in a Box"
Time: a long time ago, early in the history of Earth
Place: American Southwest, Kachina Pueblo
Customs: Native American dancing
Beliefs: A coyote released the sun and the moon into the sky. This action created winter.

"How the Snake Got Poison"
Story Title: "How the Snake Got Poison"
Time: probably a long time ago
Place: Earth and heaven
Customs: African American dialect
Beliefs: God gave snakes poison to protect themselves against other animals. He also gave snakes rattles to warn other animals of their approach.

p. 322 Reading/Writing Connection
Sample response: Some stories have a character who tries to exploit other characters. He will often convince others to trust him. He might interact with others in a normal way, but he is really trying to trick them.

p. 322 Note-taking Guide
Sample response:

Effect/Cause 1: They want to borrow the sun and moon, so Eagle grabs the box and flies off.

Effect/Cause 2: Coyote wants the box, so he pleads to carry it. He says his family will think badly of him for not helping. He promises not to open the box.

Effect/Cause 3: Eagle gives Coyote the box. Coyote cannot control his curiosity.

Effect/Cause 4: Coyote opens the box, and the sun and moon escape into the sky.

p. 323 Activate Prior Knowledge
Students may be familiar with the Greek legend of the god Apollo and his twin sister Artemis. When Apollo rode his golden chariot across the sky, he was the sun. When Artemis rode her silver chariot across the sky, she was the moon. Students also may be familiar with the Bible's account of God's creation of the sun, moon, and earth.

p. 323 Reading Skill
Sample response: Coyote does not do things well and expects Eagle to help him. Eagle is strong and helps Coyote.

p. 323 Read Fluently
Students should underline "they opened the box enough to let the sun peek out" and "they let the moon look out."

p. 323 Build English Skills
Students should circle *flew*, *sat*, and *saw*.

p. 324 Vocabulary and Pronunciation
Students should circle "Verb."

p. 324 Literary Analysis
Sample response: Eagle says that if Coyote had acted responsibly, they could have always enjoyed summer. The story treats winter as a bad and unpleasant season. Ancient people probably did not like winter as much as summer. They had a hard time finding food and staying warm in the winter.

p. 324 Reading Check
Students should circle "He could not curb his curiosity."

p. 325 Apply the Skills
1. Sample response: Eagle may have decided that Coyote must be serious because of his constant begging to carry the box.
2. Sample response: Eagle shares responsibility. Eagle knew that he should not trust Coyote, but he let him carry the box anyway.
3. **Graphic Organizer**
Sample response:
Coyote: lazy, sneaky, irresponsible
Eagle: strong, responsible, trusting

Both: Both want the box with the sun and the moon; both want to carry the box.
4. Sample response: The Kachinas were Native Americans who lived in the American Southwest. This detail shows that Native Americans from the Southwest told this story.

p. 327 Reading/Writing Connection
Sample response: Most people communicate by talking and writing. When people interact in different settings they behave in different ways. Language helps them comprehend what other people are doing and thinking.

p. 327 Note-taking Guide
Sample response:
Snake: complains to God because he has no protection; takes the poison and kills anything that tries to step on him; explains that he cannot tell who is an enemy and who is a friend
Varmints: tread on snakes and kill them; complain to God when snake gets poison because snake starts killing everything

p. 328 Apply the Skills
1. Sample response: The varmints and the snake are afraid of each other. They dislike and misunderstand each other because of their past actions.
2. Sample response: This answer might reflect how people ignore each other unless there is a threat of harm. It might also show that two people sometimes need a third party to help them solve their differences.
3. **Graphic Organizer**
Sample response:
Snake: living on the ground without protection from other animals; has no poison, rattle, legs, or claws; can see only feet
Varmints: can't see, smell, or hear the snake in the bushes; step on snake and kill its kind
Both: do not see enemies clearly; accidentally kill too many of the other's kind
4. The use of dialect helps readers understand that the folk tale comes from the African-American oral tradition.

Reading Informational Materials: Editorials

p. 330 Graphic Organizer
Sample response:

Animals in Zoos: do not learn the survival techniques needed to live in the wild; provide entertainment; are protected; educate visitors

Animals in the Wild: learn how to survive in their natural habitat; have better chances of success and reproduction; are free to behave naturally

p. 331 Reading Editorials
Sample response: The title suggests that there is a question to be answered. It shows that the author will be expressing an opinion.

p. 331 Reading Skill
The writer compares the zoo to a place of captivity where a person is deprived of his or her natural home and put on display.

p. 331 Read Fluently
Students should circle all instances of *your, you're, you, and they*. Sample response: Most of these pronouns are in second person. They connect the editorial to the reader. They make the discussion personal.

p. 332 Reading Skill
The writer compares and contrasts how animals behave in zoos and how they behave in the wild. Students should underline "but" and "although."

p. 332 Culture Note
Student responses will vary. Students should answer yes or no. If students answer yes, then they should describe their visit.

p. 332 Reading Editorials
The writer supports this point by mentioning that the San Diego Zoo has four shows each day.

p. 333 Reading Editorials
Sample response: The paragraph says that zoos are supposed to be places to learn about and enjoy nature and animals, but that zoos do not live up to these ideals. The author explains that zoos take care of animals, but they do not treat animals with the respect they deserve.

p. 333 Reading Informational Materials
Some students may say that the editorial showed them that zoos are not as good as they thought they were. The article explains that it is not fair to keep animals in small pens and cages. It also explains how animals in zoos do not act as they would in their natural habitats. Therefore, people cannot go to the zoo and learn how animals act in their natural habitats. Other students may think zoos are good places to keep animals. The author admits that zoos take care of animals and protect them.

p. 333 Reading Check
Students should underline "look at the enclosure of the tigers and watch the seals balance a ball on their noses, and then think about what you are really learning from your day at the zoo."

p. 334 Apply the Skills
Thinking About the Editorial
1. The writer claims that zoos neither help endangered animals nor educate the public about animals' authentic behavior.
2. The writer would claim that a film showing lions in the wild is more educational because it shows how lions really behave in their natural environment.

Reading Skill
3. Animals learn survival techniques in the wild.
4. Animals are better off in the wild than in a zoo.

"The People Could Fly"
Virginia Hamilton

"All Stories Are Anansi's"
Harold Courlander

p. 335 Graphic Organizer
Sample response:
"The People Could Fly"
Character 1: Toby: has wings, is an old man, helps Sarah, teaches Sarah and other slaves to fly, says the magic words
Character 2: Sarah: sheds her wings; is a young woman, is a mother, is afraid, has no heart to comfort her baby, is whipped, is weak, is sad, is starving, appeals to Toby for help
Both: slaves, fly away

"All Stories Are Anansi's"
Character 1: Mmoboro: are hornets; fly into a gourd

Character 2: Onini: is a python; gets tied to a pole
Both: are caught by Anansi and taken to the Sky God

p. 336 Reading/Writing Connection
Sample response:
1. Children may not <u>appreciate</u> their stories until they grow older.
2. Families that share stories <u>establish</u> their history.
3. Stories from long ago help <u>define</u> the past for younger generations.

p. 336 Note-taking Guide
Sample response:
What Character Says: "I must go soon"; "Now, before it's too late. . . . Now, Father!"
What Character Does: works in the field; is not able to soothe baby; is whipped by driver; falls down; bleeds; appeals to Toby; flies away
What Character Thinks: She thinks that she does not have the heart to soothe her child.
What Others Say about Character: Driver: "Get up, you black cow." Toby: "Yes, Daughter, the time is come. . . . Go, as you know how to go!"

p. 337 Activate Prior Knowledge
Sample response: "Cinderella" is a tale portraying the enslavement of a young girl at the hands of her stepmother. The tale ends with the girl's freedom.

p. 337 Vocabulary and Pronunciation
b. Some cats <u>shed</u> their fur.

p. 337 Reading Check
Students should underline "But they lost that ability when they were enslaved."

p. 338 Read Fluently
Students should circle "across the babe" and "to the earth."

p. 338 Stop to Reflect
Students may say that they would feel hopeless and depressed. They may think that the Driver is a cruel person who cares only about himself and does not care who he hurts.

p. 338 Reading Skill
Sample response: Sarah is concerned about the welfare of her child; the Driver is not concerned about the welfare of Sarah's child.

p. 339 Reading Check
Students should underline ". . . *buba yali . . . buba tambe . . .*"

p. 339 Build English Skills
Too means "also" in the underlined sentence.

p. 339 Literary Analysis
Students should underline "The Overseer told it."

p. 339 Reading Skill
The Overseer told the story as the narrator tells it. The Master said the story was a lie. The Driver did not say anything.

p. 340 Literary Analysis
The slaves who could not fly away told their children the story. These children told their own children, and so on.

p. 340 Reading Check
Students should circle "The slaves who could not fly told about the people who could fly to their children."

p. 340 Culture Note
Students should list one or more stories or folk tales that have been passed down in their culture. Students from Africa may mention the story of the lazy donkeys or a story about Anansi the trickster.

p. 341 Apply the Skills
1. Sample response: The author uses the African words to represent the free life to which the slaves hope to return. The words represent their history and heritage.
2. "Flying" is a metaphor for being free and living a free life in one's own culture.
3. Sample response: Toby is helpful, caring, and powerful in an unexpected way. The Overseer is brutal, violent, and mean. Both men are leaders, but Toby leads quietly and effectively. The Overseer has to use fear and pain to force people to do what he wants.
4. **Graphic Organizer**
Sample response:
Evil: the Master, the Overseer, the Driver, and their cruelty toward the slaves
Lesson: Remembering your past or your heritage will give you strength; hope and faith are powerful.
Theme: Freedom comes to those who remember how important it is.

p. 343 Reading/Writing Connection

Sample response:

1. Trickster tales require a clever trickster.
2. The trickster will demonstrate cunning and intelligence.
3. Good tricksters exhibit sneakiness.

p. 343 Note-taking Guide

Sample response:

What does Anansi do to the hornets?

Anansi pours water on himself and the hornets' nest. He then tells them to get out of the rain. He convinces them to fly into a gourd. He traps them in the gourd and takes them to the Sky God.

What does Anansi do to the python?

Anansi challenges the python to stretch alongside a bamboo pole. Anansi ties the python to the pole and takes him to the Sky God.

What does Anansi do to the leopard?

Anansi digs and covers a hole into which the leopard falls. Anansi says he will help the leopard and ties the leopard to a bent tree. Anansi cuts the rope holding the tree. The leopard hangs from the tree. Anansi kills him and takes him to the Sky God.

p. 344 Apply the Skills

1. Sample response: Students may infer that all of the animals trust Anansi.
2. Sample response: Anansi is selfish. He will do and say anything to get what he wants.
3. The animals are different in that the hornets are afraid of rain, the python is vain, and the leopard is too trusting. They are similar in that all of the animals are bigger and stronger than Anansi, and yet all are tricked by Anansi.
4. **Graphic Organizer**

Students may notice that elements of good and evil are not very clear in this tale.

Sample response:

Evil: All of the animals are motivated by self-interest.

Lesson: Do not be too trusting; learn to think for yourself.

Theme: Intelligence is more powerful than physical strength or size.

READER'S NOTEBOOK

Using a Dictionary

p. V8

1. Students should circle "n." The "v." stands for verb; "adv." stands for adverb; "adj." stands for adjective; and "prep." stands for preposition.
2. Students should underline "[ME *lymon* < Mfr *limon* < Ar *laimun* < Pers *limun*]." "MFr" stands for Middle French.
3. Students should draw a box around the pronunciation.
4. There are four noun definitions for the entry.
5. Definition four is slang.
6. Definition four is used in the sentence.

p. V9 Activity

1. **Pronunciation:** (lit′ ər ə chər)
Main Part of Speech: noun
Original Language(s): ME *litterature* < OFr < L *litteratura* < *littera*
1st Meaning: books, plays, etc. that are considered very good and that people have liked for a long time
Other Meanings: printed information produced by organizations that want to sell something or tell people about something
2. **Pronunciation:** (laŋ′gwij)
Main Part of Speech: noun
Original Language(s): ME < OFr *langage* < *langue*, tongue < L *lingua*, tongue, language, altered (by assoc. with *lingere*, to lick) < OL *dingwa* < IE *dnghwa* > OE *tunge*, TONGUE
1st Meaning: a system of words, phrases, and grammar, used by people who live in a country or area to communicate with each other
Other Meanings: the use of words, grammar, etc. to communicate with other people; the kind of words that someone uses, or that are used when talking or writing about a particular subject; a system of instructions used in computer programs; any system of signs, movements, sounds, etc. that are used to express meanings or feelings

p. V9 Activity
Sample response:
Moment: A *moment* is a "short portion or point of time." The perfect moment passed me by.
Popular: *Popular* means "commonly liked or approved." Logan wanted to sit with the popular students during lunch.
Remedy: A *remedy* is "a medicine or treatment that cures an illness." Ariel discovered a remedy for her grandmother's illness.
Blur: A *blur* is "a stain or smear that obscures." I couldn't see through the window because of the blur on it.
Lazy: *Lazy* means "not energetic." My brother is lazy because he doesn't do any chores or his homework.

Unit 1: Academic Vocabulary Words

p. V12 A. True/False
1. T
2. F; Sample response: If you had a previous experience playing on a team, you do not need to be introduced to the rules of the game.
3. T
4. T
5. F; Sample response: If you have an appointment prior to the first class in the morning, you cannot go after lunch.
6. F; Sample response: When learning new words as you read, pay attention to the context of the paragraph.
7. F; Sample response: If you are giving a surprise party for a friend, it is best to not reveal your plan to him.
8. T
9. F; Sample response: If something has significance, it is very important.
10. T

p. V13 B. Completion
Sample response:
1. It is important to know the *background* of an author to write a research report on him or her.
2. You can use an explanation to *clarify* the meaning of a term.

3. The *context* of a word is the information that surrounds it.

4. If you want to *establish* a good reputation in school, you should always complete your homework on time and follow the rules.

5. Three of my *previous* teachers were my teachers in primary school.

6. One advantage of having *prior* knowledge of a story is that you already know the general plot.

7. I like to *recall* my favorite poem, which is "The Raven" by Edgar Allan Poe.

8. If you *reveal* the secret location of the meeting, the spy will know where to go.

9. Please, explain the *significance* of the blue sweater in the mystery novel.

10. To *verify* your identity, it is important to carry your driver's license.

Unit 2: Academic Vocabulary Words

p. V14 A. True/False

1. F; Sample response: Matthew says that he is able to anticipate what will happen tomorrow.

2. T

3. F; Sample response: As the leaves changed colors, Sam began to conclude that autumn was here.

4. T

5. T

6. T

7. T

8. F; Sample response: Please, indicate which dishes are dirty after you are through eating.

9. T

10. F; Sample response: You can predict that a car is going to turn left if the left blinker is on.

p. V15 B.

Sample response:

Anticipate: We anticipate that there will be a large crowd, given the ticket sales.

Conclude: I can conclude that the necklace is Jackie's because I have seen her wearing it.

Credible: Evan told a credible story about his trip to Alaska.

Indicate: Please indicate which pencil you want me to use.

Object: I saw the object in the kitchen.

Perspective: I read the story to discover the author's perspective.

Plot: The plot of the story had many unexpected twists and turns.

Predict: I predict that our team will win the volleyball tournament.

Subject: The subject of the article is endangered species.

Verify: I need to verify the statement to figure out whether it is true.

Unit 3: Academic Vocabulary Words

p. V16 A. Completion

Sample response:

1. The *almanac* contained information about events in 2005.

2. Go back to the house and *check* that the stove was turned off.

3. The test is meant to *evaluate* your skills in grammar.

4. Read the paragraph and *identify* the main idea.

5. The boy felt *insignificant* when he was not chosen for the team.

6. The inspector will *investigate* the building to look for clues to the crime.

7. The most *irrelevant* information I have learned in school is how to diagram sentences.

8. The most *relevant* information I have learned in school is the history of the United States of America.

9. The most *significant* event of the day was when I was awarded the medal.

10. A *valid* reason to go to school is that my education will help prepare me for the future.

p. V17 B.

Sample response:

Almanac: I looked in the almanac to find information about events in 1998.

Check: I will check to see whether we turned the lights off in the house.

Evaluate: I will evaluate whether I liked the article or not.

Identity: I use my passport to prove my identity at the airport.

Insignificant: The detail of the iron kettle was insignificant in the plot of the story.

Investigate: We will investigate the case of the missing stereo.

Irrelevant: Duncan revealed information that was irrelevant to our case.

Relevant: The relevant information Carrie received helped her finish her science project.
Significant: My history teacher tells me about significant events in American history.
Valid: Her reasons for not being in school were valid.

Unit 4: Academic Vocabulary Words

p. V18 A. True/False

1. T
2. F; Sample response: A list that highlights someone's strengths would indicate all the accomplishments the person has achieved.
3. F; Sample response: To emphasize your point, it is best to speak clearly.
4. T
5. F; Sample response: To paraphrase the words of a song for an audience, put the lyrics in your own words.
6. F; Sample response: Reading a passage of a story will not take as much time as reading the whole story.
7. T
8. F; Sample response: If your friend came in to the classroom soaking wet, you might correctly infer there was a thunderstorm.
9. T
10. T

p. V19 B. Completion

Sample response:

1. If you see that the door is open and the lights are on you can *conclude* that people are home.
2. A bloodhound uses its nose to *detect* people's scents.
3. When giving an oral report, it is important to *emphasize* the important points and supporting details.
4. If you see dark clouds in the sky, you can *infer* that a storm is coming.
5. You would *highlight* sentences in a book that may help you study for a test.
6. When you *paraphrase* a poem, you restate the poem in your own words.
7. When I come across a long *passage* in a story, I try to focus on the main ideas.
8. To find information on snakes, I would *refer* to an encyclopedia.
9. If you were to *restate* what you heard at a meeting, you would summarize the information.

10. A magician is able to *transform* a watch into a dove.

Unit 5: Academic Vocabulary Words

p. V20 A. True/False

1. F; Sample response: Most assumptions turn out to be inaccurate.
2. T
3. F; Sample response: Chronological order goes from first event to last event.
4. T
5. F; Sample response: When you write a critique of a poem, you write facts and opinions.
6. F; Sample response: It is not a good idea to watch television while you are studying to help you focus.
7. T
8. F; Sample response: An appropriate reaction to a scary movie is screaming.
9. T
10. F; Sample response: When you summarize a story, you tell only the important events.

p. V21 B. Completion

Sample response:

1. Student *involvement* in a classroom is good because people learn more when they participate.
2. If you change the *sequence* of steps in a process, the end result might be surprising.
3. We can't wait to see the movie again because our *reaction* the first time was one of excitement and pleasure.
4. After my friend *summarized* the story, I knew all the important events.
5. In a movie I liked, there was a *conflict* between the two main characters.
6. An important *characteristic* of a rain storm is thunder.
7. Writers can use *critiques* of their work to improve their work in the future.
8. When you tell the *chronological* story of someone's life, the first event is birth.
9. One thing that can help you *focus* as you read is placing yourself in a quiet room.
10. One *assumption* people often make about children is that they are fast learners.

Unit 6: Academic Vocabulary Words

p. V22 A. Code Name

1. unique
2. effect
3. consequence
4. alter
5. detail
6. analyze
7. affect
8. occur
9. characteristic
10. aspect

p. V23 B. True/False

1. F; Sample response: We saw the unique hat on only one boy in the park.
2. T
3. F; Sample response: The effect of the car crash was a dented hood on the car.
4. F; Sample response: If they do not get here in time, the meeting will occur without them.
5. T
6. T
7. F; Sample response: To alter the plot, the writer changed several items.
8. T
9. F; Sample response: Eating too much ice cream affected my stomach.
10. T

READER'S NOTEBOOK ADAPTED VERSION

Using a Dictionary

p. V8

1. Students should circle "n." The "v." stands for verb; "adv." stands for adverb; "adj." stands for adjective; and "prep." stands for preposition.
2. Students should underline "[ME *lymon* < Mfr *limon* < Ar *laimun* < Pers *limun*]." "MFr" stands for Middle French.
3. Students should draw a box around the pronunciation.
4. There are four noun definitions for the entry.
5. Definition four is slang.
6. Definition four is used in the sentence.

p. V9 Activity

1. **Pronunciation:** (lit′ ər ə chər)
Main Part of Speech: noun
Original Language(s): ME *litterature* < OFr < L *litteratura* < *littera*
1st Meaning: books, plays, etc. that are considered very good and that people have liked for a long time
Other Meanings: printed information produced by organizations that want to sell something or tell people about something
2. **Pronunciation:** (laŋ′gwij)
Main Part of Speech: noun
Original Language(s): ME < OFr *langage* < *langue*, tongue < L *lingua*, tongue, language, altered (by assoc. with *lingere*, to lick) < OL *dingwa* < IE *dnghwa* > OE *tunge*, TONGUE
1st Meaning: a system of words, phrases, and grammar, used by people who live in a country or area to communicate with each other
Other Meanings: the use of words, grammar, etc. to communicate with other people; the kind of words that someone uses, or that are used when talking or writing about a particular subject; a system of instructions used in computer programs; any system of signs, movements, sounds, etc. that are used to express meanings or feelings

p. V9 Activity

Sample response:
Moment: A *moment* is a "short portion or point of time." The perfect moment passed me by.
Popular: *Popular* means "commonly liked or approved." Logan wanted to sit with the popular students during lunch.
Remedy: A *remedy* is "a medicine or treatment that cures an illness." Ariel discovered a remedy for her grandmother's illness.
Blur: A *blur* is "a stain or smear that obscures." I couldn't see through the window because of the blur on it.
Lazy: *Lazy* means "not energetic." My brother is lazy because he doesn't do any chores or his homework.

Unit 1: Academic Vocabulary Words

p. V12 A. True/False

1. T
2. F; Sample response: If you had a previous experience playing on a team, you do not need to be introduced to the rules of the game.
3. T
4. F; Sample response: When learning new words as you read, pay attention to the context of the paragraph.
5. F; Sample response: If something has significance, it is very important.

p. V13 B. Completion

Sample response:
1. You can use an explanation to *clarify* the meaning of a term.
2. The *context* of a word is the information that surrounds it.
3. Three of my *previous* teachers were my teachers in primary school.
4. I like to *recall* my favorite poem, which is "The Raven" by Edgar Allan Poe.
5. Please, explain the *significance* of the blue sweater in the mystery novel.

p. V13 C.

Sample response: The words *legend*, *concentration*, and *declined* were words I did not recognize. A *legend* is "a key that goes with a map." *Concentration* is the "ability to think carefully." *Declined* means "decreased in quantity."

Unit 2: Academic Vocabulary Words

p. V14 A. True/False

1. F; Sample response: As the leaves changed colors, Sam began to conclude that autumn was here.
2. T
3. T
4. T
5. F; Sample response: You can predict that a car is going to turn left if the left blinker is on.

p. V15 B.

Sample response:

Conclude: I can conclude that the necklace is Jackie's because I have seen her wearing it.
Object: I saw the object in the kitchen.
Predict: I predict that our team will win the volleyball tournament.
Subject: The subject of the article is endangered species.
Verify: I need to verify the statement to figure out whether it is true.

p. V15 C.

Sample response: The words *eerie, mourned,* and *microchip* were words I did not recognize. *Eerie* means "spooky or weird." Someone who *mourned* is "very sad about something." A *microchip* is a "computer chip."

Unit 3: Academic Vocabulary Words

p. V16 A. Completion

Sample response:

1. The test is meant to *evaluate* your skills in grammar.
2. The boy felt *insignificant* when he was not chosen for the team.
3. The most *irrelevant* information I have learned in school is how to diagram sentences.
4. The most *significant* event of the day was when I was awarded the medal.
5. A *valid* reason to go to school is that my education will help prepare me for the future.

p. V17 B.

Sample response:

Evaluate: I will evaluate whether I liked the article or not.
Insignificant: The detail of the iron kettle was insignificant in the plot of the story.

Irrelevant: Duncan revealed information that was irrelevant to our case.
Significant: My history teacher tells me about significant events in American history.
Valid: Her reasons for not being in school were valid.

p. V17 C.

Sample response: The words *survive, communal,* and *eternal* were words I did not recognize. Someone who *survives* "lives through a difficult time." *Communal* means "shared by a group of people." *Eternal* means "continuing forever."

Unit 4: Academic Vocabulary Words

p. V18 A. True/False

1. F; Sample response: To emphasize your point, it is best to speak clearly.
2. F; Sample response: To paraphrase the words of a song for an audience, put the lyrics in your own words.
3. T
4. F; Sample response: If your friend came in to the classroom soaking wet, you might correctly infer there was a thunderstorm.
5. T

p. V19 B. Completion

Sample response:

1. When giving an oral report, it is important to *emphasize* the important points and supporting details.
2. If you see dark clouds in the sky, you can *infer* that a storm is coming.
3. When you *paraphrase* a poem, you restate the poem in your own words.
4. To find information on snakes, I would *refer* to an encyclopedia.
5. A magician is able to *transform* a watch into a dove.

p. V19 C.

Sample response: The words *oregano, luminous,* and *brooch* were words I did not recognize. *Oregano* is "a plant used in cooking, especially Italian cooking." *Luminous* means "giving off light." A *brooch* is a "large ornamental pin."

Unit 5: Academic Vocabulary Words

p. V20 A. True/False

1. F; Sample response: Chronological order goes from first event to last event.
2. F; Sample response: When you write a critique of a poem, you write facts and opinions.
3. T
4. F; Sample response: An appropriate reaction to a scary movie is screaming.
5. F; Sample response: When you summarize a story, you tell only the important events.

p. V21 B. Completion

Sample response:

1. Student *involvement* in a classroom is good because people learn more when they participate.
2. We can't wait to see the movie again because our *reaction* the first time was one of excitement and pleasure.
3. After my friend *summarized* the story, I knew all the important events.
4. Writers can use *critiques* of their work to improve their work in the future.
5. When you tell the *chronological* story of someone's life, the first event is birth.

p. V21 C.

Sample response: The words *contraption*, *bitterly*, and *flickers* were words I did not recognize. A *contraption* is a "machine." *Bitterly* means "very cold." *Flickers* are "unsteady lights that go on and off quickly."

Unit 6: Academic Vocabulary Words

p. V22 A. Code Name

1. effect
2. alter
3. characteristic
4. affect
5. aspect

p. V23 B. True/False

1. F; Sample response: The effect of the car crash was a dented hood on the car.
2. F; Sample response: To alter the plot, the writer changed several items.
3. T
4. F; Sample response: Eating too much ice cream affected my stomach.
5. T

p. V23 C.

Sample response: The words *pathetic, veered,* and *shallow* were words I did not recognize. *Pathetic* means "sad enough to cause pity or tenderness." *Veered* means "changed directions." *Shallow* means "measuring only a short distance from the top to the bottom."

Using a Dictionary

p. V8

1. Students should circle "n." The "v." stands for verb; "adv." stands for adverb; "adj." stands for adjective; and "prep." stands for preposition.
2. Students should underline "[ME *lymon* < Mfr *limon* < Ar *laimun* < Pers *limun*]." "MFr" stands for Middle French.
3. Students should draw a box around the pronunciation.
4. There are four noun definitions for the entry.
5. Definition four is slang.
6. Definition four is used in the sentence.

p. V9 Activity

1. **Pronunciation:** (lit′ ər ə chər)
Main Part of Speech: noun
Original Language(s): ME *litterature* < OFr < L *litteratura* < *littera*
1ˢᵗ Meaning: books, plays, etc. that are considered very good and that people have liked for a long time
Other Meanings: printed information produced by organizations that want to sell something or tell people about something
2. **Pronunciation:** (laŋ′gwij)
Main Part of Speech: noun
Original Language(s): ME < OFr *langage* < *langue*, tongue < L *lingua*, tongue, language, altered (by assoc. with *lingere*, to lick) < OL *dingwa* < IE *dnghwa > OE *tunge*, TONGUE
1ˢᵗ Meaning: a system of words, phrases, and grammar, used by people who live in a country or area to communicate with each other
Other Meanings: the use of words, grammar, etc. to communicate with other people; the kind of words that someone uses, or that are used when talking or writing about a particular subject; a system of instructions used in computer programs; any system of signs, movements, sounds, etc. that are used to express meanings or feelings

p. V9 Activity
Sample response:
Moment: A *moment* is a "short portion or point of time." The perfect moment passed me by.
Popular: *Popular* means "commonly liked or approved." Logan wanted to sit with the popular students during lunch.
Remedy: A *remedy* is "a medicine or treatment that cures an illness." Ariel discovered a remedy for her grandmother's illness.
Blur: A *blur* is "a stain or smear that obscures." I couldn't see through the window because of the blur on it.
Lazy: *Lazy* means "not energetic." My brother is lazy because he doesn't do any chores or his homework.

Unit 1: Academic Vocabulary Words

p. V12 A. True/False

1. T
2. F; Sample response: If you had a previous experience playing on a team, you do not need to be introduced to the rules of the game.
3. T
4. F; Sample response: When learning new words as you read, pay attention to the context of the paragraph.
5. F; Sample response: If something has significance, it is very important.

p. V13 B. Completion
Sample response:
1. You can use an explanation to *clarify* the meaning of a term.
2. The *context* of a word is the information that surrounds it.
3. Three of my *previous* teachers were my teachers in primary school.
4. I like to *recall* my favorite poem, which is "The Raven" by Edgar Allan Poe.
5. Please, explain the *significance* of the blue sweater in the mystery novel.

p. V13 C.
Sample response: The words *legend*, *concentration*, and *declined* were words I did not recognize. A *legend* is "a key that goes with a map." *Concentration* is the "ability to think carefully." *Declined* means "decreased in quantity."

Unit 2: Academic Vocabulary Words

p. V14 A. True/False

1. F; Sample response: As the leaves changed colors, Sam began to conclude that autumn was here.
2. T
3. T
4. T
5. F; Sample response: You can predict that a car is going to turn left if the left blinker is on.

p. V15 B.

Sample response:

Conclude: I can conclude that the necklace is Jackie's because I have seen her wearing it.
Object: I saw the object in the kitchen.
Predict: I predict that our team will win the volleyball tournament.
Subject: The subject of the article is endangered species.
Verify: I need to verify the statement to figure out whether it is true.

p. V15 C.

Sample response: The words *eerie, mourned,* and *microchip* were words I did not recognize. *Eerie* means "spooky or weird." Someone who *mourned* is "very sad about something." A *microchip* is a "computer chip."

Unit 3: Academic Vocabulary Words

p. V16 A. Completion

Sample response:

1. The test is meant to *evaluate* your skills in grammar.
2. The boy felt *insignificant* when he was not chosen for the team.
3. The most *irrelevant* information I have learned in school is how to diagram sentences.
4. The most *significant* event of the day was when I was awarded the medal.
5. A *valid* reason to go to school is that my education will help prepare me for the future.

p. V17 B.

Sample response:

Evaluate: I will evaluate whether I liked the article or not.
Insignificant: The detail of the iron kettle was insignificant in the plot of the story.

Irrelevant: Duncan revealed information that was irrelevant to our case.
Significant: My history teacher tells me about significant events in American history.
Valid: Her reasons for not being in school were valid.

p. V17 C.

Sample response: The words *survive, communal,* and *eternal* were words I did not recognize. Someone who *survives* "lives through a difficult time." *Communal* means "shared by a group of people." *Eternal* means "continuing forever."

Unit 4: Academic Vocabulary Words

p. V18 A. True/False

1. F; Sample response: To emphasize your point, it is best to speak clearly.
2. F; Sample response: To paraphrase the words of a song for an audience, put the lyrics in your own words.
3. T
4. F; Sample response: If your friend came in to the classroom soaking wet, you might correctly infer there was a thunderstorm.
5. T

p. V19 B. Completion

Sample response:

1. When giving an oral report, it is important to *emphasize* the important points and supporting details.
2. If you see dark clouds in the sky, you can *infer* that a storm is coming.
3. When you *paraphrase* a poem, you restate the poem in your own words.
4. To find information on snakes, I would *refer* to an encyclopedia.
5. A magician is able to *transform* a watch into a dove.

p. V19 C.

Sample response: The words *oregano, luminous,* and *brooch* were words I did not recognize. *Oregano* is "a plant used in cooking, especially Italian cooking." *Luminous* means "giving off light." A *brooch* is a "large ornamental pin."

Unit 5: Academic Vocabulary Words

p. V20 A. True/False
1. F; Sample response: Chronological order goes from first event to last event.
2. F; Sample response: When you write a critique of a poem, you write facts and opinions.
3. T
4. F; Sample response: An appropriate reaction to a scary movie is screaming.
5. F; Sample response: When you summarize a story, you tell only the important events.

p. V21 B. Completion
Sample response:
1. Student *involvement* in a classroom is good because people learn more when they participate.
2. We can't wait to see the movie again because our *reaction* the first time was one of excitement and pleasure.
3. After my friend *summarized* the story, I knew all the important events.
4. Writers can use *critiques* of their work to improve their work in the future.
5. When you tell the *chronological* story of someone's life, the first event is birth.

p. V21 C.
Sample response: The words *contraption*, *bitterly*, and *flickers* were words I did not recognize. A *contraption* is a "machine." *Bitterly* means "very cold." *Flickers* are "unsteady lights that go on and off quickly."

Unit 6: Academic Vocabulary Words

p. V22 A. Code Name
1. effect
2. alter
3. characteristic
4. affect
5. aspect

p. V23 B. True/False
1. F; Sample response: The effect of the car crash was a dented hood on the car.
2. F; Sample response: To alter the plot, the writer changed several items.
3. T
4. F; Sample response: Eating too much ice cream affected my stomach.
5. T

p. V23 C.
Sample response: The words *pathetic*, *veered*, and *shallow* were words I did not recognize. *Pathetic* means "sad enough to cause pity or tenderness." *Veered* means "changed directions." *Shallow* means "measuring only a short distance from the top to the bottom."

Idioms

p. V46 A. Hypothesize
Sample response:
1. If someone "broke the ice," he or she showed friendliness by starting a conversation.
2. A *copycat* is someone who imitates other people's clothes, behavior, and so on.
3. If people are "horsing around," they are playing in a rough and silly way.
4. If someone "let the cat out of the bag," he or she told a secret without intending to do so.
5. If I "cross my fingers," I am hoping that something will happen the way I want it to.

p. V47 Graphic Organizer
Sample response:
Idiom: just fly away
Explanation: Sometimes when people are upset, they wish they could "just fly away." This means that they wish they could escape from their troubles or worries.
Sample Sentence: After seeing the poor grade on my test, I wished I could just fly away.
Idiom: throw yourself
Explanation: If you throw yourself into an activity, you give it all of your energy. You do not literally throw your body.
Sample Sentence: You have to throw yourself into school projects if you want to earn good grades.
Idiom: it has stuck
Explanation: If something has stuck, it has been accepted.
Sample Sentence: Everyone called Brooke "Bella" in grade school, and the name stuck throughout her life.
Idiom: keep the ball rolling
Explanation: If a person keeps the ball rolling, he or she keeps an activity or event in motion.

Sample Sentence: Patrick bailed out at the last minute, and it was my job to keep the ball rolling.

Idiom: live in the past

Explanation: If a person lives in the past, he or she thinks only of past events or people. The person does not concentrate on possibilities or events in his or her present life or future life.

Sample Sentence: It is not healthy to live in the past because you forget to experience life today and tomorrow.

Idiom: dead as a doornail

Explanation: This idiom suggests immediate finality.

Sample Sentence: Mr. Hunley was dead as a doornail.

Idiom: open their hearts to each other

Explanation: This idiom means that a person allows himself or herself to care for and be cared for by others in a spirit of love and friendship.

Sample Sentence: At Christmas time, people open their hearts to one another.

Idiom: cold heart

Explanation: If someone has a cold heart, he or she is unkind and cruel.

Sample Sentence: Scrooge had a cold heart.

Idiom: win me

Explanation: If a man is trying to win a woman, he is trying to make her love or marry him.

Sample Sentence: Oswald tried to win me with gifts and poetry.